W9-ASC-231

SEP 1984

RECEIVED
OHIO DOMINICAN
COLLEGE LIBRARY
COLUMBUS, OHIO

SOCIAL MEASUREMENT

SOCIAL MEASUREMENT
Current Issues

George W. Bohrnstedt
Edgar F. Borgatta
Editors

SAGE PUBLICATIONS   Beverly Hills   London

300.724
B677₂
1981

Copyright © 1981 by Sage Publications, Inc.

All rights reserved. No part of this book may be reproduced or utilized in any form or by any means, electronic or mechanical, including photo-copying, recording, or by any information storage and retrieval system, without permission in writing from the publisher.

For information address:

SAGE Publications, Inc.
275 South Beverly Drive
Beverly Hills, California 90212

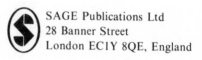

SAGE Publications Ltd
28 Banner Street
London EC1Y 8QE, England

Printed in the United States of America

Library of Congress Cataloging in Publication Data

Main entry under title:

Social measurement.

    Bibliography: p.
    1. Social sciences—Statistical methods—Ad-
dresses, essays, lectures. 2. Social sciences—
Mathematical models—Addresses, essays, lectures.
I. Bohrnstedt, George W. II. Borgatta, Edgar F.,
1924-
HA29.S638   300'.724   81-8954
ISBN 0-8039-1595-0   AACR2
ISBN 0-8039-1596-9 (pbk.)

FIRST PRINTING

Chapters 1, 5, 6, 7, 8, and 9 reprinted from *Sociological Methods and Research,* Volume 9, Number 2 (November 1980).

CONTENTS

Foreword
    GEORGE W. BOHRNSTEDT
    EDGAR F. BORGATTA   9

Part I. Philosophy of Measurement Models   21
1. Level of Measurement: Once Over Again
    EDGAR F. BORGATTA
    GEORGE W. BOHRNSTEDT   23

2. The Generalizability of Indirect Measures to Complex
   Situations: A Fundamental Dilemma
    PAUL H. WILKEN
    H. M. BLALOCK, Jr.   39

Part II. Techniques for Estimating Measurement Models   63
3. Analyzing Models with Unobserved Variables:
   Analysis of Covariance Structures
    EDWARD G. CARMINES
    JOHN P. McIVER   65

4. Latent Trait Modeling of Attitude Items
    MARK REISER   117

5. The Factor Analysis of Ipsative Measures
    DAVID J. JACKSON
    DUANE F. ALWIN   145

Part III. Empirical Examples   167
6. Response Errors in Self-Reported Number of Arrests
    GORDON A. WYNER   169

7. Children's Reports of Parental Socioeconomic Status:
   A Multiple Group Measurement Model
    ROBERT D. MARE
    WILLIAM M. MASON   187

120919

8. Sex Differences in Measurement Error in
   Status Attainment Models
   MARY CORCORAN   209

9. Occupational Characteristics and Classification
   Systems: New Uses of the *Dictionary of Occupational
   Titles* in Social Research
   KENNETH I. SPENNER   229

Foreword

This volume presents a set of papers that illustrate the state of measurement in the social sciences. The papers fall into three classes: the philosophy of social measurement, techniques for estimating measurement models, and empirical examples. With the publication of this volume we hope to achieve two major goals: (1) the stimulation of further theoretical research in the area of sociological measurement, and (2) the provision of examples showing how these techniques can be applied in research settings.

The growth in interest in measurement in the social sciences is relatively recent. While textbooks in methodology have long argued for the assessment of reliability and validity, until recently it has been rare to see any data on reliability and validity reported in research papers, and even more rare for these reports to reflect sophisticated procedures. Even a casual inspection of a volume such as Robinson and Shaver's (1973) *Measures of Social Psychological Attitudes* underscores this point. Although scores of measures are reported, the information available on their reliability and validity is sparse.

To understand why researchers paid mere lip service to measurement concerns in the past, as opposed to launching frontal attacks on them, one must understand that during the 1950s and early 1960s the tenor of the times was considerably different from what it is now. In particular, the dominant methodological issue at that time was the inappropriateness of using parametric statistics to analyze presumed nonintervallevel data. Because the major techniques for assessing reliability and validity assume an underlying continuous variable, most of the techniques were seen as inappropriate and therefore were rarely applied. Many social scientists working at the time can attest that anyone using factor analysis during this period was viewed with some suspicion.

The introduction of causal modeling to the social sciences played an important role in shifting attitudes about the use of parametric statistics. Especially important in this regard were Blalock (1963, 1964, 1969a, 1969b, 1971) and Duncan (1966). With the continuing shift in attitude toward the use of parametric statistics in the social sciences, there has been a growing interest in formal measurement models as well. Twenty years ago, the dominant measurement model grew out of classical test score theory (Lord and Novick, 1968). The classical model posits that an observed variable y is due to an underlying true score, τ, and an error component e:

$$y = \tau + e \qquad [1]$$

with the assumption that y and e are uncorrelated and the mean of the errors is zero; i.e., the errors are random rather than systematic. Under this formulation, the true score for a given observation is simply the expected value (mean) of y given an infinity number of repeated measurements on a given observation. That is, it is not assumed that τ is a "true" score in some existential sense. Rather, it is simply defined as an expected value across repeated measurements; i.e., $\tau_i = E(x_i)$ for individual i.

Obtaining reliability estimates from the classical model shown in equation 1 above has required assumptions that are somewhat unrealistic with respect to the kind of data usually collected in the social sciences. There have been two major approaches: (1) the use of test-retest correlations, and (2) the use of internal consistency measures employing two or more parallel items. Test-retest estimates of reliability suffer from problems of respondent memory, differing estimates of reliability as a function of the test-retest interval, the correlation of measurement errors across time, and the problem of distinguishing true change from unreliability (Bohrnstedt, 1970, forthcoming). Fortunately, by adding a third wave of observations, some of these problems have been overcome, as the work of Heise (1969), Wiley and Wiley (1970), and Werts et al. (1971) shows. The use of parallel measures required the researcher to assume that (1) the errors across measures were uncorrelated with one another, and (2) the measures had equal measurement error variances. When one combines these restrictions with the simplicity of the model shown in equation 1, it is clear why this approach to the assessment of unreliability is of limited use.

A less restrictive set of assumptions is associated with what Lord and Novick (1968: 49-50) define as τ-equivalent measures. Two measures are τ-equivalent if they share the same latent true score. Unlike parallel measures, there is no restriction that the measurement error variances be equal. Lord and Novick (1968: 90) show that coefficient alpha (Cronbach, 1951), the most popular internal consistency measure of reliability, equals the reliability of the measure (rather than being merely a lower bound) if one can assume measures are τ-equivalent. This demonstration was important, since it meant that coefficient alpha, to be an accurate estimate of reliability, did not depend upon parallel scores, which are difficult to construct, as anyone who has tried knows. As we shall see below, an even more useful conceptualization of measurement (Jöreskog, 1971a) is available.

Exploratory factor analysis has long been used as a device to select items that presumably have the same underlying true score. More recently, there have been formal attempts to link factor analysis to scores or scales constructed from the items factor analyzed (Heise and Bohrnstedt, 1971; Allen, 1974; Armor, 1974; Smith, 1974a, 1974b; Greene and Carmines, 1980), but not until Jöreskog (1969) developed confirmatory factory analysis was the most useful link made between the two, complete with statistical tests of significance. In con-

firmatory factor analysis, one hypothesizes which items will
load on which factors and what the interrelationships among
the factors themselves will be. The technique is flexible
enough to allow one to fix some of the parameters (e.g., to fix
some loadings or factor correlations to zero), to constrain
selected parameters to be equal to one another, and to estimate
freely the remaining parameters. After hypothesizing the
structure to account for the observed covariances or correlations, one can then test for the goodness of fit between the
observed covariance matrix and that implied by the hypothesized models.

Jöreskog (1971a) wed confirmatory analysis to reliability
theory by defining congeneric measures. Variables $x_1, x_2 \ldots$
x_n are defined as congeneric if their true scores $\tau_1, \tau_2 \ldots \tau_n$
correlate perfectly with each other, with the implication that a
random variable τ exists such that all of the τ_i are linearly related
to it. More formally, the model is

$$\tau_i = \mu_i + \beta_i \tau \qquad [2]$$

Now, because y_i equals $\tau_i + e_i$, it follows that

$$y_i = \mu_i + \beta_i \tau + e_i \qquad [3]$$

for the ith congeneric measure. The usual assumptions of test
score theory are also made; that is, τ and e_i are assumed to be
uncorrelated and all e_i are assumed to have means of zero.
Finally, the errors across measures are also assumed to be
uncorrelated. Equation 3 in vector form is

$$y = \mu + \beta\tau + e \qquad [4]$$

If Σ is the covariance matrix of y and θ^2 is a diagonal matrix of
variance associated with e, then $E(yy') = \Sigma$ and

$$\Sigma = \beta\beta' + \theta^2 \qquad [5]$$

Equation 5 is the basic equation for a single-factor model. If the distribution of the y is multivariate normal, then parameters in equation 5 can be estimated by Jöreskog's confirmatory factor analysis. The method yields standard errors for the parameter estimates and an overall chi-square statistic that allows one to test whether the y_i are indeed congeneric. Jöreskog then goes on the develop a measure of the reliability of each of the items constituting a composite, as well as that of the composite itself.

Quite obviously, congeneric measures conform much more closely to assumptions we are able to make about our measures compared to those associated with either parallelism or τ-equivalence. That is, the items may differentially affect the true score (captured by the β_i) and may differ in their location along the true score (captured by the μ_i). Even though the assumptions underlying the estimation of reliability with congeneric measures conform far more closely to practice (when compared to the restrictive assumption of parallel measures), those who have used the Jöreskog (1971a) procedure are almost uniformly disappointed in how poorly their items fit the congeneric model. To achieve good fits one is reduced to building scores with only a few items. While some of this poor fit is due to the sensitivity of the chi-square goodness-of-fit statistic to sample size, good fits for as many as eight to ten items are difficult to observe, even when using the less sensitive Tucker and Lewis (1973) coefficient. The researcher is faced with a Hobson's choice. One can build a score with a few factorially pure items; but since reliability is partially a function of the number of items in the score, the score may be quite unreliable. Or one can choose to ignore the issue of factorial homogeneity and add together items that are intercorrelated, regardless of why. This latter approach can display substantial reliability, but unfortunately at the expense of validity, since the items will likely be related to several underlying true scores rather than to a single one. It is significant that this dilemma was not created by, nor is it due to, the method of congeneric scores. Rather, the dilemma results from the difficulty of constructing adequate measures in the social sciences. As Alwin and Jackson (1980) point out, it is difficult to imagine measures so pure in content that variation in them is due to a single construct. Other substantive constructs and reliable methods factors may also be involved. These problems make it clear why special efforts and care are needed in constructing measures in the social sciences. It is our impression that many of the measures in the social sciences were not developed as the result of a systematic attempt to sample items from content domain (Nunnally, 1967; Bohrnstedt, 1970, forthcoming), which are then cross-validated in new samples. Rather, they often appear to be the result of spending a short time writing new items or of borrowing extant indicators. Furthermore, often the only criterion for deciding to include an item seems to be whether it appears to have face validity. When a slapdash method is used to construct a measure, it is little wonder that statistical models do not fit it well.

The social sciences appear to have reached a point where the quality of the models available to evaluate the measures far outstrip the quality of the measures themselves. This statement is not intended to disuade methodologists from developing new methods. Rather, it is intended to encourage researchers to approach development of measures with more care and forethought. Good measures may take years to develop, not days or weeks.

The chapters in this book are divided into three parts. The first contains two studies that fall broadly within the realm of the philosophy of science. The first, by Borgatta and Bohrnstedt, notes that in spite of the shift toward parametric and away from so-called nonparametric statistics, questions continue about the appropriateness of parametric techniques for analyzing "soft" social variables (see, for example, Blalock, 1974). Numerous attempts to assess the utility of "ordinal" measures of association for causal analysis and regression procedures have appeared in recent years (Blalock, 1976; Ploch, 1974; Leik, 1976a, 1976b). Given the continuing concern about analyzing ordinal-level data with parametric statistics, it seemed appropriate to include a chapter on the topic in this volume. Therefore, in the article "Level of measurement: Once Over Again," we argue that even though some of the manifest data in the social sciences may be collected at the ordinal level, most of the variables of interest to us as sociologists can be thought of as continuous (and therefore interval) at the latent level. And since most of the variables are constructs (as opposed to operational definitions), why not also assume that the latent constructs in sociology are reasonably well distributed. Accordingly, the analysis of most sociological data with multivariate statistical procedures is appropriate, particularly since most of the alternate analysis techniques make the same and often more restrictive assumptions.

In a well-known paper, Blalock (1968) argued that a researcher needs to specify carefully his or her *auxiliary theory* in a given research situation. Most researchers begin with a general set of theoretical propositions involving abstract concepts. An auxiliary theory specifies the relationships between one's operations in a given research situation and the underlying theoretical concepts. Blalock argues that the indirect nature of much measurement in the social sciences requires an explicit attempt to estimate the relationships between the indicators and the concepts as well as the relationships among the concepts themselves. Wilken and Blalock, in a follow-up to the original Blalock chapter, argue that indirect measurement procedures require auxiliary measurement theories that may well vary across research situations when testing the same theory. They point out that moving from simple to more complex situations may be difficult because of the confounding of the auxiliary theory and the more general substantive theory being tested. They illustrate the dilemma with the problem of measuring utilities and subjective probabilities in social psychology.

The second part of the book contains three reports on estimating measurement models. The first, by Carmines and McIver, provides an introduction to the analysis of models with unobserved variables. It shows how the models developed

16

Foreword

by Karl Jöreskog can be used to test whether a given set of
items are congeneric or not, or whether the more restrictive
assumptions associated with τ-equivalent or parallel measures
can be assumed. They illustrate the approach by analyzing
Rosenberg's (1965) popular self-esteem measure. They conclude that the items that constitute it cannot be adequately
represented by a congeneric model, apropos of our earlier
discussion about the difficulty in achieving this goal. In the last
section of the chapter, Carmines and McIver present Jöreskog's
approach to estimating simultaneously *measurement* and
structural models in the test of a set of theoretical propositions. The measurement model is a set of equations linking the
observed indicators in a research setting to a set of underlying
unobserved concepts. The structural model is a set of equations linking the unobserved theoretical concepts to one
another. The authors show how Jöreskog and Sörbom's
LISREL computer program can be used to estimate the
parameters of both models simultaneously. The measurement
model is, in fact, a kind of auxiliary theory of the type argued
for by Wilken and Blalock in their chapter.

In the second chapter of this part of the volume, Reiser
introduces a latent trait model for the analysis of attitude
items. The latent trait model he presents assumes a single,
underlying, unobserved variable that can account for the
covariation among a set of items. The maximum likelihood
estimation procedure used not only provides estimates of an
item's ability to discriminate along the underlying variable,
but an estimate of where the item is operating along the
continuum as well. Although models of the sort Reiser introduces have become widely used in educational measurement,
they are virtually unknown to social scientists. As Reiser's
analysis of items from NORC's General Social Survey demon-
strates, latent trait models show promise for the analysis of
social science measures.

The final chapter in this section, by Jackson and Alwin,
presents a model for the factor analysis of ipsative measures.
An ipsative transformation centers a set of variables about an

individual's mean. Popular examples of ipsative measures are the Allport, Vernon, and Lindzey (1951) values measures and Kohn's (1976) measures of parental values. The authors show that the assumptions appropriate for the common factor model, especially that of uncorrelated disturbances, do not hold for the analysis of ipsative variables. Then Jackson and Alwin develop a factor model for ipsative variables under the assumption that a hypothetical, nonipsative set of measures exists that corresponds to the set of ipsative measures, and show that the model can be estimated using Jöreskog's (1969) confirmatory factor analysis. This application is yet another example of how important Jöreskog's methods have become for the assessment of measurement in the social sciences.

Part III of the volume provides a set of empirical examples in which various measurement models are applied.

Most of the variables in the social sciences are latent, unobservable constructs with no naturally occurring metrics. There are some variables of interest to social scientists, however, that are indeed more tangible. For this reason, there is justification for pursuing an alternative definition of true scores. In this conceptualization it is argued that the true score is potentially, if not actually, observable. Sutcliffe (1965) defines these as *platonic true scores*. One does not assume that the true scores and errors are uncorrelated or that the errors are necessarily random when assuming platonic true scores. Wyner (1976) has explored platonic measurement models and applies them in the first chapter of this section, "Response Errors in Self-Reported Number of Arrests." Wyner shows that there are substantial response errors in self-reported arrests and that these errors are *not* independent of the number of actual arrests, nor are they random.

Jöreskog (1971b) has generalized his method of confirmatory factor analysis to allow one to test whether a factor structure is general or varies in several populations. Part III contains two creative applications of this generalization. Mare and Mason, in "Children's Reports of Parental Socioeconomic Status: A Multiple Group Measurement Model," show similarities and differences in children's reports of parental socio-economic status as a function of the child's grade level. Corcoran employs the methodology to show that young women's reports of mother's education are significantly more reliable than young men's reports, in her essay, "Sex Differences in Measurement Error in Status Attainment Models." The final chapter of this volume is an example of applied measurement. Spenner, in "Occupational Characteristics and Classification Systems: New Uses of the *Dictionary of Occupational Titles* in Social Research," develops a new set of indicators for measuring routinization and closeness of supervision in work. This article should be especially important for researchers working in the status attainment area.

This volume takes one step toward achieving our stated goals of stimulating more theoretical and empirical work in the area of measurement. Much remains to be done, but we are confident that the kind of work represented in this volume will serve as a solid base on which to build.

—George W. Bohrnstedt
Indiana University

Edgar F. Borgatta
University of Washington

REFERENCES

ALLEN, M. P. (1974) "Construction of composite measures by the canonical factor regression method," pp. 51-78 in H. L. Costner (ed.) Sociological Methodology: 1973-74. San Francisco: Jossey-Bass.
ALLPORT, G. W., P. E. VERNON, and G. LINDZEY (1951) A Study of Values. Boston: Houghton-Mifflin.
ALWIN, D. F. and D. J. JACKSON (1980) "Measurement models for response errors in surveys: issues and applications," pp. 68-119 in K. F. Schuessler (ed.) Sociological Methodology: 1980. San Francisco: Jossey-Bass.
ARMOR, D. J. (1974) "Theta reliability and factor scaling," pp. 17-50 in H. L. Costner (ed.) Sociological Methodology: 1973-74. San Francisco: Jossey-Bass.
BLALOCK, H.M., Jr. (1976) "Can we find a genuine slope analog?" pp. 195-229 in D. R. Heise (ed.) Sociological Methodology: 1976. San Francisco: Jossey-Bass.

_____(1974) "Beyond ordinal measurement: weak tests of stranger theories," pp. 424-455 in H. M. Blalock, Jr. (ed.) Measurement in the Social Sciences. Chicago: AVC.

_____[ed.] (1971) Causal Models in the Social Sciences. Chicago: AVC.

_____(1969a) Theory Construction: From Verbal to Mathematical Formulations. Englewood Cliffs, NJ: Prentice-Hall.

_____(1969b) "Multiple indicators and the causal approach to measurement error." Amer. J. of Sociology 75 (September): 264-272.

_____(1968) "The measurement problem: a gap between the languages of theory and research," pp. 5-27 in H. M. Blalock and A. B. Blalock (eds.) Methodology in Social Research. New York: McGraw-Hill.

_____(1965) "Some implications of random measurement error for causal inferences." Amer. J. of Sociology 71 (July): 37-47.

_____(1964) Causal Inferences in Nonexperimental Research. Chapel Hill: Univ. of North Carolina Press.

_____(1963) "Making causal inferences for unmeasured variables from correlations among indicators." Amer. J. of Sociology 69 (July): 53-62.

BOHRNSTEDT, G. W. (forthcoming) "Measurement," in J. Wright and P. Rossi (eds.) Handbook of Survey Research. New York: Academic.

_____(1970) "Reliability and validity assessment in attitude measurement." pp. 80-99 in G. Summers (ed.) Attitude Measurement. Skokie, IL: Rand-McNally.

CRONBACH, L. J. (1951) "Coefficient alpha and the internal structure of tests." Psychometricka 16: 297-334.

DUNCAN, O. D. (1966) "Path analysis: sociological examples." Amer. J. of Sociology 72: 1-16.

GREENE, V. L. and E. G. CARMINES (1980) "Assessing the reliability of linear composites," pp. 160-175 in K. F. Schuessler (ed.) Sociological Methodology: 1980. San Francisco: Jossey-Bass.

HEISE, D. R. (1969) "Separating reliability and stability in test-retest correlation." Amer. Soc. Rev. 34 (February): 93-101.

_____and G. W. BOHRNSTEDT (1971) "Validity, invalidity and reliability," pp. 104-129 in E. F. Borgatta and G. W. Bohrnstedt (eds.) Sociological Methodology: 1971. San Francisco: Jossey-Bass.

JÖRESKOG, K. G. (1971a) "Simultaneous factor analysis in several populations." Psychometrika 36 (December): 409-426.

_____(1971b) "Statistical analysis of sets of congeneric tests." Psychometrika 36: 109-134.

_____(1969) "A general approach to confirmatory maximum likelihood factor analysis." Psychometrika 34: 183-202.

KOHN, M. L. (1976) "Social class and parental values: another confirmation of the relationship." Amer. Soc. Rev. 41: 538-545.

LEIK, R. K. (1976a) "Monotonic regression analysis for ordinal variables," pp. 250-270 in D. R. Heise (ed.) Sociological Methodology: 1976. San Francisco: Jossey-Bass.

_____(1976b) "Causal models with nominal and ordinal data: retrospective," pp. 271-275 in D. R. Heise (ed.) Sociological Methodology: 1976. San Francisco: Jossey-Bass.

LORD, F. M. and M. R. NOVICK (1968) Statistical Theories of Mental Test Scores. Reading, MA: Addison-Wesley.

20 Foreword

NUNNALLY, J. C. (1967) Psychometric Theory. New York: McGraw-Hill.

PLOCH, D. H. (1974) "Ordinal measures of association and the general linear model," pp. 343-368 in H. M. Blalock, Jr. (ed.) Measurement in the Social Sciences. Chicago: AVC.

ROSENBERG, M. J. (1965) Society and the Adolescent Self-image. Princeton, NJ: Princeton Univ. Press.

ROBINSON, J. P. and P. R. SHAVER (1973) Measures of Social Psychological Attitudes. Ann Arbor: University of Michigan Institute of Social Research.

SMITH, K. W. (1974a) "Forming composite scales and estimating their validity through factor analysis." Social Forces 53 (December): 168-180.

———(1974b) "On estimating the reliability of composite indexes through factor analysis." Soc. Methods and Research 2 (May): 485-510.

SUTCLIFFE, J. P. (1965) "A probability model for errors of classification. I. General considerations." Psychometrika 30: 73-96.

TUCKER, L. R. and C. Lewis (1973) "A reliability coefficient for maximum likelihood factor analysis." Psychometrika 38: 1-10.

WERTS, C. E., K. G. JÖRESKOG, and R. L. LINN (1971) "Comment on the estimation of measurement error in panel data." Amer. Soc. Rev. 36 (February): 110-112.

WILEY, D. F. and J. A. WILEY (1970) "The estimation of measurement error in panel data." Amer. Soc. Rev. 35: 112-117.

WYNER, G. A. (1976) "Sources of response error in self-reports of behavior." Ph.D. dissertation, University of Pennsylvania.

PART I

Philosophy of Measurement Models

CHAPTER ONE

Level of Measurement
Once Over Again

EDGAR F. BORGATTA
University of Washington
GEORGE W. BOHRNSTEDT
Indiana University—Bloomington

I f those who already believe do not need to be convinced, and those who are skeptics will not believe, then a lot of preaching goes on without purpose. Therefore, we hope what follows is less a matter of preaching and more a matter of pursuing the consistency and appropriateness of one position on the "level of measurement" issue in the social sciences. The position taken here is that the question of measurement assumptions in statistical applications often has been treated inappropriately, and, more to the point, erroneously. As we look back, we see resulting misinformation that can be described as a hindrance to the development of the social and psychological sciences. Our objective here is to emphasize the misinformation and the errors, with some historical reference. We hope to ease the minds of those researchers who have been "mindlessly" applying parametric statistics to social variables. As we will show, this practice has been a wise one.

Most discussions of the level of measurement issue can be traced back to the work of Stevens (1966). While many people have written about the ideas of measurement, the variety of approaches that are involved is still impressive. Essentially, one's objective determines, to some extent, how one enters the argument. To begin with, no one enters this arena without some experience with numbers and ideas of measurement; therefore, there are few neutral persons involved in the debate.

As one works more and more with Stevens' concepts, aspects of circularity involved in definitions and refinements of concepts become evident. In at least part of our presentation, we shall follow Stevens not only as a matter of convenience, but also to maintain continuity with presentations that have been made earlier by other writers. Following common convention, Stevens defines measurement thusly: "A rule for the assignment of numerals (numbers) to aspects of objects or events creates a *scale* [of measurement]" (1966: 22). More simply measurement is the assignment of numbers to objects according to rules. Stevens (1966: 23) proceeds directly to a discussion of types of scales, a set of distinctions that has received much attention:

> The type of scale achieved when we deputize the numerals to serve as representatives for a state of affairs in nature depends upon the character of the basic empirical operations performed on nature. These operations are limited ordinarily by the peculiarities of the thing being scaled and by our choice of concrete procedures, but once selected the procedures determine that there will eventuate one or another of four types of scale: nominal, ordinal, interval or ratio. Each of these classes of scales is best characterized by its range of invariance—by the kinds of transformations that leave the "structure" of the scale undistorted. And the nature of the invariance sets limits to the kinds of statistical manipulation that can legitimately be applied to the scaled data. This question of the applicability of the various statistics is of great practical concern to several of the sciences.

Stevens presents the four types of scales as ordered in a cumulative sense. The nominal scale requires the determination of equality for placement in the classes implied; the ordinal scale additionally requires a determination of "greater than" or "less than" for objects; the interval scale in addition requires determination of equality of differences between scale intervals; and the ratio scale further requires determination of a true zero point. The ratio scale, of course, has all the qualities of the three previously named scales. It is appropriate to go over the meanings associated with these scales in terms of the elaboration by Stevens.

NOMINAL SCALES

Stevens sees two types of nominal scales: the type used for purposes such as numbering individuals for identification as one, and a scale used for classification into types where those who are placed within the type are given the same number as the other. The former is a special case of the latter. Nominal scales are seen as a primitive type of scale, one in which the basic rule is that the same numeral is not assigned to different classes. A class is defined as or based on the demonstration of equality in respect to some characteristic of the object. We shall bypass here the question of the logical definition of equality, although this is an important issue in itself.

According to Stevens (1966) "the *ordinal scale* arises from the operation of rank ordering." It is at this point that Stevens appears to have gone astray, possibly because of the direction from which he approached the subject matter. And, indeed, the most serious misdirection that has developed in the area of measurement resulted from this statement. Stevens (1966: 26) asserts:

As a matter of fact, most of the scales used widely and effectively by psychologists are ordinal scales. In the strictest propriety, the ordinary statistics involving means and standard deviations ought not to be used with those scales, for these statistics imply a knowledge of something more than the relative rank order of data.

The quarrel here is simple and direct. Most of the scales used widely and effectively by psychologists (and other social scientists) simply are not ordinal scales; the procedures used by social scientists usually fit badly to an interval scale, but they certainly are not ordinal scales. In other words, we measure latent continuous variables with error at the manifest level.

Stevens appears aware of the limitations associated with the idea of ordinal scales, but unfortunately was distracted from pursuing this matter:

> In earlier discussions (e.g., Stevens, 1946) I expressed the opinion that rank-order correlation does not apply to ordinal scales because the derivation of the formula for this correlation involves the assumption that the differences between successive ranks are equal. My colleague, Frederick Mosteller convinces me that this conservative view can be liberalized, provided that the resultant coefficient (e.g., Spearman's ρ or Kendall's τ) is *interpreted only* as a test function for a hypothesis about *order* [1966: 26].

If only Stevens had not been convinced, the enormous wasted energy and misdirection of the fads and fashions of so-called nonparametric or distribution-free statistics might possibly have been avoided. This extremely important point will receive specific and special attention below.

INTERVAL SCALES

An interval scale is identified by Stevens as what we ordinarily think of when we consider quantitative procedures. An interval scale is subject to a linear transformation with invariance, and is represented by many common measures, such as the Fahrenheit and Celsius temperature scales. With minor limitations, these are subject to all the algebraic operations with which we are ordinarily concerned in science. The transition to a ratio scale is easily handled by the fact that operations on the interval scale can conveniently fix a true zero.

Stevens (1966: 28) goes astray in discussing interval measurement relative to the work of psychologists:

> The variability of a psychological measure is itself sometimes used to equalize the units of a scale. This process smacks of a kind of magic—a rope trick for climbing the hierarchy of scales. The rope in this case is the assumption that in the sample of individuals tested the trait in question has a canonical distribution (e.g., "normal"). Then it is a simple matter to adjust the units of the scale so that the assumed distribution is recovered when the individuals are measured. But this procedure is obviously no better than the gratuitous postulate behind it.

Stevens recognizes that "the fact remains that the assumption of normality has the advocacy of a certain pragmatic usefulness in the measurement of many human traits," but he does not pursue this point, we shall do later in this essay.

STEVENS MORE RECENT POSITION

In another treatment of measurement, Stevens (1975) takes a position that is emphasized here and leads to quite a different global interpretation of the measurement process as appropriate for the social and psychological sciences. Stevens notes that "it is helpful . . . to regard measurement as a two-part endeavor, consisting on the one hand of manipulations and on the other of models. You do something, you perform a sequence of operations, and afterwards you invoke a model or a schema to stand for what you have done." He observes that there are really two aspects to the idea of measurement: the everyday operations involved, and the model of measurement used to rationalize these operations. What is most important is a kind of circularity. That is, scientists go through operations and invoke models, then go through additional operations and invoke additional models. We eventually enter an area in which there are many models and many sets of possible operations. Stevens (1975: 47) continues: "The model used in measurement is usually the system of numbers bequeathed to us by mathematics. The empirical operations may vary enormously, however, depending on what is to be measured."

It should be noted here that this emphasis on models is somewhat in contrast to the negative comment relative to earlier assumptions made by Stevens (1966: 28) and noted here.

In dealing with measurement, then, one may begin wherever one pleases, but one must give attention, as has been suggested by Stevens and many others, to the correspondence between what one does and an underlying model. Of course, however, there is no reason that one should not begin with a model, then design operations which conform to it within given bounds of error. It is exactly this approach that we take here.

A SUGGESTED MODEL

The variables of greatest interest to social scientists are latent unobserved constructs rather than constructs that are operationally defined. And most of these constructs are conceptualized to be continuous at the latent level, even though they are usually manifestly measured as discrete variables. Examples of this include the constructs of industrialization, social status, power, authoritarianism, and self-esteem. If the constructs are continuous, they must also be interval.

Importantly, the use of inferential regression analysis, factor analysis, and other multivariate techniques require that one's dependent variables be continuous and distributed normally (multivariate normality for multiple dependent variables) for each outcome associated with the independent variable(s). It is worth emphasizing here that level of measurement is not a requirement for the use of parametric statistics, as was suggested by Stevens. For a recent discussion of this point and a brief history of this issue, see Gaito (1980).

Because most of the variables that interest us as researchers are continuous at the conceptual level and are reasonably close to normally distributed in the population of interest, there is no reason to eschew the use of parametric statistics.

And why not also assume that most of these latent variables are roughly bell-shaped in the population? For most constructs, does it not make sense to assume that the bulk of observations in the population lie close to the mean, with relatively few cases falling at the extremes? It should be pointed out that Chebycheff's well-known theorem guarantees that the probability of observing a given outcome increases the closer that outcome is to the population mean. While the theorem in no sense guarantees that the distribution will be normal, it is well known that regression and regression-like procedures tend to be relatively robust even if the assumption of normality is violated (Bohrnstedt and Carter, 1971).

To summarize this argument, most of the central constructs in the social sciences are conceptualized as continuous, and their distributions are such that the application of parametric statistics to their analyses will not result in seriously biased estimates. And if the variables are continuous, they must also by definition, be interval.

IMPERFECT INTERVAL-LEVEL MANIFEST SCALES

At the manifest, observed level, our measures are likely to be imperfect interval-level scales. Social measurement is crude. Unlike the physicist, who can measure with high precision through the use of pointer and meter readings which reflect agreed-upon international standards, social scientists are likely to generate measures which are (1) unquestionably discrete, rather than continuous, and (2) likely to result in measures with intervals which are not truly equal. However, if we have been careful in developing our measures (e.g., item and indicator development procedures that are extensive and systematic) we should be able to assume that there is a monotonic relationship between the manifest scale and the underlying latent construct. That is, a positive difference between two points on the manifest scale reflects a positive difference on the latent scale as well, even though the intervals on the manifest scale may not be isomorphic.

This is another way of saying that our measures contain error. Measurement error is defined, of course, as a function of the fit between the manifest scale and the latent construct. Importantly, measurement error will have an effect on parameter estimates. But the fact that our observations do not correspond perfectly to the underlying model in no way implies that ordinal level statistics are required to analyze the data.

ORDINALITY?

We think the emphasis on using ordinal statistics in the social sciences is misplaced for two reasons. First, we do not visualize a model in which each and every individual in the population is ordered (ranked) relative to each and every other individual, nor do we think most social scientists visualize such a model. Indeed, the notion that ranking is a "natural" and appropriate way of thinking about most variables in social and psychological science is simply nonsense.

Second, let us examine how a manifest, well-ordered scale is modified in order to arrive at an ordinal scale. In practice, this occurs by the allocation of unit distances between individuals, independently of how they might be distributed on a variable. For example, if on an interval scale 3 persons have scores of 1, 3, and 14, the procedure of converting the scale to a set of ordered ranks is to revalue them as 1, 2, and 3. Ordinal scaling, then, may be thought of as a form of scaling in which the interval information is lost. Presumably, because the ordinal scale does not have appropriate allocation of numbers relative to the interval scale, it cannot be handled with all the convenient properties that would otherwise accrue. Nunnally (1967: 18) states this without ambiguity: "With ordinal scales, none of the fundamental operations of algebra may be applied. In the use of descriptive statistics, it makes no sense to add, subtract, divide, or multiply ranks." Blalock (1979: 17) puts it as follows: "When we translate order relations into mathematical operations, we cannot, in general, use the usual operations of addition, subtraction, multiplication, and division."

Here we will make some immediately relevant comments, the first of which may be extremely disturbing to researchers who have been persuaded they are making no assumptions in using nonparametric statistics or distribution-free statistics. According to the statements by Nunnally and Blalock quoted above, computing a tau, a rank correlation statistic, or a Wilcoxon Test makes no sense at all if one thinks one is dealing with ordinal-level measurement. However, in computing these statistics, the ranks are added—and more. This means that least one important error is involved: the researcher has erroneously labeled the scale as ordinal. The other obvious error may be that the person is applying the operations of algebra where they should not be applied. If the operations are examined, it is clear that a form of interval measurement is being utilized that presumably distorts the true interval measurement, because the ordinary integer number system is usually applied directly to the so-called ranks. In particular, a unit distance is being placed between each of the elements or observations.

Let us illustrate the point simply. Assume that we have 3 individuals of different heights, and by observing them we can order them into ranks 1, 2, and 3. Furthermore say that 3 is greater than 2 is greater than 1. That is, we observe that 3 is some height greater than 2, which is some height greater than 1. However, information about distance either is not recorded or is discarded, and only the information concerning greater than and less than is retained. If anything is to be done with this set of ranks, numbers are allocated, and these numbers are in terms of unit differences between the ranks. The operations most people carry out, and all ordinal scales, should not be thought of as having only some intrinsic quality of greater than and less than. Often, in fact, they are simply very poorly devised interval scales which result from the method of collecting or analyzing the information. Does the fact that people are given rank order in height in any way vitiate the idea that height is to be measured in the population as an interval scale? Emphatically, no. Skeptics should try to compute ordinal statistics using the alphabet, which can also be ordered, but resists addition and subtraction. If greater than and less than are all that is involved, the substitution should be simple.

SOME OPERATIONS AND
THE MODEL OF MEASUREMENT

The issue of an appropriate model of measurement has been dealt with briefly, and now we can progress to some operations that may be seen to generate measures that, for various reasons, will be convenient. Suppose that we think of a latent variable X on which we wish to order individuals. This variable presumably can be tapped in a number of ways. But let us assume that the items will be answered as simple dichotomies—yes or no. Assume also that we can find dichotomies that measure this variable with reasonable reliability. In addition, for the sake of convenience, the variables are all chosen so that each divides the population exactly in half on the variable X. (It is clear that we have a special case with perfectly reliable data, none of which has ever been known, and that some other observations could be detailed here.)

Because the variables are not perfect measures of X, if we assume that each is answered independently of each other, then we could expect a certain progression of events. First, those persons who are exactly at the middle point of the population would have a hard time deciding whether they are yeses or nos. Thus, for that particular group, one might expect that yeses and nos might be given randomly. Indeed, the expectation would be that over a long series of questions, half would be answered yes and half would be answered no.

On the no side, the closer that one is to the decision point on the dimension—that is, the amount of the dimension which is measured that divides the population in half—the closer the individual would be in a long series of responses of giving half yeses and half nos, but one would expect more nos than from those who are exactly at the division point. It then follows immediately that the further a person is in the direction of no on the latent variable X, the higher the proportion of no answers he would be expected to give. Indeed, if it is assumed that individuals are distributed in some way along the latent X axis, a smooth curve that will unavoidably remind one of the normal curve will manifest itself. In fact, even if the questions were totally unreliable, the Central Limit Theorem guarantees that as the number of items increases, the distribution of their sum approaches normality. The point here is that if we deal with the assumption of a large number of dichotomous items assumed to be equally reliable, for a variable X, we expect a subsequent distribution that has characteristics approaching those of a normal curve. We use the weak language at the end of the sentence because it is appropriate to generalize this immediately. Suppose all the variables are not at exactly one-half the cutting point of the population—what would happen? The answer, relatively simply, is that whatever was operating in the original example would continue to operate, but because of the different cutting points and the possibility that quite different combinations of items might be included, the resulting curve could be spread, flattened, made irregular, or distorted in other ways. The distortion, however, is not likely to be enormous if there are many items and if the items do not deviate radically from dividing the population in half. And, if we approximate such normally distributed scores, it is difficult to argue that the assumptions for parametric analyses are not approximately satisfied. It is granted without question that the measures are not exactly isomorphic with the normal model, and therefore efficiency will be lost to the extent that there is a lack of correspondence. But, again, this may be thought of as a form of measurement error, and in no way suggests that ordinal level statistics are more appropriate to analyze the data.

Measurement error may be increased by using fewer items. For example, assuming 20 equally reliable items, the measure must be better than if there are 10. It follows that 5 items would be worse, 2 even worse, and 1 item would represent the worst possible condition. But what is absolutely clear is that what was true of 20 items, of 10 to a lesser extent, of 5 to a still lesser extent, must still be true, although to an even lesser extent, of the single item. It is still a measure corresponding to a model which would produce a normal distribution, but it is a degenerate case in which the measurement has become as poor as possible—the single item dichotomy. The underlying model has not changed; all that has occurred is that in developing the scale, the researcher has elected, either out of ignorance or by design, to use a single item, and therefore the score that is generated is less good'that it could have been.

It is now possible to generalize the above results. If trichotomies or fourfold response categories are utilized, using large numbers of items, the distribution generated by their sum will also be roughly normal. But because more precision is possible by using the additional cutting points, one can expect a more efficient (more reliable) score X than we would expect if using an equal number of dichotomies (assuming that question content is held constant and only the response categories are changed). The important point here is that a bell-shaped distribution will be generated by the arbitrarily scored dichotomies as well as with items with more ordered categories.

In building scales, it is rather a ridiculous question to ask why one should arbitrarily allocate the value 0 to no and 1 to yes, then raise the question of why one should not be able to allocate the values of 0 to no, 1 to maybe, and 2 to yes, on the grounds that ostensibly equal distances do not exist between the midpoints of those categories of response. The question is not whether or not there is error in such an allocation of numbers, but whether or not using that allocation contributes to the unreliability of the resulting measure. In other words, persons who had been following the common sense procedure should not have felt guilty about doing so.

INAPPROPRIATE CRITICISMS OF INTERVAL MEASURES

The problem of making an appropriate distinction between ordinal and interval measurement is commonplace, and unfortunately, among some scholars, it may be highly visible and influential in presentation. For example, Blalock (1979) apparently draws his distinction between ordinal and interval from Cohen and Nagel (1934). The latter writers, however, draw a distinction between what they call intensive and extensive qualities, and in the former designation they include temperature and density, while in the latter they include lengths, time intervals, areas, angles, electric current, and electric resistance. The distinction made by Cohen and Nagel, which is not discussed here, is the distinction between nonratio (less than ratio) and ratio measurement. Confusion of this distinction with definitions of ordinal and interval is visible in Blalock's thinking (1979: 18) when he states that "this means that it is possible to add or subtract scores in an analogous manner to the way we can add weights on a balance or subtract 6 inches from a board by sawing it in two [Reference to Cohen and Nagel]." The examples are the kind associated with ratio measurement, rather than interval measurement.

Blalock also perpetuates a common fallacious criticism of a common score encountered in social science; namely, the IQ score. This is done, however, in a manner that can only be said to reflect the lack of attention to the distinction he outlines between theoretical definitions and operational definitions. Accordingly, in one sentence (1979: 18) he states that "there are no such interval units of intelligence, authoritarianism, or prestige," but directly following that he refers to the IQ score as a specific operational measure: "Similarly, we can add the incomes of husband and wife, whereas it makes no sense to add their IQ scores." Note here that income happens to be a ratio scale, as implied, and IQ scores are an operational definition, presumably of intelligence. If it does not make sense to add IQ scores, does it make sense to add other properties of the husband and wife that can be measured at the ratio level? For example, does adding their weights make one larger, heavier person, presumably analogous to one larger total income? Does adding their ages make one older age? This simply is not the question that should be asked to determine whether weight, age, temperature, and IQ scores are interval measures.

Another point that Blalock (1979: 23) makes is interesting, but may be misleading. He states that "ideally, one should make use of a data-gathering technique that permits the lowest levels of measurement, if these are all the data will yield, rather than using techniques which force a scale on the data." The problem is raised by the word "ideally," as research never seems to be carried out under ideal conditions. More to the point, the data-gathering approach should maximize the amount of information that can be gathered given the limiting circumstances under which measurement will be carried out.

This, then, requires pragmatic decisions. For example, a method of paired comparisons may be discarded because of cumbersome procedures—procedures which, of course, may become virtually impossible if large numbers of comparisons are to be carried out. What is needed is some implicit notion of efficiency. The question is whether the more cumbersome procedure is worth the presumed increment of accuracy in ranking over the direct allocation of a set of ranks, balanced against other possible losses. However, choice of the paired comparison procedure, (or of rankings) would make sense only if more information could not be obtained by some other procedure, such as the allocation of scores implying some notion of distance (with error, of course).

SUMMARY

In our opinion, the following is worth stating: what makes an *appropriate* ordinal scale is not merely the assignment of ranks to observations. An ordinal scale is appropriate if we assume that only the properties of "greater than" and "less than" define an underlying latent construct. We doubt this is the case for most variables of interest to social scientists. As it seems to us that most constructs are conceptualized as continuous and can be thought of as reasonably distributed in the population using a bell-shaped curve as a model, we see no reason not to analyze the manifest data using parametric statistics, even though they are imperfect interval-level scales.

REFERENCES

BLALOCK, H. M., Jr. (1979) Social Statistics. New York: McGraw-Hill.
BOHRNSTEDT, G. W. and T. M. CARTER (1971) Robustness in regression analysis," pp. 118-146 in G. W. Bohrnstedt and E. F. Borgatta (eds.) Sociological Methodology. San Francisco: Jossey-Bass.
COHEN, M. R. and E. NAGEL (1934) An Introduction to Logic and Scientific Method. New York: Harcourt Brace Jovanovich.
GAITO, J. (1980) "Measurement scales and statistics: resurgence of an old misconception." Psych. Bull. 87: 564-567.
NUNNALLY, J. C. (1967) Psychometric Theory. New York: McGraw-Hill.
STEVENS, S. S. (1975) Psychophysics: Introduction to Its Perceptual, Neural and Social Prospects. New York: John Wiley.
——— [ed.] (1966) Handbook of Experimental Psychology. New York: John Wiley.

George W. Bohrnstedt is Professor of Sociology and director of the National Institute of Mental Health-sponsored Postdoctoral Training Program in Measurement at Indiana University—Bloomington. He is past co-editor (with E. F. Borgatta) of Sociological Methodology *and* Sociological Methods & Research. *He currently edits* Social Psychological Quarterly *(formerly Sociometry).*

Edgar F. Borgatta is on the faculty of the Department of Sociology and the Institute on Aging at the University of Washington. He is research director of the CASE Center for Gerontological Studies and training director of an interdisciplinary program on gerontological studies.

CHAPTER TWO

The Generalizability of Indirect Measures to Complex Situations
A Fundamental Dilemma

PAUL H. WILKEN
University of Virginia

H. M. BLALOCK, Jr.
University of Washington

The strategy of studying simple situations and then gradually moving to more complex phenomena once the principles in these simpler situations have become well understood is dependent upon the crucial assumption that measurement operations are basically similar across these situations, and that they do not depend in essential ways on the simplicity of the situation. In particular, indirect measurement procedures require auxiliary measurement theories that vary in simplicity and plausibility across situations, making it extremely difficult to move systematically from simple special cases to more complex ones because of the impossibility of

AUTHORS' NOTE: *Partial support for writing this chapter was provided by grants from the National Science Foundation (GS 37686 and SOC 72-05601 A01). We wish to thank Herbert L. Costner for his critical comments on an earlier version.*

unconfounding the auxiliary measurement theory from the substantive theory. If so, it becomes crucial to state this auxiliary theory explicitly and to work with alternative measures that can be linked to it (Blalock, 1968).

If we begin with the plausible assumption that it makes sense to follow the lead of the laboratory scientist who works toward the establishment of reasonably simple laws under conditions that approximate idealized models (such as that of the perfect vacuum), we must note that the *measurement* of the basic variables (distance, time, and mass) ordinarily does not itself depend upon this simplicity. Rather, the lack of complexity permits the testing and refinement of relatively simple laws. As simplifying assumptions are relaxed in favor of more "realistic" ones, such as those allowing for air resistance or friction, one can then modify the *equations* or laws by adding complexities allowing for these disturbances. For example, if a body is falling toward the earth, the path of its trajectory can be studied and modifications introduced to allow for friction produced by air currents. But the fundamental measurements of the basic variables are not altered.

If it becomes necessary to substitute one operation for another because the latter is not feasible in the more complex situation, one must rely on an auxiliary theory to make this substitution. These auxiliary theories are usually precise ones in the physical sciences, however, and sometimes they are based on strictly mathematical (logical) equivalences. For example, if it is impractical to measure the height of a mountain the same way we measure the height of a desk, the surveyor may calculate this height by relying on the properties of triangles, combined with simpler research operations such as the measurement of other distances and angles. The important point is that the auxiliary measurement theory is presumed to be well established empirically and also *invariant* across situations (Coleman, 1964).

Of course, there are occasions in the physical sciences in which operations must be shifted, and where the auxiliary measurement theories may be called into question. If, for example, one must "measure" the mass of a heavenly body by observing its trajectory through space, one may experience the same confounding of law with measurement that we shall argue occurs frequently in the social sciences. If one accepts Newton's laws of motion as valid, and if one is aware of the presence of a specific number of planetary bodies and is willing to assume the essential isolation of the solar system from others, one may indeed infer the mass of a given planet.

If the laws themselves are questioned, however, as occurred historically with the rise of Einstein's Special and General Theories of Relativity, then any measurement theory based on these laws may become inappropriate under certain circumstances. Indeed, the paradox that a body's "mass," as measured in this way, becomes indefinitely large as the body's velocity relative to the observer's approaches the speed of light, can be interpreted as a confounding of a theoretical law with a measurement theory based on it. Clearly, our intuitive conception of mass is violated by the notion that mass changes as velocity relative to the observer changes. If we wish to retain a conception of "mass" that is invariant with respect to relative velocities, then our operations for measuring mass must reflect this fact in some way. If these operations are not linked with a theory, we shall have no deductive or systematic way of explaining what is going on. That is, if *both* the operations and the situations being compared are different, we will not be able to decide how to modify the substantive law in question, since the measurement and substantive theories will be hopelessly confounded.

Measurement operations may have to differ from situation to situation, and the substantive laws may also differ. But it does *not* follow that if we keep the operations nearly identical we can then establish differences in the laws. This can be done *only if* the auxiliary measurement theory also remains identical. For example, the same research operations conducted in several different societies or small groups may have different relationships with the theoretical constructs in these different settings. An I.Q. test identically administered to whites and blacks may give different results, either because the true intelligence levels are different or because it is a better measure of intelligence for one group than the other. Voting behavior may be a better indicator of political participation in one society than in another.

Przeworski and Teune (1970) refer to this phenomenon as "system interference." We prefer to think in terms of differential measurement error. But, regardless of the terminology used, the basic idea is that the equation linking the "true" and measured variables is not a constant across all situations. If so, we cannot guard against this kind of difficulty by blindly using the same measurement operations in all contexts.

Many of our measurement procedures are highly indirect and therefore require complex auxiliary theories. Ideally, such theories should be explicitly stated, so that hidden assumptions are brought out into the open. In very simple situations, however, many of these assumptions are sufficiently plausible so that if they remain implicit this creates no special difficulties. In these instances, the explicit portions of the theories can remain much simpler than in the case of more complex situations. Ideally, it is desirable to use the same auxiliary measurement theory in different settings so that particular simplifications can be treated as special cases of a more general theory. To formulate such a general theory, however, we will probably need to employ several alternative measurement procedures that require different sets of auxiliary assumptions. Undoubtedly, one procedure will be preferable in a given setting, whereas a second will be more realistic for other situations. If so, it will obviously be advantageous to use several distinct kinds of measurement procedures *simultaneously* in different settings.

In the illustrations that follow, we shall focus on measurement problems that involve the interrelationship between certain types of behaviors and postulated internal states. We must emphasize, however, that the fundamental issues involved are not peculiar to social psychological research in general, or experimental studies in particular. If anything, the measurement of macrolevel concepts presents even greater problems, if only because it seems more difficult to develop plausible causal models of measurement errors in the case of highly aggregated data.

In the next section, we turn to the measurement and classification of behaviors, a problem that appears to be much more complex than one might expect in the case of supposedly "directly observed" phenomena. Our concern will be with those types of behaviors that are defined in terms of presumed motives or apparent consequences (Blalock, 1979). In the following section, we focus on the measurement of two important kinds of internal states, utilities and subjective probabilities.

BEHAVIORS DEFINED IN TERMS
OF INTERNAL STATES

All of the measurement problems that will be discussed in this and the following section involve a basic kind of causal model that contains a set of stimuli or environmental impacts (S_i), another set of postulated internal states (I_j), and a third set of responses (R_k). If the stimuli, internal states, and responses could be connected in simple one-to-one relationships, we would encounter no special difficulties even in instances where certain of the variables—commonly the I_j— could not be directly measured. However, as is clearly recognized, the models interrelating these three kinds of variables will ordinarily be much more complex and of the type illustrated by the model of Figure 1. Even ignoring possible feedbacks from behaviors to stimuli or internal states, we note a number of complexities, including (a) possible intercorrelations among stimuli; (b) the potential linkage of each stimulus with each internal state; (c) possible causal connections among the internal states; and (d) multiple links between internal states and behaviors. Of course, we do not expect all of these complexities to occur in every instance.

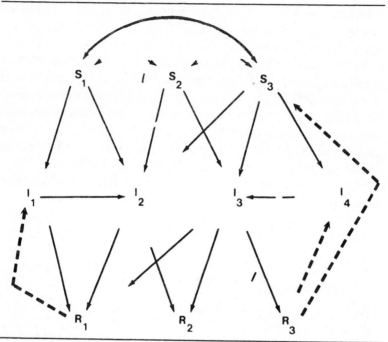

Figure 1

Perhaps the most familiar kind of measurement problem is that of inferring internal states on the basis of behavioral responses. Often these responses are of no theoretical interest in their own right, in which case we seldom bother to give them behavioral labels (other than the generic term "response"). Thus, if factor analysis is used to infer attitudes or abilities on the basis of response patterns, the conceptual labels are attached to the internal states, rather than the behaviors.

In the present section our concern will be with the labeling and aggregation of behaviors in order to obtain behavioral measures. Since the range of human behaviors is extremely great, however, interests of parsimony require that they be grouped in a relatively small number of ways and labeled as instances of the same kinds of behaviors. Thus, there are many "forms" of aggression. According to what rationale should all of these very dissimilar acts be grouped together under the single label of aggression, and what instructions would a social scientist give an observer who is attempting to record instances of aggression in several different kinds of groups? If aggression has been defined theoretically as "behavior the purpose of which is to injure another party," or as "behavior that generally results in the injury of another party," then there must be an auxiliary (causal) theory linking these and other specific acts to either "purpose" or "results."

If the study involves a very simple situation, such as the observation of young children in a contrived laboratory experiment, this auxiliary theory may also be rather simple. For instance, if we assume that children know that kicking, biting, scratching, or slapping another person causes pain, and if we also assume away *other* possible motivations for slapping another person, then the process of going from the theoretical definition of aggression, as involving intent to injure, to a listing of aggressive acts is relatively simple.

If we wish to extend the study into one involving a much longer duration, sophisticated adults, and a complex situation in which injury may be accomplished by much more subtle means, the operations, too, must change to admit this complexity. Linking acts to motives in a one-one fashion also becomes more problematic. We recognize this clearly when we admit to exceptions and try to identify these exceptions in terms of slight differences in behavior. For example, a shooting that appears to have been an accident is not considered aggression. If a supervisor gives a subordinate a poor rating, we do not know whether or not injury was intended, but we might infer this if the act were accompanied by hostile remarks.

In other examples, we find that manifestly similar behaviors are distinguished theoretically by tacking on a qualifying phrase containing a reference to some internal state. "Avoidance" behavior usually involves movement away from another actor, but it also often includes the connotation that the movement is intended to reduce contact. If we see a white resident moving away from an area, and if we say that he or she is "avoiding" contact with blacks, we imply that the motivation is to reduce these contacts. Actually, the reasons for the move may be quite different, but observation of the behavior alone could not uncover this fact. Therefore, we might use the term "movement away from" to refer to a larger class of behaviors, with "avoidance" being a subclass of these behaviors that also involves a desire to reduce contacts. But if we did so, then the research operations for distinguishing "avoidance" behavior would require something over and above those needed to class the behavior as "movement away from." Furthermore, they would have to allow for the possibility that an actor may also avoid someone by a different means, such as erecting barriers against that person.

We encounter a similar difficulty in attempts to define and measure "discrimination" as a behavioral process. The theoretical notion of discrimination typically involves two ideas: There is some kind of differential treatment of individuals, and this treatment is "because of" or "based on" race, sex, or some other characteristic of the individual that is "irrelevant" to the decision involved. This kind of judgment requires a complex auxiliary theory that usually must allow for correlations between relevant and irrelevant criteria. For instance, if whites tend to score higher than blacks on a screening exam, does this automatically mean that the screening exam is ipso facto discriminatory? This would imply that the actor is using this test primarily in order to discriminate, rather than as a relevant criterion for making the judgment. We would either need to get inside that actor's head or else infer the motivation on other grounds, perhaps through a series of replications involving many applicants. We would then have to be assured that the applicants have been equated on all relevant characteristics. Clearly, this would require a theory varying in its complexity according to the nature of the situation being studied.

These few illustrations exemplify the problem, but they cannot indicate how common it is, for a rather obvious reason. We often fail to specify our concepts with sufficient clarity so that a reader can tell whether or not some internal state is essential to the definition, or which behaviors should be grouped together *even if complete knowledge of the relevant internal states is at hand.* That is, a distinction such as the one between "avoidance" and "movement away from" may not have been made at all. The investigator is then left with a fundamental ambiguity concerning the exact class of behaviors to be included, even under ideal conditions. Furthermore, if two researchers use different implicit definitions, it will be difficult, even with perfect knowledge of the motivational structures of the actors, to reconstruct their respective auxiliary measurement theories. Their research operations may be identical, but their *interpretations* may differ. One social scientist may infer that a "retreat" to the white suburbs is primarily due to a wish to avoid blacks, whereas the second may stop with the observation that increasing segregation is occurring.[1]

MEASUREMENT OF UTILITIES AND SUBJECTIVE PROBABILITIES

The problems involved in retaining the same auxiliary theory while moving to more complex situations can be illustrated by two variables for which the problems accompanying indirect measurement have been well identified. These are utilities, or subjective values, and subjective probabilities, both of which involve the measurement of an internal state by means of a behavioral indicator. Typically, this indicator has been choices between gambles and events that occur with certainty.

Although most sociologists are not very familiar with the procedures for measuring these two variables, those procedures are quite similar to attitude measurement techniques, which also use behavioral indicators of internal states, often consisting of choices between fixed alternatives as in a Likert scale. Furthermore, the two concepts are virtually synonymous with more common sociological concepts. Utility may be equated with subjective value (Siegel, et al., 1964), which occupies an important place in sociological theories, such as equity or status value theory. Likewise, sociologists often make use of the concept of expectations, which can be translated into subjective probabilities. Thus, attempts to measure subjective values and expectations should confront problems similar to those encountered in measuring utilities and subjective probabilities.

We will describe the auxiliary theories for the measurement of utilities and subjective probabilities in terms of the assumptions that must be met in the simplest choice situations, and then note the complications likely to appear in more complex situations. Since these assumptions become difficult to meet as complexity increases, the use of alternative measurement procedures with less stringent auxiliary theories appears a necessity, and we make some suggestions in that regard.

UTILITIES

Utilities generally have been measured by choices between elementary behaviors under tightly controlled laboratory conditions. The justification for this procedure has been that individuals are unable to provide meaningful estimates of utility if asked questions such as, "How much money will make you twice as happy as $20"? This indirect measurement procedure involves a number of implicit assumptions, however, even in very simple choice situations.

The most general assumption is that the model of choice behavior on which the procedure is based is valid. One of the most widely used choice models has been the subjective expected utility model, according to which the subjective expected utility (SEU) of a behavioral alternative equals the sum of the products of the subjective probabilities of the outcomes. This model can be represented as follows for the general case:

$$SEU = \sum_{i=1}^{k} p_i U_i \qquad [1]$$

In the simplest case, involving two mutually exclusive outcomes, and in which it can be assumed that the subjective probability of one outcome, p_2, equals $(1 - p_1)$, the equation becomes

$$SEU = p_1 U_1 + (1 - p_1) U_2 \qquad [2]$$

Since this equation involves three unknowns, it is necessary to assign values to some of them in order to estimate subjective expected utility. In the original Mosteller and Nogee design (1951), this was accomplished by giving subjects a series of choices between playing a gamble and receiving a specific amount of money with certainty. Indifference between playing the gamble and receiving the money was assumed to indicate that the subjective expected utilities of the two choices were equal. And since the probability of receiving the money without playing the gamble was assumed to equal one, it was possible to create equations of the form

$$U_3 = p_1 U_1 + (1 - p_1) U_2 \qquad [3]$$

Values then were assigned to the probability terms and two of the utility terms, leaving only one utility term to be estimated. The utility functions derived from numerous choices of this type, involving varying probabilities and amounts of money, were then used to predict choices in new situations.

We will use the subjective expected utility model as the basis for our analysis of the assumptions required for the measurement of utilities, because it generally is considered more realistic than other models of choice behavior (Coombs, et al., 1967).[2]

Maximization. The first major assumption required by this model is that subjects maximize their subjective expected utilities. This assumption, which is necessary whether one uses the Mosteller-Nogee approach or a derivative of it and whether subjects are given choices between gambles and events occurring with certainty or between gambles, very likely is met in quite simple situations, but in more complex situations it becomes tenuous. Other decision strategies, such as satisficing, the choice of an alternative offering satisfactory subjective expected utility (Simon, 1957), may be used. In choices involving outcomes affecting others, it is probable that their perceived utilities will be taken into account. One may simultaneously attempt to maximize own and minimize other's utilities, or one may alternate maximizing own and other's utilities.[3] Thus, the assumption of maximization is questionable in more complex choice situations.

Equality of objective and subjective probabilities. The values typically assigned to the unknown probability terms in the subjective expected utility equation have been the objective probabilities structured into the measurement situation by the investigator, a practice that requires the assumption that these in fact equal the subjects' subjective probabilities. Not only does this contradict the major reason for using subjective probabilities in a choice model, but there also is substantial experimental evidence that people do not equate the two types of probability (Wyer and Goldberg, 1970; Lee, 1971; Coombs et al., 1970; Luce and Suppes, 1965). Furthermore, in more complex real-world situations objective probabilities often will have little meaning, so that one will be unable even to "guesstimate" them. Thus, this assumption appears shaky in elementary choice situations and indefensible in more complex ones.

Independence of utilities and subjective probabilities. A third assumption is that utilities and subjective probabilities are independent determinants of subjective expected utility. If they are not independent, then outcomes will vary in utility, depending on the subjective probabilities associated with them, and utility estimates will be influenced by the specific probabilities included in the measurement procedure. This has proven to be a difficult assumption, even in elementary choice situations. Two types of nonindependence have been detected (Edwards, 1962): Outcomes with high utilities have been assigned subjective probabilities higher than their objective probabilities (what might be called "wishful thinking"), and utilities for a given outcome have been higher when its subjective probability is relatively low, suggesting a possible effect of perceived scarcity of outcomes on utilities.

Equal weights of utilities and subjective probabilities. The assumption that all of the terms in the equation have equal weights is perhaps less obvious than some of the preceding assumptions. For gambles this assumption is that the probabilities of winning and of losing are weighted equally, and for all alternatives it is that positive and negative utilities have equal weights. There is evidence, however, that subjects' winning and losing probabilities are not weighted equally (Slovic and Lichtenstein, 1968), so it is likely that this assumption is not tenable in complex choice situations.[4]

Knowledge of signs. With the procedure for measuring utilities that we are describing, it also is necessary to determine whether the unknowns in the equation should be given positive or negative values. This probably is not difficult for monetary outcomes, since it may be assumed that gains have positive utility and losses negative utility. But in situations in which nonmonetary outcomes are involved, it may not always be possible to make such an a priori judgment.

Unidimensionality of outcomes. The measurement procedure also presumes that outcomes have only one dimension. In other words, there is only one source of utility associated with each outcome. For instance, the utility associated with the outcome "win $x" is assumed to be the utility of $x. What this overlooks is that subjects also may regard winning as a source of utility, so that an estimate of the utility of "winning $x" will include both the utility of winning and the utility of $x. This, of course, will yield a biased estimate of either utility.

This assumption appears particularly problematic in more complex situations, especially those involving outcomes having both *consummatory* and *status* value.[5] Outcomes will be multidimensional if they are perceived to offer both types of subjective value.[6] Furthermore, it should not be assumed that both types will have the same sign for a given outcome.[7] Recipients of outcomes may obtain positive consummatory value from them, but also may simultaneously perceive that they have *negative* status value if they do not meet the standards of their peers.

No missing outcomes. Not only may there be sources of utility associated with a given outcome that are unknown to the investigator, but there also may be additional outcomes of which he or she is unaware. Even in the elementary situation involving a gamble, subjects may anticipate outcomes in addition to "winning $x" and "losing $y"—for example, that the investigator will approve or disapprove of their choices.[8]

Multiple outcomes, which may occur either simultaneously or sequentially, are even more probable in more complex situations. One who assists another may simultaneously receive approval from him or her and disapproval from someone he or she has not assisted. Or immediate approval from the recipient may be accompanied with an anticipation of a future reciprocal act of assistance. In either case, the utility of the additional outcome will have to be included in the choice model or the estimate of utility for the other outcome will be biased. This also means, of course, that the model will contain more unknowns.

Therefore the possibility of multiple multidimensional outcomes plays an important role in the problem of the comparability of "similar events" discussed earlier. Events or outcomes can be assumed to be similar only if they and their dimensions are identical in different situations.

Constancy. A last assumption is that utilities remain constant for some amount of time. If they change during the measurement process, then subjects' choices will be intransitive and/or inconsistent, and if they change between their measurement and their use to predict behavior, then the measurement procedure hardly is satisfactory.

This assumption is hard to sustain if one makes the quite reasonable assumption that utilities are affected by deprivation and satiation.[9] Since levels of deprivation and satiation will change over time as the result of the outcomes one does or does not experience, it appears more realistic to assume that utilities will change than that they will remain constant over an extended time period.

Conclusions. We have noted a few possible modifications of the subjective expected utility model to reflect the complications we have described, and it is conceivable that more of these could be incorporated in the model if their precise influence were known.[10] But we also have seen that even relatively simple assumptions are quickly rendered suspect as one moves to even slightly more complex choice situations. Hence, a procedure for measuring utilities that is applicable to situations of varying complexity is necessary.

Several researchers have attempted to measure utilities more directly by magnitude estimation procedures, for example, that use both verbal and written responses (Galanter, 1962; Hamblin, 1971; Shinn, 1971). These techniques are more direct than the technique we have described, and they involve a much less complex auxiliary theory, basically consisting of the assumption that subjects are able to estimate utilities.[11]

It would be particularly beneficial if this procedure and the effect-indicator approach both were used to measure utilities in the elementary situations we have described. Systematic comparison of the results obtained from the two procedures would provide insights regarding their potential in more complex situations. In light of our discussion, however, it appears that the more direct magnitude estimation procedures will prove preferable by default in more complex choice situations.

SUBJECTIVE PROBABILITIES

Researchers have been more willing to use relatively direct methodologies, like magnitude estimation, to measure subjective probabilities than utilities, no doubt because subjective probabilities can be assumed to have limits of zero and one and thus be less likely to have serious measurement errors. Measuring them indirectly from choices involves basically the same procedure we have described for the measurement of utilities, except of course that they constitute the unknowns in the equations of the choice model. Thus, many of the assumptions we have described, including the validity of the choice model itself, maximization, the independence and the equal weighting of utilities and subjective probabilities, and their constancy over a reasonable period of time apply also to them.

Several of the assumptions we have described must be modified somewhat for the measurement of subjective probabilities, however. For instance, the assumption of equal objective and subjective probabilities becomes the assumption of equal objective and subjective values. Despite this change, the problem of the disparity between objective and subjective variables discussed earlier still exists. Second, the knowledge of signs assumption does not apply directly, but has an analogue in the reasonable assumption that all nonzero subjective probabilities are positive. Third, the assumption of unidimensionality of outcomes can be dropped, since the subjective probability of an outcome presumably will be the same whether it is unidimensional or multidimensional.

The assumption of no missing outcomes is crucial for the measurement of subjective probabilities, though. If subjects perceive outcomes in addition to those controlled by the investigator, then each of these outcomes will require a subjective probability estimate, just as each requires a utility estimate. The example cited above of the subject's anticipating both winning or losing the gamble and receiving approval or disapproval from the investigator would require four different subjective probabilities for the four possible combinations of outcomes.

Situations become still more complex if one allows for the possibility that outcomes will be dependent on one another, in which case it would be necessary to use *conditional* probabilities in the choice model. For example, if one anticipates that giving another assistance will result in approval from the recipient and that the recipient's action will influence whether a nonrecipient gives approval or disapproval, then *six* subjective probabilities must be included in the model: of recipient's approval, recipient's disapproval, nonrecipient's approval given recipient's approval, nonrecipient's approval given recipient's disapproval, nonrecipient's disapproval given recipient's approval, and nonrecipient's disapproval given recipient's disapproval.[12] With this many unknowns it will be impossible to obtain subjective probability estimates unless one makes radical use of an assumption that is implicit in elementary choice situations.

Summation to a constant. We noted previously that the assumption, $P_2 = (1 - p_1)$, was a basic simplification in the subjective expected utility model. This assumption reflects the more basic assumption that the subjective probabilities of exhaustive mutually exclusive events sum to a constant, usually one. In simple choice situations, involving outcomes that obviously are exhaustive and mutually exclusive, this appears a reasonable assumption.[13] But in situations that are more complex, involving outcomes that are neither mutually exclusive nor exhaustive, it becomes much more difficult to meet. In the above case with six subjective probabilities, for example, it is possible to reduce the number of unknowns by one-half by assuming that the subjective probabilities of exhaustive mutually exclusive events sum to one. The only alternative for further reducing the number of unknowns is to set them equal to zero or one, or to each other.

Chance outcomes. A second assumption, perhaps applicable only to the measurement of subjective probabilities, is that the outcomes included in the measurement procedure are not under the subjects' influence.[14] The outcome, receiving $x for certain, is under the investigator's control, for example, and the outcome of a gamble is the result of chance factors. In more complex real-world situations, however, subjective probability estimates will in many cases be based on perceived capacity to influence outcomes. Thus, the generalizability of this procedure to situations involving nonchance outcomes obviously is questionable, a conclusion reinforced by experimental evidence of differences in subjective probability estimates in chance and nonchance situations (Howell, 1971; Masterson, 1973).

Conclusion. The possibility of retaining an auxiliary theory as one moves from simple to complex choice situations appears just as remote for subjective probabilities as for utilities. It may be possible to incorporate some of the complications in the choice model, as we suggested in regard to utilities, but at present there is not sufficient evidence to indicate exactly how to do so. Therefore a more direct procedure of measurement, such as magnitude estimation, appears essential in relatively complex situations. As with utility measurement, it and the effect-indicator methodology should be used together in elementary choice situations to provide information regarding their relative validity and generalizability.

IMPLICATIONS

In the previous section we have deliberately focused in some detail on two measurement problems for which there are explicit auxiliary theories. These auxiliary theories had to be kept very simple to reduce the number of unknowns. The implied dilemma is that of either forcing unrealistic assumptions on the theory to obtain some sort of measure or of limiting one's attention to situations that are simple enough to yield accurate indirect measures. If one follows the first alternative, biases in the measurement procedure can almost certainly be expected. But if one follows the second, measurement accuracy is achieved at the expense of generalizability. In effect, then, a procedure that may work very well in extremely simple situations, for which a simple auxiliary theory is justified, may be much less satisfactory than alternative procedures whenever the measurement theory must be modified to handle difficulties encountered in more complex situations.

It appears much more difficult than is sometimes realized to provide theoretical definitions of behaviors that are not dependent on at least one of the following: (1) certain internal states, (2) causal assumptions of one kind or another, or (3) the notion of replications under "similar" circumstances (Blalock, 1979). No matter which of these three alternatives one uses, certain untested assumptions will be required to link the construct with an operational procedure. The complexity and plausibility of these assumptions will vary from situation to situation, however. This must be recognized if we are to arrive at definitions that are sufficiently broad to make the concepts theoretically useful. Therefore, if we are ever to resolve the basic problem, we must first develop the habit of attempting to state these assumptions as explicitly as possible.

In connection with the distinction between internal states and "objective" behaviors, it would seem wise to rely whenever possible on theoretical definitions that do not confound the two. This implies, for example, that it would be preferable to use the concept "withdrawal," meaning "moving away from," rather than "avoidance," as defined in terms of the actor's intent. But, if so, it then becomes necessary to include in the *substantive* theory a separate set of variables referring to various internal states involving different motivations for "withdrawal" behaviors, as well as additional behaviors that may be alternative means of achieving the same objective. This makes the substantive theory much more complex than one that merely *defines* avoidance behavior as involving movements away from other persons in order to reduce contact.

We note a tradeoff between the relative complexities of the substantive and auxiliary measurement theories. Also, we see that the goals of achieving relatively simple measurement theories, on the one hand, and generalizability, on the other, may be incompatible. In view of the extremely wide variety of possible behaviors and contexts, generalizability seems absolutely essential. This may turn out to imply that measurement theories will have to be highly tentative and filled with untested assumptions. But if they are, then the tests we can make of these theories will have to be very weak ones indeed.

Our primary suggestion is that we take advantage of the fact that there will usually be several ways in which a given variable may be measured. If one of these seems more "valid" (i.e., less subject to distortions produced by nonrandom measurement errors) than the others, but also is more dependent upon the simplicity of the situation, then we would suggest the use of *both* procedures in the same piece of research. The usual practice in social psychological and sociological research seems to be to use what is deemed to be the best *single* measure for the purpose at hand, without regard to its general applicability. But if several procedures are used, their relationship can be examined. Furthermore, it becomes possible to study the *conditions* under which they yield similar or different results.

If one is willing to assume that the more valid but less generalizable procedure can be used as a criterion for assessing the validity of the second measure, it then becomes possible to develop a theory through which biases in the second measure may be corrected. In brief, the suggestion is to use both kinds of measures in simple settings, so that the knowledge gained can be utilized in more complex situations in which only the less "valid" measure can be employed. In the example of utility measurement, this would imply that in simple situations subjects should also be asked directly about their utilities, since in more complex situations this latter method may be the only means by which utilities can be estimated.

This process requires that the assumptions made in going from a conceptual definition to a set of research operations be made explicit in the form of an auxiliary measurement theory. The common practice is to provide a theoretical discussion of a concept, and perhaps an explicit definition, and then merely to announce by fiat that certain research procedures are being used to measure the variable in a particular context. This makes replication extremely difficult unless *precisely* the same research procedures can be followed. This kind of "exact" replication is highly desirable (Duncan, 1969), but it neglects the problem of generalizability. In short, unless the measurement theory is made explicit—implying, of course, that the measurement processes are embedded in a larger theoretical framework—substantive differences and measurement noncomparability will be hopelessly confounded.

These remarks imply certain desiderata with respect to journal reporting procedures. They suggest the need for more space devoted to results using alternative measurement procedures, for the explicit statement of theoretical definitions and the assumptions needed to link these to the research operations, and for more attention to the implications of these definitions for generalization to more complex situations. In short, they imply the need for special efforts to go beyond the particular data and setting at hand. These suggestions are obvious ones, but unfortunately they run counter to the practical factors that limit journal space and readers' patience. However, unless we keep these problems in mind, practical expediencies—which may be functional for disseminating knowledge about the largest number of *individual* pieces of research—will work against the systematic cumulation of knowledge.

NOTES

1. Before concluding this section, we should take note of a theoretical device that avoids reference to postulated internal states, instead relying on the notion of replication of "similar events." Let us consider the notion of "rewarding behavior," which may be defined either in terms of behavior that satisfies some goal (such as reducing hunger) or that can be identified by watching an actor behave in such a fashion that he or she receives the "reward" a high proportion of the time "under similar circumstances." The latter kind of definition, which is common in the behavior modification literature, avoids any reference to internal states. But it requires replications that often do not occur outside the laboratory setting. More correctly stated, the naturally occurring replications are not well controlled, so that they are much less similar than in manipulated settings. In this case, one has to make a series of assumptions about "similarities," presumably as they are perceived or experienced by the actor. As one moves from rather simple situations to more complex ones, these auxiliary assumptions about similar events also must become more complex and much less plausible. We shall note below a comparable problem with variations in outcomes perceived by investigators and subjects.

2. We already have called attention to two assumptions: (a) $P_2 = (1 - p_1)$; (b) indifference between alternatives indicates equality of their subjective expected utilities. We will discuss the former in the context of the measurement of subjective probabilities. The latter is specific to the Mosteller-Nogee technique and we therefore do not discuss it here.

3. Meeker (1971) has suggested several decision strategies for dyadic situations, including reciprocity, equity, competition, and altruism.

4. These weights could be applied to the probability terms as follows, where W_1 represents the winning, and W_2 the losing, weight:

$$SEU = W_1 \, p_1 \, (U_1) + W_2 \, (1 - P_1) \, (U_2)$$

5. This distinction, emphasized in the literature on equity and distributive justice by the exchange and status value theorists respectively (Cook, 1975), is very likely relevant to a variety of more complex situations.

6. The total utility, U_i, of a multidimensional outcome can be represented as a function of component utilities, as follows:

$$U_i = u_{i1} + u_{i2} + u_{i3} + \ldots + u_{ik}$$

where the u_{ij} represent the amount of utility derived from the ith outcome on the jth dimension and the dimensions represent the different sources of utility.

7. Thus, this assumption may become confounded with the knowledge of signs assumption discussed above.

8. Consequently in this situation there would be four possible combinations of outcomes: winning and approval, winning and disapproval, losing and approval, losing and disapproval.

9. The assumption of decreasing marginal utility incorporates the effects of satiation on utilities.

10. Attempts to take these complicating factors into account have involved including terms in choice models representing utilities for gambling (Luce and Suppes, 1965; Tversky, 1967a), choice variability (Siegel, 1959), equity (Ofshe and Ofshe, 1970), and actors' preferences for the variances rather than the values of gambles (Lee, 1971; Coombs and Pruitt, 1960).

11. The work of S. S. Stevens (1959, 1966) and his associates has provided support for this assumption. It also is noteworthy that on the basis of this measurement approach Hamblin (1971, 1974) has claimed that the utility of money is a power function of its objective value. Tversky (1967b) has come to the same conclusion via a completely different route—additive conjoint measurement based on gambles—which is a distant relative of the effect-indicator approach we have described.

12. It would be more accurate to allow three possible responses for the recipient and the nonrecipient—approval, disapproval, and indifference—but this would increase the number of subjective probabilities to twelve!

13. This assumption and the assumption that there is no utility for gambling are incompatible in the subjective expected utility model, according to Tversky (1967a).

14. We do not discuss here the possibility that utilities are affected by the manner in which an outcome is obtained.

REFERENCES

BLALOCK, H. M. (1979) "Measurement and conceptualization problems: the major obstacle to interpreting theory and research." Amer. Soc. Rev. 44 (December): 881-894.

———(1968) "The measurement problem: a gap between the languages of theory and research," Chapter 1 in H. M. Blalock and A. B. Blalock (eds.) Methodology in Social Research. New York: McGraw-Hill.

WILKEN, BLALOCK 61

COLEMAN, J. S. (1964) Introduction to Mathematical Sociology. New York: Free Press.

COOK, K. S. (1975) "Expectations, evaluations, and equity." Amer. Soc. Rev. 40 (June): 372-388.

COOMBS, C. H. and D. G. PRUITT (1960) "Components of risk in decision-making: probability and variance preferences." J. of Experimental Psychology 60 (November): 265-277.

COOMBS, C. H., T. G. BEZEMBINDER, and F. M. GOODE (1967) "Testing expectation theories of decision making without measuring utility or subjective probability." J. of Mathematical Psychology, 4 (February): 72-103.

COOMBS, C. H., R. DAWES, and A. TVERSKY (1970) Mathematical Psychology. Englewood Cliffs, NJ: Prentice-Hall.

DUNCAN, O. D. (1969) "Toward social reporting: next steps." New York: Russell Sage.

EDWARDS, W. (1962) "Utility, subjective probability, their interaction, and variance preferences." J. of Conflict Resolution 6 (March): 42-51.

GALANTER, E. (1962) "The direct measurement of utility and subjective probability." Amer. J. of Psychology, 75 (June): 208-220.

HAMBLIN, R. L. (1974) "Social attitudes: magnitude measurement and theory," Chapter 3 in H. M. Blalock (ed.) Measurement in the Social Sciences. Chicago: AVC.

———(1971) "Ratio measurement for the social sciences." Social Forces 50 (December): 191-206.

HOWELL, W. (1971) "Uncertainty from internal and external sources: a clear case of overconfidence." J. of Experimental Psychology 89 (August): 240-243.

LEE, W. (1971) Decision Theory and Human Behavior. New York: John Wiley.

LUCE, R. D. and P. SUPPES (1965) "Preference, utility, and subjective probability," Chapter 19 in R. D. Luce et al. (eds.) Handbook of Mathematical Psychology, Volume 3. New York: John Wiley.

MASTERSON, J. H. (1973) "Expectancy changes with skill-determined and chance-determined outcomes." J. of Personality and Social Psychology 27 (September): 396-404.

MEEKER, B. F. (1971) "Decisions and exchange." Amer. Soc. Rev. 36 (June): 485-495.

MERTON, R. P. (1957) Social Theory and Social Structure. New York: Free Press.

MOSTELLER, F. and P. NOGEE (1951) "An experimental measurement of utility." J. of Pol. Economy 59 (October): 371-404.

OFSHE, L. and R. OFSHE (1970) Utility and Choice in Social Interaction. Englewood Cliffs, NJ: Prentice-Hall.

PRZEWORSKI, A. and H. TEUNE (1970) The Logic of Comparative Social Inquiry. New York: John Wiley.

SHINN, A. M., Jr. (1971) "Measuring the utility of housing: demonstrating a methodological approach." Social Sci. Q. 52 (June): 88-102.

SIEGEL, S. (1959) "Theoretical models of choice and strategy behavior: stable state behavior in the two-choice uncertain outcome situation." Psychometrika 24, 4: 303-316.

———A. E. SIEGEL, and J. M. ANDREWS (1964) Choice, Strategy, and Utility. New York: McGraw-Hill.

SIMON, H. (1957) Models of Man. New York: John Wiley.

SLOVIC, P. and S. LICHTENSTEIN (1968) "Relative importance of probabilities and payoffs in risk taking." J. of Experimental Psychology Monograph 78 (November): 1-18.

STEVENS, S. S. (1966) "A metric for the social consensus." Science 151 (February 4): 530-541.

_____(1959) "Measurement, psychophysics, and utility," Chapter 2 in C. W. Churchman and P. Ratoosh (eds.) Measurement: Definitions and Theories. New York: John Wiley.

TVERSKY, A. (1967a) "Additivity, utility, and subjective probability." J. of Mathematical Psychology 4 (June): 175-201.

_____(1967b) "Utility theory and additivity analysis of risky choices." J. of Experimental Psychology 75, 1: 27-36.

WYER, R. S., Jr., and L. GOLDBERG (1970) "A probabilistic analysis of the relationship between beliefs and attitudes." Psych. Rev. 77, 2: 100-120.

Paul H. Wilken currently is Assistant Professor of Sociology at the University of Virginia, having received his Ph.D. from the University of North Carolina at Chapel Hill. He is author of Entrepreneurship: A Comparative and Historical Study, and coauthor (with H. M. Blalock, Jr.) of Intergroup Processes: A Micro-Macro Perspective.

H. M. Blalock, Jr., is Professor of Sociology and Statistics at the University of Washington, Seattle. His interests are in conceptualization and measurement problems in sociology and in theoretical work in the area of social power and conflict.

PART II

Techniques for Estimating Measurement Models

CHAPTER THREE

Analyzing Models with Unobserved Variables
Analysis of Covariance Structures

EDWARD G. CARMINES
JOHN P. McIVER
Indiana University

Broadly speaking, there are two basic types of inferences that are relevant in the social sciences. The first is structural in nature; it focuses on the causal relationships among unobserved variables. The key question with respect to this inference is: Do changes in X produce changes in Y? To take a popular political example, does higher socioeconomic status produce more conservative political views? In order to make strong causal inferences, it is necessary to establish time precedence, functional relatedness, and nonspuriousness between cause and effect variables.

The second type of inference is concerned with measurement. While this type has received less attention from methodologists, it is no less central to social science research. Many of the most important variables in the social sciences

AUTHORS' NOTE: *We wish to express our deep appreciation to the Workshop in Political Theory and Policy Analysis, Indiana University, and to Marsha Porter and Patty Zielinski of its secretarial staff for the prepara-*

cannot be directly observed. As a consequence, they can only be measured indirectly through the use of empirical (or measured) indicators that represent the unmeasured variables (or constructs). The fundamental question with regard to measurement inferences is how validly and reliably these indicators represent the unobservables. In other words, do the measured variables, x_i's, provide an accurate, consistent, and repeatable representation of the unmeasured variables, Xs? To refer to our earlier example, does income, residential location, and/or education adequately represent socioeconomic status?

While these two types of inferences are logically related and empirically interdependent, they have developed along separate methodological paths. Structural inferences have been studied most extensively by econometricians. In contrast, psychometricians have made the greatest contribution to understanding measurement inferences. They have developed a variety of factor analysis models that can be used to estimate the relationship between measured indicators and unobserved constructs.

Methodologies for estimating parameters of structural (dependent and interdependent) equation systems and of factor analytic models were developed in isolation from one another. Social scientists interested in examining causal relationships among unobserved variables found themselves in a methodological no-man's-land. The practical "solution" to this problem has usually involved a two-step sequential procedure in which (1) each set of measured variables is factor analyzed to obtain a single derived composite, and (2) these factor-generated composites then serve as variables in the causal modeling process.

tion of the manuscript. George Bohrnstedt, James Kuklinski, and Robert Luskin provided valuable comments on earlier drafts of this manuscript. We would like to thank Roberta Sigel for making the data analyzed in this chapter available to us. Carmines would like to acknowledge the financial support provided by his department, university, and the Workshop so that he could attend an Abt Associates Workshop on Structural Equation Models conducted by Karl G. Jöreskog, Cambridge, Massachusetts, June 28 through July 1, 1979. The authors were supported by the National Science Foundation under grant SOC-7907543 during the preparation of this chapter.

The problems with this approach, however, are severe and readily apparent. Theoretically, this procedure treats measurement and causal inferences as completely separate and distinct instead of intimately related to one another. Methodologically, the approach is essentially ad hoc and lacks an explicit statistical justification. As a result, the properties of the parameter estimates derived from this procedure are unknown.

Recognizing these difficulties, social science methodologists in the late 1960s began to formulate models expressing both structural and measurement relations. A satisfactory method for estimating these models, however, was not forthcoming until the ground-breaking work completed by Karl G. Jöreskog and his collaborators (1967, 1969, 1970, 1973a, 1973b, 1974, 1977, 1978).

Over the past 10 years, Jöreskog has developed a general system for analyzing covariance structures. In its most general form, the approach provides for the efficient estimation of structural equation models containing unobserved variables. Specifically, his approach permits the simultaneous estimation of both the parameters linking empirical indicators to latent, unobserved variables (the measurement equations) and the parameters linking the unobserved variables to each other (the structural equations). The model allows for reciprocal causation among variables and correlated measurement error. The method also permits the researcher to impose a variety of constraints on the various parameters of the structural and measurement models.

The purpose of this chapter is to present an introduction to this method for analyzing covariance structures. The chapter is divided into two basic sections. The first section outlines the underlying logic and statistical foundations of this method, paying particular attention to the issues of identification, estimation, and model assessment. This general model for analyzing covariance structures encompasses a number of more specific models as special cases. In the second part of the chapter, we analyze data from a political socialization study to illustrate how measurement theory models, factor analysis models, and structural equation models containing unobservables represent special applications of this general method. Our basic purpose is to show how

Jöreskog's general system for analyzing covariance structures provides a coherent and unified approach to the estimation and evaluation of structural and measurement models.

THE GENERAL METHOD

LOGIC AND STRATEGY

As its name implies, the basic idea behind this method is that by analyzing the information contained in the sample variance-covariance matrix, one can obtain estimates of a hypothetical structure. A variance-covariance matrix is simply an unstandardized correlation matrix. Each entry in the correlation matrix is recoverable from the variance-covariance matrix by the equation

$$\rho_{ij} = \frac{\sigma_{ij}}{\sqrt{\sigma_i^2} \ \sqrt{\sigma_j^2}}$$

Alternatively, the variance-covariance matrix may be obtained from the correlation matrix if one also knows the standard deviation of each item using the information $\sigma_{ij} = \rho_{ij}\sigma_i\sigma_j$. If the theoretical model is scale-free and if the units of measurements in the variables are arbitrary or irrelevant, then a correlation matrix may be analyzed instead of a variance-covariance matrix.

While the method can be applied in purely exploratory investigations, it is most useful when the study is at least partly confirmatory. In these latter instances, by examining the form of the hypothesized model, the researcher can generate some predictions about the sample data. The hypothesis implies very specific consequences for the population (predicted) variance-covariance matrix. Sample data are then used to generate parameter estimates of the proposed model. If the hypothesized model generates a variance-covariance matrix that reproduces the sample data with a high degree of accuracy, then the model is retained as a plausible representation of the underlying process. If the model turns out to provide a poor approximation of the sample data, then it is rejected, and alternative theoretical structures can then be investigated. One or more of these structures may provide a closer fit to the sample data, but because of the possibility of "capitalizing on chance," it is preferred that the retained model be tested on data from a new sample before much confidence be placed in it. Given the cost of data collection in many situations, Jöreskog suggests splitting the original sample and using half of the data to evaluate the new model. This type of cross-validation is less powerful, however, than replication with an entirely new sample.

Thus, the general strategy one follows in conducting a confirmatory analysis of covariance structures can be broken down into the following steps:

(1) Specify the structural form of the hypothesized model.
(2) Generate the relevant predictions from the structural hypothesis.
(3) Examine the correspondence between the variance-covariance matrix produced by the proposed model, Σ, and the sample variance-covariance matrix, S.
(4) If there is a close fit between Σ and S, retain the model for further investigation.
(5) If the model is inconsistent with the sample data, i.e., Σ is not approximately equal to S, reject it and investigate other plausible models beginning with step 1 above.

STATISTICAL MODEL

The general model for analyzing covariance structures can be broken down into two segments or submodels, expressing, respectively, the structural and measurement relations (Jöreskog, 1970, 1973a).

The structural model specifies the causal relationships among the latent or unmeasured variables (e.g., party identification, social status). Variables within a structural model are divided into two groups: "endogenous" (or "dependent") variables, and "exogenous" (or "independent") variables. The relationships among the endogenous variables distinguish two basic types of structural models: recursive and nonrecursive. Very simply, recursive models have two defining characteristics. First, the causal paths among the endogenous variables run in only one direction and no feedback loops exist. Second, the disturbances in recursive models are uncorrelated.

Nonrecursive causal systems exhibit the characteristics recursive equation systems do not. In particular, reciprocal relationships may exist among the endogenous variables and disturbances may be correlated. Ability to model reciprocal relationships and correlated disturbances is not without a price, however. Identification of the uniqueness of parameter estimates is not guaranteed (as it is for recursive models). On the contrary, a series of necessary and sufficient conditions for identification must be examined prior to estimation. Nonrecursive models are not discussed further in this chapter. An extensive econometrics literature covers this subject. See, for example, Johnston (1972), Theil (1971), Fisher (1966), and Mosbaek and Wold (1970).

The simplest structural relationship involves a single equation with one dependent variable (η_1) and one independent variable (ξ_1):

$$\eta_1 = \gamma_{11}\xi_1 + \zeta_1 \qquad [1]$$

where γ_{11} is a parameter signifying the relationship between η_1 and ξ_1 —it may be thought of as the estimate of the regression of η_1 on ξ_1 —and ζ_1 is the disturbance term.

An elementary system of equations is this two-equation recursive model:

$$\eta_1 = \gamma_{11}\xi_1 + \zeta_1 \qquad [2]$$

$$\eta_2 = \beta_{21}\eta_1 + \gamma_{21}\xi_1 + \zeta_2$$

where γ_{ij} is a parameter describing the structural relationship between an endogenous variable η_i and an exogenous variable ξ_j, and β_{ij} signifies the causal effect of endogenous variable η_j on η_i.

With

$$\underset{\sim}{\eta}' = (\eta_1, \eta_2 \ \cdots \ \eta_m) \ \text{and} \ \underset{\sim}{\xi}' = (\xi_1, \xi_2 \ \cdots \ \xi_n)$$

representing random vectors of latent dependent and independent variables, a general system of linear structural equations may be expressed as

$$\underset{\sim}{B}\underset{\sim}{\eta} = \underset{\sim}{\Gamma}\underset{\sim}{\xi} + \underset{\sim}{\zeta} \qquad [3]$$

where $B\,(m \times m)$ and $\Gamma\,(m \times n)$ are coefficient matrices, and $\underset{\sim}{\zeta}' = (\zeta_1, \zeta_2 \cdots \zeta_m)$ is a random vector of residuals (errors in equations, random disturbance terms).

Our two- equation system may be written in matrix form as follows. First, rearrange the equations so that all dependent (or endogenous) variables are on the left side of the equals signs:

$$\eta_1 = \gamma_{11}\xi_1 + \zeta_1 \qquad [4]$$

$$-\beta_{21}\eta_1 + \eta_2 = \gamma_{21}\xi_1 + \zeta_2$$

Then the coefficient matrices $\underset{\sim}{B}$ and $\underset{\sim}{\Gamma}$ may be read from these rearranged equations. Combining these coefficient matrices with the three vectors of dependent, independent, and error variables yields

$$\begin{bmatrix} 1 & 0 \\ -\beta_{21} & 1 \end{bmatrix} \begin{bmatrix} \eta_1 \\ \eta_2 \end{bmatrix} = \begin{bmatrix} \gamma_{11} \\ \gamma_{21} \end{bmatrix} \begin{bmatrix} \xi_1 \end{bmatrix} + \begin{bmatrix} \zeta_1 \\ \zeta_2 \end{bmatrix} \qquad [5]$$

or

$$\underset{\sim}{B} \qquad \underset{\sim}{\eta} \quad = \quad \underset{\sim}{\Gamma} \quad \underset{\sim}{\xi} \ + \ \underset{\sim}{\zeta}$$

Alternatively, to read any single equation from this system of matrices, one reads across the coefficient matrices (B and Γ) and down the variable vectors (η and ξ) and adds the disturbance term (ζ).

A measurement model, alternatively a factor model, describes the relationship of an unmeasured construct (or constructs) and measured indicators of the construct. A simple three-indicator model of a single latent factor, η, is written as:

$$y_1 = \lambda_1 \eta + \epsilon_1 \tag{6}$$

$$y_2 = \lambda_2 \eta + \epsilon_2$$

$$y_3 = \lambda_3 \eta + \epsilon_3$$

where y_i is an empirical indicator of the unmeasured variable η, λ_i is a parameter ("factor loading") describing the relationship between the y_i and η, and ϵ_i is the error of measurement in y_i. These equations may be simplified in matrix notation:

$$
\begin{bmatrix} y_1 \\ y_2 \\ y_3 \end{bmatrix}
=
\begin{bmatrix} \lambda_1 \\ \lambda_2 \\ \lambda_3 \end{bmatrix}
\begin{bmatrix} \eta \end{bmatrix}
+
\begin{bmatrix} \epsilon_1 \\ \epsilon_2 \\ \epsilon_3 \end{bmatrix}
\tag{7}
$$

or

$$ y = \Lambda \; \eta \; + \; \epsilon $$

In the general analysis of covariance structures, there are two measurement equations specifying the relationships between the measured variables (x's and y's) and latent dependent and independent variables (η and ξ). They are

$$y = \Lambda_y \eta + \epsilon \tag{8}$$

and

$$x = \Lambda_x \xi + \delta \tag{9}$$

CARMINES, McIVER

73

where the matrices Λ_y and Λ_x are regression matrices of $\underset{\sim}{y}$ on $\underset{\sim}{\eta}$ and of $\underset{\sim}{x}$ on $\underset{\sim}{\xi}$, and $\underset{\sim}{\epsilon}$ and $\underset{\sim}{\delta}$ are vectors of errors of measurement in $\underset{\sim}{y}$ and $\underset{\sim}{x}$.

The advantage of this model (equations 3, 8, and 9) over conventional structural equation models (either recursive or nonrecursive) is that it does not assume perfectly measured variables. For too many years, social scientists have thought of structural equation models as a means of expressing relationships among variables whose operational characteristics were equated with their "true" characteristics. Here we make explicit the fact that theoretical variables are distinct from their indicators and that we are concerned with the structural relationships of the theoretical variables. In addition to the structural relationships among the latent or unmeasured endogenous and exogenous variables, this general model for the analysis of covariance structures provides for the measurement relations between both the endogenous and the exogenous variables and their respective empirical indicators.

Combining the structural and measurement equations 3, 8, and 9 into a single system, one can represent the general variance-covariance matrix of all measured variables as

$$
\underset{\sim}{\Sigma} = \left[
\begin{array}{c|c}
\Lambda_y (\underset{\sim}{B}^{-1}\Gamma\Phi\underset{\sim}{\Gamma}'\underset{\sim}{B}'^{-1} + \underset{\sim}{B}^{-1}\Psi\underset{\sim}{B}'^{-1})\underset{\sim}{\Lambda}'_y + \Theta_\epsilon & \Lambda_y\underset{\sim}{B}^{-1}\Gamma\Phi\underset{\sim}{\Lambda}'_x \\
\hline
\Lambda_x\Phi\Gamma'\underset{\sim}{B}'^{-1}\underset{\sim}{\Lambda}'_y & \Lambda_x\underset{\sim}{\Phi}\underset{\sim}{\Lambda}'_x + \Theta_\delta
\end{array}
\right] \quad [10]
$$

where Φ is the covariance matrix of the true independent variables ($\underset{\sim}{\xi}$), Ψ is the covariance matrix of the errors in structural equations ($\underset{\sim}{\zeta}$), Θ_ϵ is the covariance matrix of errors in measurement for the dependent variables ($\underset{\sim}{\epsilon}$), and Θ_δ is the covariance matrix of errors in measurement for the independent variables ($\underset{\sim}{\delta}$). In other words, the population variance-covariance matrix $\underset{\sim}{\Sigma}$ can be represented completely by the functions of the elements of the parameter matrices Λ_y, Λ_x, $\underset{\sim}{B}$, Γ, Φ, Ψ, Θ_ϵ, and Θ_δ. Note that the population variance-covariance matrix as presented is partitioned into four submatrices. The upper left-

TABLE 1
Variables and Matrices Used in the Analysis of Covariance Structures

	Symbol	Definition
I. Observed Variables	y	observed dependent variable/ indicators of unobserved dependent variable
	x	observed independent variable/ indicators of unobserved independent variable
II. Unobserved Variables	η (eta)	unobserved dependent variable
	ξ (xi)	unobserved independent variable
	ζ (zeta)	errors in structural equation
	ϵ (epsilon)	errors in measurement of dependent variable
	δ (delta)	errors in measurement of independent variable
III. Matrices	β (beta)	coefficient matrix of unobserved dependent variables
	Γ (gamma)	coefficient matrix of unobserved independent variables
	Λy (lambda y)	factor matrix of y on η
	Λx (lambda x)	factor matrix of x on ξ
	Φ (phi)	variance-covariance matrix of unobserved independent variables
	Ψ (psi)]	variance-covariance matrix of structural errors (variance-covariance matrix of factors in factor analytic models)
	θ_ϵ (theta epsilon)	variance-covariance matrix of errors of measurement of observed dependent variables
	θ_δ (theta delta)	variance-covariance matrix of errors of measurement of observed independent variables

hand cluster of parameter matrices describes the variances and covariances among the y_i's (Σ_{yy}), the lower left and upper right sets of parameter matrices describe the interrelationships among the y_i's and x_i's (Σ_{yx}), and the lower righthand group of matrices delineates the variances and covariances of the x_i's (Σ_{xx}). Table 1 provides a summary of the variables and matrices used in this model.

Equation 10 may be simplified considerably in given research situations. For example, if the researcher is only interested in examining a particular factor analysis model, then equation 10 reduces to

$$\Sigma = \Lambda \Psi \Lambda' + \Theta_\epsilon \qquad [11]$$

In this case, there is no ξ, Γ, δ, Λ_x, Φ, and Θ_δ; B must be set to I, the identity matrix. Similarly, for structural equation models where all variables are assumed to be measured without error, the equation of interest is equation 3. In this case, $y \equiv \eta$ and $x \equiv \xi$. The model is specified by setting Λ_y and Λ_x to I, the identity matrix. Both Θ_ϵ and Θ_δ are zero matrices. In short, in many realistic applications of this general model, the researcher may not be interesed in analyzing all of these parameter matrices, but only a selected subset of them. The initial complexity of the general variance-covariance matrix, therefore, should not be intimidating.

More generally, some or all of the elements of any of the eight parameter matrices included in equation 10 may be known a priori or set equal to some other parameter in the model. Specifically, the elements in Λ_y, Λ_x, B, Γ, Φ, Ψ, Θ_ϵ, and Θ_δ may be of three types: (a) *fixed parameters* that have been preassigned specific values; (b) *constrained parameters* that are unknown, but equal to one or more other parameters in the model; and (c) *free parameters* that are unknown and not constrained to be equal to any other parameter (i.e., are completely estimated in the analysis). In general, the assignment of given parameters as being either fixed, constrained, or free should be based on explicit theoretical considerations.

IDENTIFICATION

Before discussing the procedures for estimating the parameters of specific models, the identification issue must be examined. Basically, the identification status of any model is determined by the correspondence between the amount of information contained in the observed data (usually the variance-covariance matrix) and the number of model parameters that need to be estimated. The latter is, of course, a function of the number and type of restrictions that are placed on the general model. Models cannot be usefully analyzed if they are underidentified—meaning, generally, that Σ can be generated by more than one Θ, a vector of all unknown parameters to be estimated.[1] Under these circumstances there is no unique set of parameter estimates; i.e., Θ is not uniquely determined by Σ. Rather, the parameters of the model can take on many values, and hence cannot be satisfactorily estimated. All identified models contain a unique set of parameters. That is, Σ is generated by one and only one Θ. If the model is just identified, then the number of parameters is equivalent to the number of observed variances and covariances. While such a just identified model can be estimated (its parameters have unique values), it is not scientifically interesting because it can never be rejected. Instead, it can be fit to any sample data. The model has no discriminative power. In order for a model to be most useful, it must be overidentified, meaning, loosely speaking, that the number of parameters is less than the number of observed variances and covariances. In this situation, the proposed model can be rejected by discovering data that are inconsistent with it. This often takes the form of one or more covariances that are expected to be zero under the conditions of the model that turn out in actuality to have nonzero values. Although overidentified models can be rejected given certain data configurations, they cannot be considered valid merely because they are consistent with the sample data. This asymmetric situation arises because it is always possible that other models can also reproduce the variance-covariance matrix of the sample data, perhaps even providing a closer fit.

In sum, underidentified models cannot be estimated, just identified models can be estimated but not rejected, and overidentified models can be estimated and possibly rejected, but not confirmed. For this reason, overidentified models are the most interesting and useful from a theory testing standpoint.[2]

ESTIMATION

Assuming the model is identified, one is then in a position to estimate its parameters. As stated, it is presumed that the population variance-covariance matrix is a function of the parameters contained in equation 10. In practice, at least some of the parameters are assumed to be unknown and must be estimated from the sample variance-covariance matrix $\underset{\sim}{S}$. Three general methods for estimating the unknown parameters have been proposed, normally unweighted least squares (ULS), generalized least squares (GLS), and maximum likelihood (ML). Since standard errors are difficult to compute for ULS estimators and since it has been shown that ML and GLS estimators are asymptomatically equal (Lee, 1977), we will confine our discussion to maximum likelihood estimation.[3] This is also the estimation method used in LISREL, a computer program written by Jöreskog and Sörbom (1978) to estimate covariance structures.

In fitting $\underset{\sim}{\Sigma}$ to $\underset{\sim}{S}$, maximum likelihood minimizes a complex mathematical function with respect to the unknown parameters. Specifically, the maximum likelihood method minimizes the function

$$L(\underset{\sim}{\Theta}) = \log|\underset{\sim}{\Sigma}| - \log|\underset{\sim}{S}| + tr(\underset{\sim}{\Sigma}^{-1}\underset{\sim}{S}) - p \qquad [12]$$

with respect to $\underset{\sim}{\Theta}$, the parameter vector. Unfortunately, this function cannot be solved analytically, but it can be minimized numerically by several methods (see Gruvaeus and Jöreskog, 1970). Basically, this estimation procedure operates as follows. $L(\Theta)$ is a positive value that we are attempting to minimize. We start with a vector of initial parameter values that are used to generate the predicted covariance matrix $\underset{\sim}{\Sigma}$. $\underset{\sim}{\Sigma}$ is then compared to our sample covariance matrix in the above function. Assuming the initial set of parameter values does not perfectly reproduce S, we generate a second set of parameter estimates (based on certain mathematical properties of the $L(\Theta)$ function) to provide us with a closer fit between Σ and $\underset{\sim}{S}$. This process continues until we can no longer improve the fit between $\underset{\sim}{\Sigma}$ and $\underset{\sim}{S}$. We can see the logic of this process by examining the components of the loss function: As the predicted and sample covariance matrices become identical, $\log|\underset{\sim}{\Sigma}| - \log|\underset{\sim}{S}|$ goes to zero as does $tr(\underset{\sim}{\Sigma}^{-1}\underset{\sim}{S}) - p$.

The parameter values that provide the lowest value of $L(\Theta)$ are the maximum likelihood estimates. If the distribution of the observed variables is multivariate joint normal, then these parameter estimates are "consistent." That is, the parameter

estimates approach the true parameter values as sample size
increases. In addition, the parameter estimates are also
"asymptotically efficient"; i.e., these estimates have the minimum variance of any consistent estimator in large samples. In
most instances, however, whether or not the sample data are
properly distributed is not questioned. And, unfortunately,
little is known about the properties of these estimates if the
data are not multivariate normal.[4]

This maximum likelihood method provides asymptotic
estimates of the standard errors for all parameter estimates as
well as a likelihood ratio test for the entire model that is
distributed in large samples as a χ^2 distribution with appropriate
degrees of freedom.

ASSESSMENT

How can the researcher tell if the proposed model adequately
fits the observed data? A test of the overall goodness of fit
between the proposed model and the sample variance-covariance matrix is provided by a chi-square or likelihood ratio
test. This chi-square test may be regarded as a comparison of
the specified model against the general alternative that Σ is any
positive definitive matrix, i.e., that the observed variables, the
x_i's and y_i's, are correlated to an arbitrary extent. The
goodness-of-fit value is equal to (N-1) times the minimum
value of the function L (see equation 12) with

$$df = \tfrac{1}{2}p\,(p + 1) - t \qquad\qquad [13]$$

where p is the number of variables, and t is the number of
unknown parameters to be estimated under the specification of
the model. Given comparable degrees of freedom, relatively
small χ^2 values indicate that the model closely fits the
observed data, while relatively large χ^2 values show that the
model is empirically inadequate. It should be emphasized that

this is just the opposite from typical use. Generally, the researcher wants to obtain high χ^2 values, thus indicating that the theoretical relationship differs from the null hypothesis of no relationship. But in the present instance, we are comparing the variance-covariance matrix implied by the theoretical model with the observed variance-covariance matrix, and hence, small χ^2 values indicate the close correspondence between model and sample data.

In many situations, the researcher may be interested in evaluating several plausible models rather than a single hypothesis. If these models are nested (hierarchical), meaning that model M_o can be obtained by constraining one or more parameters of model M_1, then the models can be compared by examining differences in their χ^2 values; these differences in χ^2 are themselves distributed as χ^2. Thus, a set of *nested* models can be evaluated by computing their likelihood ratio tests and comparing them as follows:

$$\chi^2 d = \chi^2 m_1 - \chi^2 m_o \qquad [14]$$

with

$$df_d = df_{m_1} - df_{m_o}$$

Commenting on this strategy for evaluating competing models, Jöreskog (1978:448) suggests that

if the drop in χ^2 is large compared to the difference in degrees of freedom, this is an indication that the change made in the model represents a real improvement. If, on the other hand, the drop in χ^2 is close to the difference in number of degrees of freedom, this is an indication that the improvement in fit is obtained by "capitalizing on chance" and the added parameters may not have any real significance or meaning.

The fact that the likelihood ratio test is sensitive to sample size (as are all chi-square statistics) proves to be something of a double-edged sword. If, on the one hand, the sample is too small, even an inadequate model is likely to fit the data. The more typical situation, however, especially in regard to large survey studies, is that the sample will be so large that even reasonable theories will be rejected by using the chi-square test. Focusing specifically on factor analysis models, Burt (1973:148) observes that

> for extremely large sample sizes . . . almost no theoretical structure will be adequate unless every possible factor is retained in the final structure (i.e., unless the number of unobserved variables equals the number of observed variables). In such a case, the factor analytic model loses its ability to make parsimonious statements based on the covariance of a set of observed variables.

Because of these difficulties in using the χ^2 test as a measure of goodness of fit, Wheaton et al. (1977) suggest that the researcher also compute a *relative* chi-square (χ^2/df). As they indicate, this statistic takes sample size into consideration in assessing goodness of fit. They suggest a ratio of approximately five or less "as beginning to be reasonable." In our experience, however, χ^2 to degrees of freedom ratios in the range of 2 to 1 or 3 to 1 are indicative of an acceptable fit between the hypothetical model and the sample data. We report chi-square for each of the models discussed below.

Tucker and Lewis (1973) provide an alternative to the likelihood ratio test for assessing the relative fit *for factor models* that is less sensitive to sample size. Their statistic, $\hat{\rho}$, is a measure of the proportion of covariance in the data explained by a proposed model. Their measure may be expressed as follows:

$$\hat{\rho} = (M_o - M_R) / (M_o - 1) \qquad [15]$$

where $M_o = \chi_o^2/df_o$ and $M_R = \chi_R^2/df_R$. The χ^2 values and degrees of freedom are those obtained from maximum likelihood factor analyses for zero and R common factors.

The Tucker-Lewis coefficient is not without weaknesses. Most important, its sampling distribution is unknown. As a consequence, it must be considered a descriptive and not a "test" statistic. Tucker and Lewis suggest that models are "adequate" if $\hat{\rho}$ is greater than 0.9. This is an arbitrary cutoff, however. Model adequacy is best evaluated, as in the case of χ^2, in terms of relative fit rather than against any absolute standard.[5]

Applying both the likelihood ratio test and the Tucker-Lewis statistic to a model, the researcher may determine the fit is a poor one. What can be done? Neither test indicates what part of the proposed model does not accurately represent the structure underlying the data. Several suggestions for modifying deficient models have been offered. No one approach is unambiguous in its application:

(1) Identification of which sample covariances the model is unable to predict is possible through examination of the residual variance-covariance matrix (Σ-S). Both Costner and Schoenberg (1973) and Sörbom (1975) have argued, however, that this information may be misleading.

(2) Nested models may be evaluated one coefficient at a time using the likelihood ratio test described above. A first-order derivative test, proposed by Sörbom (1975), identifies the parameter constraint that may be relaxed to produce the greatest likelihood ratio test improvement. It is possible, however, that freeing this particular parameter may be inappropriate from a theoretical standpoint. Furthermore, use of Sörbom's first derivative test without examination of this residual matrix may lead to faulty inferences about the underlying structure.

(3) Confidence intervals may be constructed for each parameter estimate for a specific model in order to examine its statistical significance. Standard errors of each estimate are computed by the LISREL program. Those parameters that are insignificant may be eliminated, thus improving the *relative* fit of the model. This approach will not, however, improve the *absolute* fit of the model, which can only be done by freeing rather than fixing parameters.

Specification of plausible alternative models in addition to the proposed model will greatly facilitate testing and evaluation and will assist interpretation of a final solution. It is not difficult to analyze a set of data using LISREL without any preconceived expectations of underlying structure and generate complex statistical models. Substantive interpretation of such models may be considerably more difficult, however.

MEASUREMENT THEORY MODELS

The previous section has outlined a general method for the analysis of covariance structures. It can be used to assess theoretical models that can be represented by sample variance-covariance data. We shall illustrate how this method can be used to make inferences about covariance structures, focusing on progressively more complex models. This section deals with measurement theory models in which multiple indicators are designed to measure a *single* unobserved variable. The following section focuses on the more general situation involving the measurement of multiple unobserved variables (i.e., factor analysis models). Finally, we analyze the most general case—a multivariate causal model containing unobserved variables, each of which is measured by a set of empirical indicators. In each instance, we emphasize the hypothesis-testing capability of this method by specifying and assessing alternative theoretical models.

The data analyzed below come from a large-scale study of the political orientations, psychological predispositions, and sociological characteristics of adolescents. The data consist of a stratified random sample of 1000 high school seniors attending 25 public schools in Pennsylvania.[6] The students were interviewed during April and May 1974 by trained interviewers from the Institute for Survey Research at Temple University. Each interview lasted approximately 50 minutes. Three weeks later, 868 of the original sample completed a follow-up questionnaire administered by high school personnel. Both sources of data are used in the following analyses.

Classical test theory is based on a set of simple assumptions about empirical measurements (Lord and Novick, 1968; Carmines and Zeller, 1979). Most important, it is assumed that the observed (i.e., measured) score is composed of two quantities: a true score, one that would be obtained if there were no measurement error; and random measurement error. Thus, the basic equation of classical test theory can be represented as

$$y_i = \eta_i + \epsilon_i \qquad [16]$$

where y_i is the observed score, η_i is the true score and ϵ_i is random measurement error.

What relationships should hold among multiple indicators assumed to measure the *same* construct? Jöreskog (1969) has suggested a congeneric measurement model.[7] A set of indicators or test items is considered to be congeneric if their true scores all correlate perfectly. Each item can be represented as

$$y_i = \mu_i + \lambda_i \eta + \varepsilon_i \qquad [17]$$

where μ_i is a location parameter that permits each y_i to vary in its position on the continuum of the underlying true score η; λ_i denotes the effect of η on y_i; ϵ_i is random measurement error. For a set of p congeneric tests, let y, μ, Λ, and ϵ represent four column vectors of order p. This set of equations can be represented in matrix form by

$$y = \mu + \Lambda \eta + \varepsilon \qquad [18]$$

With this model of congeneric tests we can estimate the relationships among the items and true scores relying on the assumptions of classical measurement theory. The basic set of assumptions required by classical test theory is:

(1) The expectation of each measurement error is 0.
(2) The true score and error component of each measurement are uncorrelated.

(3) The correlation between error components of any two measures is zero.

Then, the variance-covariance matrix of the test scores may be expressed in terms of the model parameters

$$E(\underset{\sim}{y}\underset{\sim}{y}') = E[(\underset{\sim}{\Lambda}\eta + \underset{\sim}{\varepsilon})(\underset{\sim}{\Lambda}\eta + \underset{\sim}{\varepsilon})'] = \underset{\sim}{\Lambda}\underset{\sim}{\Lambda}' + \underset{\sim}{\Theta} \qquad [19]$$

where $E(\underset{\sim}{\varepsilon}\underset{\sim}{\varepsilon}') = \underset{\sim}{\Theta}$, a diagonal matrix with variances of the error terms on the diagonal.

This model, as may be obvious by now, is a special case of the general factor analytic model; i.e., we hypothesize that a single factor underlies the interrelationships among the set of test scores (Figure 1). Alternatively, in the language of a classical test theory, we hypothesize that the true scores are perfectly correlated with one another. The LISREL program efficiently estimates $\underset{\sim}{\Lambda}$, the matrix of factor loadings and $\underset{\sim}{\Theta}$, the item uniquenesses.

Before actually estimating this model with some real data, we briefly discuss two special cases of congeneric measures: tau-equivalent measures and parallel measures.

Tau-equivalent measures have equal true score variances, i.e., $\lambda_i^2 = \lambda_j^2$ for all i and j but may have different error variances. That is, each tau-equivalent item is written

$$y_i = \mu_i + \lambda\eta + \varepsilon_i \qquad [20]$$

A set of tau-equivalent measures may be represented as

$$\underset{\sim}{y} = \underset{\sim}{\mu} + \underset{\sim}{\lambda}\eta + \underset{\sim}{\varepsilon} \qquad [21]$$

where $\underset{\sim}{\lambda}$ is a vector of constants. The variance-covariance matrix of tau-equivalent tests may be written as

$$\underset{\sim}{\Sigma} = \lambda^2 \underset{\sim}{1}\underset{\sim}{1}' + \underset{\sim}{\Theta} \qquad [22]$$

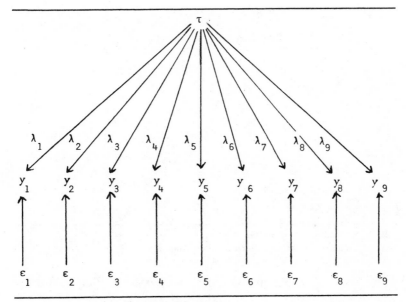

Figure 1: Measurement Model with 9 Indicators

where $\underset{\sim}{1}$ is a column vector of ones.

This is a very concise way of saying that all off-diagonal elements of the population variance-covariance matrix will equal λ^2 (i.e., the covariances among all tau-equivalent items will be identical) and that the diagonal elements of $\underset{\sim}{\Sigma}$ will equal $\lambda^2 + \theta_i$ (i.e., the diagonal entries will differ because of the unique variances of each item).[8]

On the other hand, parallel tests have both equal true score variances and equal error variances. Strictly speaking, parallel measures also have equal means. Here, we ignore modeling the structure of item means and analyze "nominally parallel" measures. In symbolic form, parallel measures are

$$y_i = \mu_i + \lambda\eta + \varepsilon \qquad [23]$$

A set of parallel items is written in matrix notation as

$$\underset{\sim}{y} = \underset{\sim}{\mu} + \underset{\sim}{\lambda}\eta + \underset{\sim}{\varepsilon} \qquad [24]$$

TABLE 2
A Summary of Test Theory Models

Models	Assumptions	Covariance Structure	Number of Parameters
I. Parallel	$\lambda_1 = \ldots = \lambda_p$	$\Sigma = \lambda^2 \underset{\sim}{1}\underset{\sim}{1}' + \Theta^2 I$	2
	$\Theta_1 = \ldots = \Theta_p$		
II. Tau-equivalent	$\lambda_1 = \ldots = \lambda_p$	$\Sigma = \lambda^2 \underset{\sim}{1}\underset{\sim}{1}' + \underset{\sim}{\Theta}^2$	$p+1$
	Θ_i unconstrained		
III. Congeneric	λ_i unconstrained	$\Sigma = \underset{\sim}{\lambda}\underset{\sim}{\lambda}' + \underset{\sim}{\Theta}^2$	$2p$
	Θ_i unconstrained		

SOURCE: Adapted from Jöreskog (1974).
NOTE: $\underset{\sim}{1}$ is a column vector with all elements equal to one.

Here, both λ and $\underset{\sim}{\varepsilon}$ are vectors of constants. The variance-covariance matrix for parallel items is

$$\underset{\sim}{\Sigma} = \lambda^2 \underset{\sim}{1}\,\underset{\sim}{1}' + \theta\,\underset{\sim}{I} \qquad [25]$$

Equation 25 indicates that all covariances among parallel items will equal λ^2 (i.e., the off-diagonal elements of $\underset{\sim}{\Sigma}$ will be identical) and also that the variances of all parallel items will be equal (i.e., all diagonal entries of the variance-covariance matrix will equal $\lambda^2 + \Theta$). Parallel items also imply equal correlations among items as well as equal covariances. Tau-equivalent measures, on the other hand, are not characterized by equal correlations.[9] A summary of all three types of measurement models is presented in Table 2. The strictest assumption we might make is that items are parallel. Only two parameters need be estimated—a common λ and a common θ^2. Tau-equivalence relaxes constraints on the error variances. Consequently, $p + 1$ parameters are estimated—one for the common λ and p error variances. The most general single-factor model assumes items are congeneric. Here, p estimates of the λ_i and p estimates of the error variances are necessary.

Which of these models is most appropriate for a given set of items? This question can be answered by a comparison of their likelihood ratio tests. Because the models are nested, the difference in χ^2 between any two models is also an χ^2 value with degrees of freedom equal to the difference in degrees of freedom between the two models. Thus, an χ^2 difference between the parallel and tau-equivalent models has p-1 degrees of freedom, as does the χ^2 difference between the tau-equivalent and the congeneric models.

As an example of the application of these measurement models, we analyze the variance-covariance matrix of nine items designed to measure adolescents' sense of self-esteem (Rosenberg, 1965).[10] (The items are presented in the appendix.)

Table 3 contains the information necessary to compare the relative fit of the various measurement models. The parallel tests hypothesis does not fit the data. The tau-equivalent model is a statistically significant improvement over the parallel model (χ^2_{diff} = 120.414 with 8 df), and the congeneric test model is a signficant improvement over the tau-equivalent model (χ^2_{diff} = 67.258 with 8 df). However, even the congeneric model fits rather poorly when the fit relative to the available degrees of freedom is taken into account. Thus, it would appear that these items are measuring some phenomenon in addition to self-esteem.

Factor analyses of the covariance matrix of the items combined with an assessment of the scale's construct validity suggest that there are two empirical factors that underlie the data, but only one of which represents the theoretical construct, self-esteem. The second factor is a methodological artifact, reflecting offsetting sources of response set due to the positive and negative wording of the items (Carmines and Zeller, 1974; Zeller and Carmines, 1976, 1980).

More generally, it is likely that few sets of measures available to social scientists fit the congeneric measurement model, let alone more restrictive models involving parallel or tau-equivalent items. In many instances, the variation in our items is due to more than a single construct. These additional

TABLE 3
Measurement Theory Results: Self-Esteem Scale

Λ	PARALLEL	TAU-EQUIVALENT	CONGENERIC
λ_1	.504 (.014)	.499 (.014)	.436 (.023)
λ_2	.504 (.014)	.499 (.014)	.509 (.026)
λ_3	.504 (.014)	.499 (.014)	.513 (.031)
λ_4	.504 (.014)	.499 (.014)	.613 (.029)
λ_5	.504 (.014)	.499 (.014)	.446 (.028)
λ_6	.504 (.014)	.499 (.014)	.535 (.026)
λ_7	.504 (.014)	.499 (.014)	.391 (.024)
λ_8	.504 (.014)	.499 (.014)	.534 (.027)
λ_9	.504 (.014)	.499 (.014)	.565 (.027)
Θ			
θ_1	:458 (.007)	.335 (.018)	.346 (.018)
θ_2	.458 (.007)	.409 (.021)	.413 (.022)
θ_3	.458 (.007)	.640 (.032)	.636 (.032)
θ_4	.458 (.007)	.525 (.026)	.489 (.026)
θ_5	.458 (.007)	.541 (.027)	.542 (.027)
θ_6	.458 (.007)	.402 (.021)	.393 (.021)
θ_7	.458 (.007)	.382 (.020)	.392 (.020)
θ_8	.458 (.007)	.451 (.023)	.440 (.023)
θ_9	.458 (.007)	.448 (.023)	.429 (.023)
χ^2	421.669	301.255	233.997
df	43	35	27
χ^2/df	9.81	8.61	8.67

NOTE: Standard errors of parameter estimates appear in parentheses.

sources of variance may be due to nonrandom measurement error or substantive causal factors. Unless these additional sources of variance are recognized, our inferences based on empirical data may be misleading. Alwin and Jackson (1979) suggest that certain procedures can lead to faulty inference about sources of common variance. Analysis of one set of items may imply the existence of a single factor. However, when these same items are analyzed in conjunction with items measuring other constructs, their single-factor structure may not persist. Consideration of multiple true score models leads us directly to the application of LISREL to factor analysis.

UNRESTRICTED AND RESTRICTED FACTOR ANALYSIS MODELS

One can find numerous examples of the application of factor analysis in the social sciences, especially in regard to exploratory investigations. The multiple factor model may be considered a special case of the general methodology for analyzing covariance matrices. In this section, we describe a series of alternative uses of the factor model for both exploratory and confirmatory analysis.

Exploratory factor analysis is usually undertaken to answer the question, how many common factors are needed to adequately describe the covariation in a set of measurements? Such analyses usually proceed on the basis of little prior knowledge about the phenomenon being examined.

Prior knowledge, theoretical or empirical, is the basis for confirmatory factor analysis. In confirmatory studies, we attempt to answer a question such as the following: Do k (where k is a specific number) common factors adequately explain the covariation in a set of measurements? Here, we will be primarily concerned with demonstrating an approach to testing a number of hypotheses about the factor structure underlying a set of measurements.

The factor model may be written as

$$y = \Lambda\eta + \epsilon \qquad [26]$$

where y is a vector of observed scores ($p \times 1$), Λ is a matrix of factor loadings ($p \times k$), η is a vector of common factors ($k \times 1$), and $\underset{\sim}{\epsilon}$ is a vector of unique scores (p $\times$ 1). Four assumptions are necessary to estimate this model:

(1) $E(\underset{\sim}{\eta}) = E(\underset{\sim}{\epsilon}) = \underset{\sim}{0}$
(2) $E(\underset{\sim}{\eta}\underset{\sim}{\epsilon}) = \underset{\sim}{0}$.
(3) $E(\underset{\sim}{\epsilon}\underset{\sim}{\epsilon}') = \underset{\sim}{\Theta}_\epsilon$, a diagonal matrix; i.e., COV $(\epsilon_i\epsilon_j) = 0$, $i \neq j$
(4) $E(\underset{\sim}{\eta}\underset{\sim}{\eta}') = \underset{\sim}{\Psi}$, the correlation matrix among the factors

On the basis of these assumptions, the model predicts the expected value of the variance-covariance matrix of the observed variables:

$$E(\underset{\sim}{y}\underset{\sim}{y}') = E(\underset{\sim}{\Lambda}\underset{\sim}{\eta} + \underset{\sim}{\epsilon})(\underset{\sim}{\Lambda}\underset{\sim}{\eta} + \underset{\sim}{\epsilon})' \qquad [27]$$

$$= \underset{\sim}{\Lambda}\underset{\sim}{\Psi}\underset{\sim}{\Lambda}' + \underset{\sim}{\Theta}_\epsilon = \underset{\sim}{\Sigma}$$

If we further assume the observed variables have been standardized, that is, $E(y) = 0$ and $Var(y) = 1.0$, $\underset{\sim}{\Sigma}$ is equal to the predicted correlation matrix among observed variables.

As an example of the use of factor analysis to test a series of related hypotheses about the structure underlying a correlation matrix, we again draw on the socialization study of Pennsylvania high school students. The questionnaire allowed the respondents to rate ten qualities in terms of their importance to good citizenship (see appendix for listing of items). One hypothesis is that student responses to this set of items are constrained by one general citizenship factor. A second hypothesis can be deduced from the content of the items— namely, that they measure three specific components of citizenship. Three items—the importance of voting, attempting to influence governmental policies, and being politically aware—are all aspects of a politically active orientation to citizenship. On the other hand, compliance with legal standards and deference to national symbols (two items) represent a passive yet still political orientation toward good citizenship. Finally, the remaining items appear to measure neighborliness (e.g., being friendly to others) in both a limited and broad sense of the term. Consequently, one might hypothesize that a three-

TABLE 4
Factor Model of the Components of Good Citizenship

Items	Factor Loadings (Λ)		
	I	II	III
Voting in most elections	λ_{11}	λ_{21}	λ_{31}
Trying to influence government	λ_{12}	λ_{22}	λ_{32}
Keeping informed about public affairs	λ_{13}	λ_{23}	λ_{33}
Volunteering for community service	λ_{14}	λ_{24}	λ_{34}
Working hard	λ_{15}	λ_{25}	λ_{35}
Being a good human being	λ_{16}	λ_{26}	λ_{36}
Being friendly	λ_{17}	λ_{27}	λ_{37}
Obeying the law	λ_{18}	λ_{28}	λ_{38}
Honoring one's country	λ_{19}	λ_{29}	λ_{39}
Not bring dishonor to the country	$\lambda_{1,10}$	$\lambda_{2,10}$	$\lambda_{3,10}$

Factor Correlations (Ψ)

	I	II	III
I	1.0		
II	ρ_{12}	1.0	
III	ρ_{13}	ρ_{23}	1.0

factor model would be more appropriate for these data. We can also posit a more restrictive hypothesis: that these three sets of items represent three sets of congeneric tests. The definition of a congeneric test—that it is the combination of a single true score and random error—implies that each of the ten citizenship items will load on one and only one of the three factors. In other words, each row of the factor pattern matrix $\underset{\sim}{\Lambda}$ should contain one and only one nonzero entry if the items are congeneric. Finally, we can examine the extent of correlations among common factors or true scores by comparing orthogonal and oblique solutions. Each of these models can be estimated by placing alternative constraints on the $\underset{\sim}{\Lambda}$ and Ψ matrices of the general factor model (Table 4).

In the first column of Table 5, we present the single-factor solution to the ten citizenship items. (All factor analyses

TABLE 5
Factor Analysis Results

Factor Loadings / Items	I 1 factor solution	II 3 Orthogonal congeneric tests			III 3 Oblique congeneric tests			IV 3 Orthogonal common factors (unrestricted)			V 3 Oblique common factors (unrestricted)			VI 3 Oblique common factors (restricted)		
1	.398	.515	.000*	.000*	.526	.000*	.000*	.466	.051	.268	.447	-.113	.223	.448	-.154	.236
2	.333	.565	.000*	.000*	.601	.000*	.000*	.534	.244	.097	.565	.108	-.023	.614	.000*	.000*
3	.452	.731	.000*	.000*	.684	.000*	.000*	.685	.183	.124	.720	.000*	.000*	.688	.000*	.000*
4	.576	.000*	.471	.000*	.000*	.546	.000*	.322	.405	.264	.305	.299	.159	.310	.266	.169
5	.485	.000*	.440	.000*	.000*	.486	.000*	.066	.387	.301	.019	.336	.241	.000*	.334	.255
6	.512	.000*	.711	.000*	.000*	.673	.000*	.005	.706	.143	.000*	.720	.000*	.000*	.729	.000*
7	.523	.000*	.751	.000*	.000*	.698	.000*	.117	.747	.057	.142	.753	-.123	.157	.730	-.118
8	.372	.000*	.000*	.435	.000*	.000*	.448	.082	.096	.422	.000*	.000*	.441	.000*	.000*	.442
9	.559	.000*	.000*	.854	.000*	.000*	.769	.022	.136	.854	-.158	-.025	.925	-.198	.000*	.918
10	.573	.000*	.000*	.644	.000*	.000*	.713	.128	.209	.605	.013	.074	.614	.000*	.000*	.663

Factor Correlations

	I	II			III			IV			V			VI		
1		1.000*			1.000*			1.000*			1.000*			1.000*		
2		.000*	1.000*		.503	1.000*		.000*	1.000*		.289	1.000*		.355	1.000*	
3		.000*	.000*	1.000*	.397	.496	1.000*	.000*	.000	1.000*	.389	.405	1.000*	.442	.419	1.000*

FIT

	I	II	III	IV	V	VI
χ²	516.32	394.87	199.44	51.44	51.44	58.33
df	35	35	32	15(18)[t]	18	24
χ²/df	14.75	11.28	6.23	3.43(2.86)	2.86	2.43

*Coefficient constrained to equal .000.

[t] Three more constraints may be placed on the Λ matrix without affecting the fit of the three common factor solution.

reported here are estimated with the LISREL program.) The likelihood ratio χ^2 (516.32 with 35 df) indicates a poor fit between the model and the data. Should these items be modeled as three sets of congeneric tests (i.e., does each item load on one and only one factor)? The "orthogonal three true scores" model (column 2) does not fit the data either. However, permitting correlations among true scores (column 3) improves the fit of the model significantly ($\chi^2_{improvement}$ = 195.43 with 3 df). But there are still substantial discrepancies between the predicted correlation matrix and the sample inter-item correlations.

Alternatively, we can examine the fit between the common factor model and these data. An "unrestricted orthogonal three-factor" solution is presented in the fourth column of Table 5. While we have still not explained all of the variation in our sample data, the relative fit of this model is far superior to any of the congeneric test models of these data. (The orthogonal solution presented here is arbitrary and can be rotated to any of an infinite number of configurations.) The oblique three-factor model (a "reference variables" solution) presented in column 5 is also unrestricted (only nine constraints have been placed on the Λ and Ψ matrices). Consequently, the fit of this model to the data is the same as the fit of the unrestricted orthogonal solution.

A restricted oblique three-factor solution is presented in column 6. This model is a considerable improvement over the oblique three congeneric tests model, which fails primarily because citizenship items 1, 4, 5, 7, and 9 appear related to more than one true score. This restricted factor solution also provides a relatively better fit to the data than the unrestricted factor solution. Each of the estimated parameters in the restricted model is at least twice its standard error. The χ^2 improvement of the unrestricted over the restricted solution is not significant (χ^2_{diff} = 6.89 with 6 df) and does not justify freeing six fixed coefficients in the restricted solution. Finally, the first derivative test of each fixed parameter in the restricted solution does not indicate statistically significant improvement of fit by relaxing any individual constraint. Our final solution to these data then suggests that the Pennsylvania high schoolers distinguish three aspects of citizenship—active and passive political components as well as neighborliness—in the ten questionnaire items presented to them. Five of the ten items, however, do not load on only one factor. Another way of saying this is that five items share more than one source of common variance. Because the variance of these items is attributable to more than one source, their usefulness as measuring instruments must be questioned. This is true especially of items 4 and 5. A substantial proportion of the variance of these two items is not attributable to any single factor.

STRUCTURAL EQUATION MODELS

Covariance matrices may be the product of causal relationships among a series of variables. In particular, one may posit an explicit causal structure underlying the covariation in a set of variables. This causal structure may be examined once theoretical relationships are made explicit within a mathematical model. This model may be a single-equation or a multiple-equation model. Disturbances may be correlated or not. Variables may be modeled with or without errors of measurement. Finally, the model may be recursive or nonrecursive.

The simplest model we might examine is a single-equation model in which variables are measured without error. In this case,

$$\underset{\sim}{B}\underset{\sim}{\eta} = \underset{\sim}{\Gamma}\underset{\sim}{\xi} + \underset{\sim}{\zeta} \qquad \text{[28, also eq. 3]}$$

reduces to

$$\eta_1 = \underset{\sim}{\Gamma}\underset{\sim}{\xi} + \zeta_1 \qquad \text{[29]}$$

since $\underset{\sim}{B} = \underset{\sim}{I} = 1.0$ and $\underset{\sim}{\Psi}$ is a 1×1 matrix containing the disturbance term ζ_1. This model is equivalent to the common multiple regression equation[11] and may be estimated by ordinary least squares if the assumptions underlying that model are appropriate.[12] If, in addition, the disturbance ζ_1 is normally distributed—as required for OLS significance testing—the model may be estimated by maximum likelihood procedures yielding results identical to OLS. (This is true for all recursive structural equation models.)

Models of two or more structural equations without errors of measurement may be expressed generally as equation 28 where the $\underline{B}$ matrix parameters describe the relationships among the endogenous or jointly dependent variables $\underline{\eta}$, the $\underline{\Gamma}$ matrix describes the effects of the exogenous (independent) variables $\underline{\xi}$ on the endogenous variables $\underline{\eta}$ and $\underline{\zeta}$ is a vector of disturbances. Structures that conform to equation 28 have been discussed in the social sciences under the general rubric of path analysis.

The importance of this methodology, however, does not lie in its capacity to estimate structural equation models containing perfectly measured variables. Rather, the unique contribution of this method for analyzing covariance structures is its ability to permit the simultaneous modeling of structural relationships among a set of latent or unmeasured endogenous and exogenous variables *and* the relationships of the latent variables to their respective empirical indicators.

To illustrate the use of LISREL for estimating and testing causal models containing imperfectly measured variables, we again turn to our sample of high school seniors in order to answer a key question about the relationship between personality and political participation: namely, how do personality traits influence political behavior? On the one hand, it is possible that political behavior is a mere extension of basic features of personality. As Mussen and Wyzenski (1952:80) observe, "political apathy and activity are specific manifestations of more deep-lying and pervasive passive and active orientations." In this case, we would expect to find a strong, direct effect of personality on political participation.

On the other hand, it is quite possible that instead of directly influencing political behavior, personality affects participation only through a series of intervening psychological processes. This would be consistent with McClosky's (1968:258) observation that

> personality is so complex a phenomenon that the connection between any particular activity and any source trait is bound to be extremely tenuous. The "distance" between a basic personality trait and a specific manifestation of political activity is too great and the route between them too circuitous for one to be directly engaged by the other.

These alternative theoretical propositions concerning the relationship between personality and political participation can be evaluated within the context of the structural model represented in Figure 2. This model presumes that self-esteem (ξ_3) is linked to political participation (η_4) via three intervening variables: exposure to political stimuli (η_1), comprehensive of political information (η_2), and orientation toward participant citizenship (η_3). These intervening variables are also considered to be causally linked to one another as indicated in the figure. Finally, two additional exogenous variables—the political environment of the home (ξ_1) and the school (ξ_2)—are included to specify more fully the model and to control for possible spurious effects of self-esteem on the intervening variables.

All of these variables are unobserved; each is measured by a set of empirical indicators: The relationships between the endogenous variables and their indicators are modeled within the equation

$$y = \Lambda_y \eta + \epsilon \qquad [30]$$

where Λ_y is the matrix of factor loadings that relate the observed measures to the appropriate unobserved variable, and ϵ is a vector containing errors in measurement.

This matrix equation summarizes the relationships between the four endogenous variables in the participation model and their respective indicators; see the appendix for the 15 operational measures of η_1 through η_4.

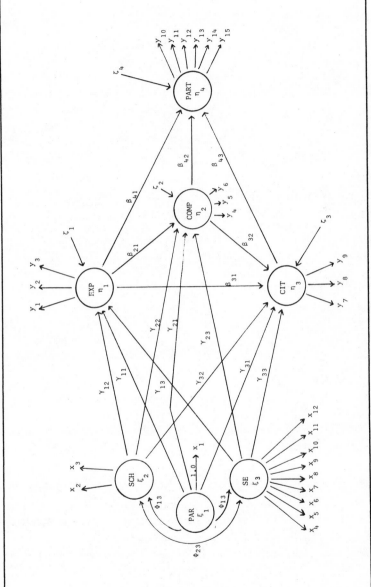

Figure 2: Determinants of Adolescent Political Participation: Recursive Structural Model with Measurement Error

97

$$y_1 = \eta_1 + \epsilon_1 \qquad\qquad y_9 = \Lambda_{93}\eta_3 + \epsilon_9 \qquad\qquad [31]$$

$$y_2 = \Lambda_{21}\eta_1 + \epsilon_2 \qquad\qquad y_{10} = \eta_4 + \epsilon_{10}$$

$$y_3 = \Lambda_{31}\eta_1 + \epsilon_3 \qquad\qquad y_{11} = \Lambda_{11,4}\eta_4 + \epsilon_{11}$$

$$y_4 = \eta_2 + \epsilon_4 \qquad\qquad y_{12} = \Lambda_{12,4}\eta_4 + \epsilon_{12}$$

$$y_5 = \Lambda_{52}\eta_2 + \epsilon_5 \qquad\qquad y_{13} = \Lambda_{13,4}\eta_4 + \epsilon_{13}$$

$$y_6 = \Lambda_{62}\eta_2 + \epsilon_6 \qquad\qquad y_{14} = \Lambda_{14,4}\eta_4 + \epsilon_{14}$$

$$y_7 = \eta_3 + \epsilon_7 \qquad\qquad y_{15} = \Lambda_{15,4}\eta_4 + \epsilon_{15}$$

$$y_8 = \Lambda_{83}\eta_3 + \epsilon_8$$

The relationships between the exogenous variables and their indicators are modeled within the comparable equation,

$$\underset{\sim}{x} = \underset{\sim}{\Lambda_x}\underset{\sim}{\xi} + \underset{\sim}{\delta} \qquad\qquad [32]$$

The twelve individual equations described by equation 32 are

$$x_2 = \xi_1 \qquad\qquad x_7 = \Lambda_{73}\xi_3 + \delta_7 \qquad\qquad [33]$$

$$x_2 = \xi_2 + \delta_2 \qquad\qquad x_8 = \Lambda_{83}\xi_3 + \delta_8$$

$$x_3 = \Lambda_{32}\xi_2 + \delta_3 \qquad\qquad x_9 = \Lambda_{93}\xi_3 + \delta_9$$

$$x_4 = \xi_3 + \delta_4 \qquad\qquad x_{10} = \Lambda_{10,3}\xi_3 + \delta_{10}$$

$$x_5 = \Lambda_{53}\xi_3 + \delta_5 \qquad\qquad x_{11} = \Lambda_{11,3}\xi_3 + \delta_{11}$$

$$x_6 = \Lambda_{63}\xi_3 + \delta_6 \qquad\qquad x_{12} = \Lambda_{12,3}\xi_3 + \delta_{12}$$

(The x_i's are described in the appendix.) We assume that parental discussion of politics is perfectly measured: The relationship between this variable and its single indicator is constrained to be 1.0; i.e., there is no error of measurement.[13]

The structural model linking the unobserved dependent variables, $\underset{\sim}{\eta}$, to the unobserved dependent variables, $\underset{\sim}{\xi}$, is represented by a system of linear equations:

$$\underset{\sim}{B}\underset{\sim}{\eta} = \underset{\sim}{\Gamma}\underset{\sim}{\xi} + \underset{\sim}{\zeta} \qquad\qquad [34]$$

The four structural equations of the participation model summarized by equation 34 are:

$$\eta_1 = \gamma_{11}\xi_1 + \gamma_{23}\xi_2 + \gamma_{13}\xi_3 + \zeta_1 \qquad [35]$$

$$\eta_2 = \beta_{21}\eta_1 + \gamma_{21}\xi_1 + \gamma_{22}\xi_2 + \gamma_{23}\xi_3 + \zeta_2$$

$$\eta_3 = \beta_{32}\eta_2 + \beta_{31}\eta_1 + \gamma_{31}\xi_1 + \gamma_{32}\xi_2 + \gamma_{33}\xi_3 + \zeta_3$$

$$\eta_4 = \beta_{43}\eta_3 + \beta_{42}\eta_2 + \beta_{41}\eta_1 + \zeta_4$$

Table 6 presents a matrix representation of both the structural and the measurement models outlined in Figure 2. The parameters to be estimated are noted by their appropriate coefficients. The zero elements in the upper triangle of B matrix indicate that the model is recursive. Finally, the placement of the zeros in the Λ_y and Λ_x matrices presumes that the measurements are congenric, i.e., each item set loads on one and only one factor.

Table 7 shows the fit of four models to the sample data. The first model (Model I), shown in row 1, may be regarded as a test of the null hypothesis of no relationship among the seven latent variables. In this case, we fit the 27 measured variables to 7 orthogonal factors. The fit is relatively poor: a χ^2 likelihood ratio of 1343.067 with 322 df. This evidence suggests that there are relationships among the seven latent variables.

The second model to be estimated (Model IV; see row 4) is a fully saturated recursive model. By fully saturated we mean that it allows for the estimation of all possible causal paths, but still retains the recursiveness of the system. This model, as expected, provides a much closer fit to the observed data. The χ^2 difference between the null model and the saturated model equals 730.946 with 18 df, indicating a relatively better fit. The saturated model with 304 df yields a χ^2 of 612.121, which is not statistically significant ($>.05$). Statistical insignificance in this case is not at all surprising, given the large sample size. The fit relative to degrees of freedom is good (2.014).

Is the saturated model, then, most appropriate for these data? Row 2 of Table 7 (Model II) suggests that this may *not* be

TABLE 6
Matrix Representation of a Recursive Structural Model of the Determinants of Adolescent Political Participation Incorporating Measurement Error

$$\beta\eta = \Gamma\xi + \zeta$$

$$
\begin{bmatrix}
1 & 0 & 0 & 0 \\
-\beta_{21} & 1 & 0 & 0 \\
-\beta_{31} & -\beta_{32} & 1 & 0 \\
-\beta_{41} & -\beta_{42} & -\beta_{43} & 1
\end{bmatrix}
\begin{bmatrix}
\eta_1 \\ \eta_2 \\ \eta_3 \\ \eta_4
\end{bmatrix}
\begin{matrix} = \\ = \\ = \\ = \end{matrix}
\begin{bmatrix}
\gamma_{11} & \gamma_{12} & \gamma_{13} \\
\gamma_{21} & \gamma_{22} & \gamma_{23} \\
\gamma_{31} & \gamma_{32} & \gamma_{33} \\
\gamma_{41} & \gamma_{42} & \gamma_{43}
\end{bmatrix}
\begin{bmatrix}
\xi_1 \\ \xi_2 \\ \xi_3
\end{bmatrix}
+
\begin{bmatrix}
\zeta_1 \\ \zeta_2 \\ \zeta_3 \\ \zeta_4
\end{bmatrix}
$$

$$y = \Lambda_y\eta + \varepsilon$$

$$
\begin{bmatrix}
y_1 \\ y_2 \\ y_3 \\ y_4 \\ y_5 \\ y_6 \\ y_7 \\ y_8 \\ y_9 \\ y_{10} \\ y_{11} \\ y_{12} \\ y_{13} \\ y_{14} \\ y_{15}
\end{bmatrix}
=
\begin{bmatrix}
1.0 & 0 & 0 & 0 \\
\Lambda_{21} & 0 & 0 & 0 \\
\Lambda_{31} & 0 & 0 & 0 \\
0 & 1.0 & 0 & 0 \\
0 & \Lambda_{52} & 0 & 0 \\
0 & \Lambda_{62} & 0 & 0 \\
0 & 0 & 1.0 & 0 \\
0 & 0 & \Lambda_{83} & 0 \\
0 & 0 & \Lambda_{93} & 0 \\
0 & 0 & 0 & 1.0 \\
0 & 0 & 0 & \Lambda_{11,\,4} \\
0 & 0 & 0 & \Lambda_{12,\,4} \\
0 & 0 & 0 & \Lambda_{13,\,4} \\
0 & 0 & 0 & \Lambda_{14,\,4} \\
0 & 0 & 0 & \Lambda_{15,\,4}
\end{bmatrix}
\begin{bmatrix}
\eta_1 \\ \eta_2 \\ \eta_3 \\ \eta_4
\end{bmatrix}
+
\begin{bmatrix}
\varepsilon_1 \\ \varepsilon_2 \\ \varepsilon_3 \\ \varepsilon_4 \\ \varepsilon_5 \\ \varepsilon_6 \\ \varepsilon_7 \\ \varepsilon_8 \\ \varepsilon_9 \\ \varepsilon_{10} \\ \varepsilon_{11} \\ \varepsilon_{12} \\ \varepsilon_{13} \\ \varepsilon_{14} \\ \varepsilon_{15}
\end{bmatrix}
$$

$$x = \Lambda_x\xi + \delta$$

$$
\begin{bmatrix}
x_1 \\ x_2 \\ x_3 \\ x_4 \\ x_5 \\ x_6 \\ x_7 \\ x_8 \\ x_9 \\ x_{10} \\ x_{11} \\ x_{12}
\end{bmatrix}
=
\begin{bmatrix}
1.0 & 0 & 0 \\
0 & 1.0 & 0 \\
0 & \Lambda_{32} & 0 \\
0 & 0 & 1.0 \\
0 & 0 & \Lambda_{53} \\
0 & 0 & \Lambda_{63} \\
0 & 0 & \Lambda_{73} \\
0 & 0 & \Lambda_{83} \\
0 & 0 & \Lambda_{93} \\
0 & 0 & \Lambda_{10,\,3} \\
0 & 0 & \Lambda_{11,\,3} \\
0 & 0 & \Lambda_{12,\,3}
\end{bmatrix}
\begin{bmatrix}
\xi_1 \\ \xi_2 \\ \xi_3
\end{bmatrix}
+
\begin{bmatrix}
0.0 \\ \delta_2 \\ \delta_3 \\ \delta_4 \\ \delta_5 \\ \delta_6 \\ \delta_7 \\ \delta_8 \\ \delta_9 \\ \delta_{10} \\ \delta_{11} \\ \delta_{12}
\end{bmatrix}
$$

TABLE 7
Comparison of Recursive Models of the Determinants of
Adolescent Political Participation (N = 776)

Model	x^2 Likelihood Ratio	Degrees of Freedom	Relative (x^2/df) Fit
I. Null Model No Structural Effects -- 7 Orthogonal Factors	1343.067	322	4.171
II. No Exogenous Effects on Participation $\gamma41=0$, $\gamma42=0$, $\gamma43=0$	618.095	307	2.013
III. No Exogenous Effects on Participation $\gamma41=0$, $\gamma42=0$, $\gamma43=0$, $\beta32=0$, $\gamma32=0$, $\gamma23=0$, $\gamma21=0$, $\gamma33=0$	623.438	312	1.998
IV. Saturated Structural Model Γ free, β lower triangular free	612.121	304	2.014

the case. In this model, we have eliminated the direct paths between the exogenous variables and participation; they have been constrained to be zero. Thus, under the conditions of the model, self-esteem (as well as the political environments of the home and school) only affects adolescent political behavior through its influence on the intervening variables. The χ^2 difference between this indirect causal model and the saturated model is not significant. Moreover, their relative degrees of fit are almost identical. In other words, the three exogenous variables, self-esteem, school politics, and parental politics, do not have a direct effect on adolescent political participation. The impact of these variables is mediated by three intervening endogenous variables: exposure to politics, comprehension, and citizenship.

The indirect causal model contains several paths that are statistically insignificant: β_{32}, γ_{21}, γ_{23}, γ_{32}, and γ_{33}. Constraining these paths to be zero leads to a slight improvement in the relative fit of the model, as seen in row 3 of Table 7

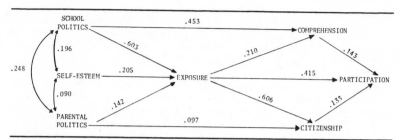

Figure 3: Model III: Standardized Structural Coefficients of the Determinants of Adolescent Political Participation (N = 776)

(Model III). In sum, on the basis of this evidence, one can conclude that the indirect causal model (Model III) provides a more appropriate representation of the process by which personality is linked to political participation. Not only does it fit the data as well as the saturated model, but it is more parsimonious and theoretically more reasonable.[14]

The standardized coefficients for Model III are presented in Figure 3. They indicate that self-esteem has its strongest impact on political participation via its effect on political exposure. Thus, adolescents with higher self-esteem are more likely to be exposed to politics, which, in turn, has a substantial effect on actual participation.

Environmental factors rather than personality are the more important determinants of political participation. Of the two environmental variables in the model, the school has a much greater impact on participation than adolescents' parents.

The total impact of each of the three exogenous variables on participation is estimated by the "reduced form" coefficients of Model III. To compute the reduced form coefficients, one simply follows the guidelines for computing effects coefficients in path analysis (Finney, 1972; Alwin and Hauser, 1975). A reduced form coefficient for recursive models is equal to the direct effect of an exogenous variable on an endogenous variable plus the sum of the products of each indirect causal path between the two variables. This procedure is instructive because it permits one to see which component paths contribute more than others. The reduced form coefficients for Model III relating the three exogenous variables to participation are .1078 (self-esteem), .3817 (school politics), and .0874 (parental politics).[15] These results are entirely consistent with our discussion of the relative importance of school politics on the political behavior of high school seniors.

Of the intervening variables in the model, exposure is by far the most important. Exposure to politics more than comprehension of the political world or acceptance of a citizenship role affects the political activity of adolescents. To the extent exposure also has a positive influence on both comprehension and citizenship, it plays a key role in this model of participatory behavior. Model III is, in many ways, a passive model of behavior. The adolescent is exposed to politics in the school, and this exposure, in turn, leads to political activity.

A final note on these analyses is necessary. Our results are a consequence of the interaction of a particular theoretical perspective and a specific set of data. Model III is the product of a comparison of two perspectives on the effect of self-esteem on political activity *and* the statistical simplification of the model. Acceptance of Model III as an appropriate representation of a process underlying adolescent political behavior will require replication of our results in another sample.

CONCLUSION

There is a duality of language that characterizes theory and research in the social sciences. On the one hand, we refer to theoretical constructs such as political participation, self-esteem, and social integration. Typically, we seek to place these theoretical constructs within an explicit causal structure— to understand the causal dynamics that surround them. But the attempt to examine the structural relations among these constructs systematically is severely hampered by our inability to observe and, hence, directly measure them. As a consequence, the empirical exploration and testing of causal theories requires the use of empirical indicators, designed to represent given theoretical constructs.

If social scientists only needed to estimate structural relationships, they could simply rely on some type of regression analysis. If they only needed to examine measurement relationships, they could turn to a variety of factor analysis models. But typically social scientists must make inferences about both types of relationships: the causal relationships among the latent theoretical constructs and the measurement relationships between the empirical indicators and their respective latent variables. And until quite recently no general statistical method for the simultaneous estimation of structural and measurement equations existed. Instead, researchers were forced to employ special ad hoc procedures, restricted both in the number of indicators per construct that could be accommodated and in the complexity of the structural relations that could be estimated (no reciprocal relationships). These procedures provided neither efficient estimates of structural parameters nor an overall test of the adequacy of the model.

The general method for analyzing covariance structures outlined in this chapter provides a general solution to this dual inference problem. It provides for the efficient simultaneous estimation of structural and measurement parameters. While the method has only been applied to recursive models here, it can also be used to estimate nonrecursive systems. The maximum likelihood estimation procedure provides a test of the statistical significance of each parameter as well as an overall goodness-of-fit test for the entire model. In short, this method provides a general procedure for analyzing models containing unobserved variables.

Actually, the method is far more general and flexible than we have been able to illustrate here. In addition to the specific applications discussed in this chapter, it can be used to analyze multitrait-multimethod data, clinical assessment ratings, variance and covariance components models, and longitudinal data (Jöreskog, 1978; see also Alwin and Jackson, 1979; Bentler, 1980; Long, 1976; McIver et al., 1980; and Wheaton et al., 1977).

The methodology has been extended to facilitate the study of other types of problems as well. Examination of the invariance of a model generating the relationships among variables in multiple populations is possible (Jöreskog, 1971; van Thilo and Jöreskog, 1970; Sörbom and Jöreskog, 1976; Alwin and Jackson, 1979: Mare and Mason, 1980; Corcoran, 1980). It is also possible to model the structure underlying sample means as well as variances and covariances (Sörbom, 1974, 1976).

There are some limitations that should be noted concerning the estimation procedures. The method assumes continuity of variables, linearity of relations, multivariate normality of data, and is based on large-sample theory. At present, there is only a rudimentary understanding of how violations of these assumptions affect the obtained estimates. A high priority for future research is to determine the relative robustness of this method through analytical (Browne, 1974) and Monte Carlo (Boomsa, 1981; Geweke and Singleton, 1980; Olsson, 1979) investigations.

Finally, we would underscore the critical role of theory in guiding applications of this methodology. It can easily be misused, negating its contribution to social analysis. If used properly, however, its potential contribution is substantial. Given well-grounded theoretical propositions and appropriate data, this general method for analyzing covariance structures should play an increasingly prominent role in the social sciences.

NOTES

1. For this discussion, we are following Jöreskog's convention of letting Θ be a vector of all the unknown parameters that are to be estimated in the model.

2. For the general model, one necessary condition for identification of all parameters is that the number of parameters to be estimated (t) be less than the number of observed variances and covariances; i.e., $t < \frac{1}{2}(p+q)(p+q+1)$ where p is the number of observed y variables and q is the number of observed χ variables. If the data are scale-free, correlations rather than variances and covariances may be analyzed. In this case, the necessary condition for identification becomes $t < \frac{1}{2}(p+q)(p+q-1)$.

Beyond this very simple necessary condition, few additional guidelines exist for the identification of the general model. Consequently, Jöreskog and Sörbom (1978) provide a numerical method for determining whether or not a model is identified. After computing the maximum likelihood coefficients of a given model, one computes the information matrix (the variance-covariance matrix of the parameter estimates) for all independent parameters. Following Silvey (1970), Jöreskog and Sörbom argue that if this information matrix is positive definite, it is "almost certain" the model is identified. But if it is singular, the model is not identified. This empirical approach to evaluating identification has been criticized by McDonald and Krane (1979), McIver (1980), and Bentler (1980).

While few guidelines exist for evaluating the identification of the general model, certain criteria have been outlined for identifying special cases of the general model. Jöreskog (1969, 1979), Dunn (1973), Jennrich (1978), and Algina (1980) discuss various criteria for computing unique factor analysis estimates. Fisher (1966) remains the definitive source for the identification of structural equation models for variables measured without error. Wiley (1973); Werts et al. (1973); Geraci (1976); Hsiao (1976); and Jöreskog (1977) provide examples of how structured equation models with imperfectly measured variables may be identified.

3. All three methods (ULS, GLS, and ML) minimize their respective function using basically the same algorithm. For a brief discussion of this algorithm, see Jöreskog, 1978. For a detailed comparison of these three estimation methods, see Jöreskog, 1976.

4. Recently, Bentler and Weeks (1980) have proposed a slightly different method for estimating covariance structures that does not assume multivariate normality.

5. Bentler and Bonett (1980) have proposed a new strategy for comparing hierarchical covariance structure models. They offer a more general solution to the sensitivity of the χ^2 test to sample size than the Tucker-Lewis reliability coefficient, $\hat{\rho}$, which is appropriate only to factor models. Unfortunately, their article appeared too late to be considered in this report.

6. Support for the study was provided by the National Science Foundation, NSF Grant SOC73-05801A01. The principal investigator was Roberta S. Sigel.

7. Actually, the common factor model is a more general model. However, in the single-factor case, the common factor and congeneric models are statistically equivalent. (This assumes, of course, that the specific variance component of the factor is assigned to the unique variance.)

8. The relationship between equation 15 and this written explanation of that equation is easily seen once it is realized that $(\underline{1}\underline{1}')$ is a square matrix (of order p) that is filled with ones. Multiplication of this matrix by λ^2 fills it with the item covariances, while addition of the diagonal matrix $\underline{\Theta}$, provides the item variances on the diagonal of $\underline{\Sigma}$.

9. If we return to our definition of a correlation as the covariance of two items divided by the product of their standard deviations, we can easily demonstrate this result. All parallel items have identical variances; $\sigma_i^2 = \sigma_j^2 = \sigma^2 = \lambda^2 + \theta$. The covariance of any two parallel measures is the same as any other pair ($\theta_{ij} = \lambda^2$ for all i and j). Thus, the correlation of any two parallel measures is $\lambda^2/(\lambda^2 + \theta) = r$. Tau-equivalent measures differ from parallel measures in that they do not have equal item variances, i.e., $\sigma_i^2 \neq \sigma_j^2$ because $\lambda^2 + \theta_i \neq \lambda^2 + \theta_j$. Consequently, the correlations among tau-equivalent items are not equal: $r_{ij} \neq r_{ik}$ because

$$\frac{\chi^2}{\sqrt{\chi^2 + \theta_i}\ \sqrt{\chi^2 + \theta_j}} \neq \frac{\chi^2}{\sqrt{\chi^2 + \theta_i}\ \sqrt{\chi^2 + \theta_k}}$$

10. Rosenberg's original scale contained ten items. However, various item analyses revealed that one of the items, "I wish I could have more respect for myself," is only weakly related to the other items in the scale. Therefore, it was removed before this analysis was undertaken.

11. This equation is usually expressed as $y = \underset{\sim}{B} \underset{\sim}{x} + e$.

12. These OLS assumptions are:

(a) The expectations of the disturbances equal zero.
(b) The variances of the disturbances are identical (i.e., they are homoscedastic).
(c) The covariances among the disturbances are zero (i.e., no serial correlation exists).
(d) The independent variables (the regressors) are fixed in repeated samples *or* they are distributed independently of the disturbances.
(e) No exact linear relationship exists between any of the independent variables (i.e., they must not be collinear).
(f) The number of independent variables in any equation is less than the number of independent pieces of information in the data (i.e., the number of independent variables in the model must be less than the rank of $\underset{\sim}{S}$).

13. In general, with only a single indicator the analyst must assume that the unobserved variable is measured without error. However, in some cases prior information can be used to estimate the reliability of single-indicator measurement models. For an example see Knoke (1979).

14. A final comment on this analysis may be useful. Because we wished to illustrate the application of the analysis of covariance structures model to structural equations with a simple example, we examined only models in which errors of measurement were assumed random. In absolute terms, however, the χ^2 test indicates that Model III does not accurately reproduce the sample variance-covariance matrix. There is some systematic variance in these data that our model is not adequately explaining. Model III might be inadequate because of its failure to account for correlated errors of measurement or methods factors. Alternatively, the model might be theoretically deficient. For example, participation may be a multidimensional phenomenon—more than one unmeasured variable may be responsible for responses to the six participation items.

Incorporating these factors into our model would provide better parameter estimates of the relationships between our unmeasured variables. Obviously, we would end up with a much more complex model. Our ability to improve model fit in this way is possible only through theoretical insight concerning the problems of our original measurement and/or of our structural models.

15. Reduced form coefficients may also be computed in matrix form as $\underset{\sim}{B}^{-1}\underset{\sim}{\Gamma}$. LISREL will provide estimates of the reduced form coefficients as the $\underset{\sim}{D}$ matrix. The interested reader can reproduce the reduced form coefficients from the path coefficients reported in Figure 3 and in this way also examine the importance of each compound path.

108 Unobserved Variables

REFERENCES

ALGINA, J. (1980) "A note on identification in the oblique and orthogonal factor analysis models." Psychometrika 45 (September): 393-396.

ALWIN, D. F. and R. M. HAUSER (1975) "The decomposition of effects in path analysis." Amer. Soc. Rev. 40 (February): 37-46.

ALWIN, D. F. and D. J. JACKSON (1979) "Measurement models for response errors in surveys: issues and application," in K. F. Schuessler (ed.) Sociological Methodology 1980. San Francisco, California: Jossey-Bass.

BENTLER, P. M. (1980) "Multivariate analysis with latent variables: causal modeling." Annual Rev. in Psychology 31: 419-456.

———and D. G. BONETT (1980) "Significance tests and goodness-of-fit in the analysis of covariance structures." Psych. Bull. 88 (November): 588-606.

BENTLER, P. M. and D. G. WEEKS (1980) "Linear structural equations with latent variables." Psychometrika 45 (September): 298-308.

BOOMSA, A. (1981) "The robustness of LISREL against small sample sizes in factor analysis models," in K. G. Jöreskog and H. Wold (eds.) Systems under Indirect Observation: Causality, Structure, Prediction.

BROWNE, M. W. (1974) "Generalized least-squares estimators in the analysis of covariance structures." South African Stat. J. 8: 1-24.

BURT, R. S. (1973) "Confirmatory factor-analytic structures and the theory construction process." Soc. Methods and Research 2 (November): 131-190.

CARMINES, E. C. and R. A. ZELLER (1979) Reliability and Validity Assessment. Sage University Paper Series on Quantitative Applications in the Social Sciences, Series 07-017. Beverly Hills, CA: Sage.

——— (1974) "On establishing the empirical dimensionality of theoretical terms: an analytical example." Pol. Methodology 1: 75-96.

CORCORAN, M. (1980) "Sex differences in measurement error in status attainment models." Soc. Methods and Research 9 (November): 199-217.

COSTNER, H. L. and R. SCHOENBERG (1973) "Diagnosing indicator ills in multiple indicator models," in A. S. Goldberger and O. D. Duncan (eds.) Structural Equation Models in the Social Sciences. New York: Seminar.

DUNN, J. E. (1973) "A note on sufficiency condition for uniqueness of a restricted factor matrix." Psychometrika 38:141-143.

FINNEY, J. M. (1972) "Indirect effects in path analysis." Soc. Methods and Research 1 (November): 175-186.

FISHER, F. M. (1966) The Identification Problem in Econometrics. New York: McGraw-Hill.

GERACI, V. J. (1976) "Identification of simultaneous equation models with measurement error." J. of Econometrics 4: 262-283.

GEWEKE, J. F. and K. J. SINGLETON (1980) "Interpreting the likelihood ratio statistic in factor models when sample size is small." J. of the Amer. Stat. Assn. 75: 133-137.

GRUVAEUS, G. and K. G. JÖRESKOG (1970) A Computer Program for Minimizing a Function of Several Variables. Princeton, NJ: Educational Testing Service.

HSIAO, C. (1976) "Identification and estimation of simultaneous equation models with measurement error." Int. Econ. Rev. 17: 319-339.

JENNRICH, R. I. (1978) "Rotational equivalence of factor loading matrices with specified values." Psychometrika 43: 421-426.

JOHNSTON, J. (1972) Econometric Methods. New York: McGraw-Hill.

JÖRESKOG, K. G. (1979) Addendum to "A General Approach to Confirmatory Maximum Likelihood Factor Analysis," in Advances in Factor Analysis and Structural Equation Models. Cambridge, Massachusetts: Abt.

_____(1978) "Structural analysis of covariance and correlation matrices." Psychometrika 43: 443-477.

_____(1977) "Structural equation models in the social sciences: specification, estimation, and testing," in P. R. Krishnaiah (ed.) Applications of Statistics. New York: Elsevier North Holland.

_____(1976) "Factor analysis by least squares and maximum likelihood methods," in K. Enslein et al. (eds.) Statistical Methods for Digital Computers. New York: John Wiley.

_____(1974) "Analyzing psychological data by structural analysis of covariance matrices," in R. C. Atkinson et al. (eds.) Contemporary Developments in Mathematical Psychology—Volume II. San Francisco, CA: Freeman.

_____(1973a) "A general method for estimating a linear structural equation system," in A. S. Goldberger and O. D. Duncan (eds.) Structural Equation Models in the Social Sciences. New York: Seminar.

_____(1973b) "Analysis of covariance structures," in P. R. Krishnaiah (ed.) Multivariate Analysis—III. New York: Academic.

_____(1971a) "Simultaneous factor analysis in several populations." Psychometrika 36 (December): 409-426.

_____(1971b) "Statistical analysis of sets of congeneric tests." Psychometrika 36: 109-133.

_____(1970) "A general method for analysis of covariance structures. Biometrika 57: 239-251.

_____(1969) "A general approach to confirmatory maximum likelihood factor analysis." Psychometrika 34 (June): 183-202.

_____(1967) "Some contributions to maximum likelihood factor analysis." Psychometrika 32 (December): 443-482.

_____and D. SÖRBOM (1978) LISREL IV—A General Computer Program for Estimation of a Linear Structural System by Maximum Likelihood Methods.

KNOKE, D. (1979) "Stratification and the dimensions of American political orientations." Amer. J. of Pol. Sci. 23 (November): 772-791.

LEE, S. Y. (1977) "Some algorithms for covariance structure analysis," Ph.D. dissertation, University of California, Los Angeles.

LONG, J. S. (1976) "Estimation and hypothesis testing in linear models containing measurement error: a review of Jöreskog's model for the analysis of covariance structures." Soc. Methods and Research 5: 157-206.

LORD, F. M. and M. R. NOVICK (1968) Statistical Theories of Mental Test Scores. Reading, MA: Addison-Wesley.

MARE, R. D. and W. M. MASON (1980) "Children's reports of parental economic status: a multiple group measurement model." Soc. Methods and Research 9 (November): 178-198.

McCLOSKY, H. (1968) "Political participation," in International Encyclopedia of the Social Sciences. New York: Macmillan.

McDONALD, R. P. and W. R. KRANE (1979) "A Monte Carlo study of local identifiability and degrees of freedom in the asymptotic likelihood ratio test." British J. of Mathematical and Stat. Psychology 32: 121-132.

McIVER, J. P. (1980) "Model specification and identification in confirmatory factor analysis—a problem for practitioners." (unpublished)

———E. G. CARMINES, and R. A. ZELLER (1980) "Multiple indicators," in R. A. Zeller and E. G. Carmines, Measurement in the Social Sciences: The Link Between Theory and Data. New York: Cambridge Univ. Press.

MOSBAEK, E. J. and H. O. WOLD (1970) Interdependent Systems: Structure and Estimation. New York: Elsevier North Holland.

MUSSEN, P. H. and A. B. WYSZNSKI (1952) "Personality and political participation." Human Relations 5: 65-82.

OLSSON, V. (1979) "On the robustness of factor analysis against crude classification of the observations." Multivariate Behavioral Research 14: 485-500.

ROSENBERG, M. (1965) Society and the Adolescent Self-Image. Princeton, NJ: Princeton Univ. Press.

SILVEY, S. D. (1970) Statistical Inference. Harmondsworth, England: Penguin.

SÖRBOM, D. (1976) "A statistical model for the measurement of change in true scores," in D. N. M. DeGruijter and L. J. Th. van der Kamp (eds.) Advances in Psychological and Educational Measurement. New York: John Wiley.

———(1975) "Detection of correlated errors in longitudinal data." British J. of Mathematical and Stat. Psychology 28: 138-151.

———(1974) "A general method for studying differences in factor means and factor structure between groups." British J. of Mathematical and Stat. Psychology 27 (November): 229-239.

———and K. G. JÖRESKOG (1976) COFAMM—Confirmatory Factor Analysis with Model Modifications. Chicago: National Educational Resources.

THEIL, H. (1971) Principles of Econometrics. New York: John Wiley.

TUCKER, L. R. and C. LEWIS (1973) "A reliability coefficient for maximum likelihood factor analysis." Psychometrika 38: 1-10.

van THILLO, M. and K. G. JÖRESKOG (1970) SIFASP—A General Computer Program for Simultaneous Factor Analysis in Several Populations. Research Bulletin 70-62. Princeton, NJ: Educational Testing Service.

WERTS, C. E., K. G. JÖRESKOG, and R. LINN (1973) "Identification and estimation in path analysis with unmeasured variables." Amer. J. of Sociology 78: 1469-1484.

WHEATON, B., B. MUTHEN, D. F. ALWIN, and G. F. SUMMERS (1977) "Assessing the reliability and stability in panel models," in D. R. Heise (ed.) Sociological Methodology 1977. San Francisco: Jossey-Bass.

WILEY, D. E. (1973) "The identification problem for structural equation models with unmeasured variables," in A. S. Goldberger and O. D. Duncan (eds.) Structural Equation Models in the Social Sciences. New York: Seminar Press.

ZELLER, R. A. and E. G. CARMINES (1980) Measurement in the Social Sciences: The Link Between Theory and Data. New York: Cambridge Univ. Press.

———(1976) "Factory scaling, external consistency, and the measurement of theoretical constructs." Pol. Methodology 3: 215-252.

APPENDIX

THE PENNSYLVANIA HIGH SCHOOL SURVEY

The questionnaire was designed to collect information about each adolescent's opinions concerning the political system and various citizenship roles, his or her participation in a wide range of conventional political activities, individual personality traits, knowledge levels, and demographic characteristics. Data from this survey are used in each of our three analyses.

Test theory models were applied to a series of nine items designed to measure the personality trait of self-esteem. Each item asks the respondent to make a positive or negative judgment about himself or herself by responding "almost always true," "often true," "sometimes true," "seldom true," or "never true" to the following statements:

(1) I feel that I have a number of good qualities.
(2) I feel I am a person of worth, at least on an equal plane with others.
(3) I feel I do not have much to be proud of.
(4) I take a positive attitude toward myself.
(5) I certainly feel useless at times.
(6) All in all, I am inclined to feel that I am a failure.
(7) I am able to do things as well as most other people.
(8) At times I think I am no good at all.
(9) On the whole, I am satisfied with myself.

The high schoolers' responses to ten questions about what makes a good citizen are the data that we explore in our example of the use of the LISREL program for factor analysis.

Below is a list of qualities some people consider important in a good citizen. For each quality, check the answer that most accurately describes how important you think it is for being a good citizen. (Each item permits five responses—extremely important, important, no opinion, not very important, not at all important.)

(1) voting in most elections
(2) trying to influence government decisions and policies
(3) keeping informed about public affairs
(4) volunteering for service to the local community
(5) working hard

TABLE A-1

Correlations Among 10 Good-Citizenship Items

	GC1	GC2	GC3	GC4	GC5	GC6	GC7	GC8	GC9	GC10
GC1	1.00									
GC2	.291	1.00								
GC3	.377	.413	1.00							
GC4	.176	.315	.340	1.00						
GC5	.163	.181	.144	.219	1.00					
GC6	.080	.185	.165	.275	.374	1.00				
GC7	.114	.239	.214	.400	.275	.536	1.00			
GC8	.219	.062	.133	.147	.194	.141	.106	1.00		
GC9	.242	.118	.150	.301	.306	.218	.152	.371	1.00	
GC10	.225	.219	.176	.300	.266	.226	.206	.208	.550	1.00

(6) being a good human being
(7) being friendly and helpful to our fellow men
(8) obeying the law
(9) honoring one's country
(10) not bringing dishonor to the country

The sample correlation matrix for these ten citizenship items is presented in Table A1.

Last, our presentation of the use of the LISREL program for analyzing structural equation models with latent and measured variables draws on our earlier analyses of self-esteem and citizenship as well as on several other series of questions asked in the Pennsylvania survey. These questions are presented here as indicators of each of the latent variables in our model of the determinants of political participation (Figure 3):

ξ_1 – Political Environment, Parents
    x_1 – Do you hear your parents talk about politics? (very often, occasionally, not at all)

ξ_2 – Political Environment, School
    x_2 – Number of civics, social studies, or current events courses. (none, one, more than one)
    x_3 – Watergate discussed in classes. (regularly, a few times, just once, never)

ξ_3 – Respondent Self-Esteem
    x_4 through x_{12} – See previous section.

η_1 — Exposure to Politics

    y_1 — Some people think about what is going on in politics and public affairs very often and others are not that interested. How much of an interest do you take in such matters? (very great deal, a lot of interest, some interest, very little interest, no interest at all)

    y_2 — Thinking about the important political issues facing the country, how well do you understand these issues? (very well, moderately well, depends on the issue, not so well, not at all)

    y_3 — Do you follow current events in the news? (almost everyday, maybe once or twice a week, very seldom, not at all)

η_2 — Comprehension of Political World

    y_4 — Number of political leaders correctly identified. (0-7)

    y_5 — Number of international political affairs items correctly answered. (0-4)

    y_6 — Number of state political questions correctly answered. (0-5)

η_3 — Citizenship Orientation to Politics (see previous section for response codes)

    y_7 — Voting in most elections.

    y_8 — Trying to influence government decisions.

    y_9 — Keeping informed about public affairs.

η_4 — Participation Index (never, once, more than once)

    y_{10} — Campaigned for a candidate.

    y_{11} — Tried to convince people how to vote.

    y_{12} — Wore a campaign button/bumper sticker on car.

    y_{13} — Stopped a candidate to talk.

    y_{14} — Complained to or made request of government official.

    y_{15} — Participated in a political demonstration.

The sample correlation matrix and item standard deviations for these items are presented in Table A2.

TABLE A-2

Correlations and Standard Deviations Among the 27 Items
of the Participation Model

	Y1	Y2	Y3	Y4	Y5	Y6	Y7	Y8	Y9	Y10
Y1	1.000									
Y2	.472	1.000								
Y3	.483	.412	1.000							
Y4	-.285	-.307	-.280	1.000						
Y5	-.225	-.234	-.277	.561	1.000					
Y6	-.272	-.259	-.261	.590	.441	1.000				
Y7	-.314	-.210	-.283	.161	.162	.161	1.000			
Y8	-.232	-.191	-.145	.070	.076	.138	.287	1.000		
Y9	-.319	-.277	-.328	.161	.164	.197	.368	.408	1.000	
Y10	-.209	-.144	-.105	.154	.114	.178	.111	.070	.097	1.000
Y11	-.282	-.227	-.219	.172	.139	.180	.203	.160	.237	.299
Y12	-.185	-.182	-.165	.193	.180	.212	.202	.180	.161	.255
Y13	-.181	-.166	-.129	.113	.077	.161	.088	.111	.106	.361
Y14	-.265	-.247	-.215	.172	.155	.223	.097	.145	.175	.174
Y15	-.148	-.139	-.060	.082	.057	.038	.057	.063	.028	.270
X1	.205	.220	.194	-.097	-.130	-.108	-.190	-.162	-.171	-.111
X2	-.175	-.187	-.174	.230	.189	.219	.106	.070	.085	.098
X3	-.276	-.253	-.230	.227	.209	.209	.103	.040	.193	.047
X4	-.202	-.183	-.157	.121	.133	.162	..151	.181	.154	.088
X5	-.226	-.201	-.234	.172	.135	.152	.094	.136	.171	.072
X6	-.073	-.097	-.048	.014	-.016	.005	.059	.054	.022	.029
X7	-.205	-.181	-.134	.056	.066	.090	.105	.091	.176	.060
X8	-.052	-.093	-.074	.006	.002	.037	.002	.071	.051	.020
X9	-.109	-.099	-.116	.083	.078	.126	.073	.067	.098	.011
X10	-.114	-.114	-.132	.045	.042	.059	.095	.097	.103	.021
X11	-.088	-.107	-.132	.063	.080	.099	.039	.059	.084	.042
X12	-.130	-.115	-.129	-.005	.009	.027	.120	.074	.149	.027

	Y11	Y12	Y13	Y14	Y15	X1	X2	X3	X4	X5
Y11	1.000									
Y12	.222	1.000								
Y13	.245	.196	1.000							
Y14	.217	.176	.257	1.000						
Y15	.204	.128	.221	.181	1.000					
X1	-.151	-.174	-.165	-.105	-.073	1.000				
X2	.159	.139	.088	.151	.003	-.088	1.000			
X3	.092	.097	.103	.162	.110	-.164	.217	1.000		
X4	.123	.035	.108	.140	.022	-.105	.051	.068	1.000	
X5	.120	.048	.080	.135	.073	-.117	.161	.152	.471	1.000
X6	.077	-.103	.039	.057	.002	-.047	.078	.015	.313	.301
X7	.120	.038	.113	.131	.045	-.044	.017	.078	.397	.403
X8	.069	.063	.098	.073	.006	-.039	-.013	.005	.255	.252
X9	.056	.021	.062	.100	.054	-.035	.034	.065	.331	.365
X10	.031	.006	.044	.088	.058	-.038	.008	.076	.374	.433
X11	.052	.023	.061	.115	.042	.006	-.024	.085	.336	.369
X12	.081	.034	.079	.105	.008	-.076	.042	.086	.419	.413

	X6	X7	X8	X9	X10	X11	X12
X6	1.000						
X7	.361	1.000					
X8	.336	.364	1.000				
X9	.443	.367	.403	1.000			
X10	.239	.340	.236	.317	1.000		
X11	.361	.399	.469	.522	.237	1.000	
X12	.325	.484	.310	.433	.381	.402	1.000

TABLE A-2 (Continued)

Standard Deviations

y_1	.7303	x_1	.5292
y_2	.7811	x_2	.6144
y_3	.9302	x_3	.7529
y_4	1.9841	x_4	.7390
y_5	1.0761	x_5	.8101
y_6	1.1050	x_6	.9407
y_7	.7672	x_7	.9326
y_8	.9124	x_8	.9730
y_9	.8520	x_9	.8311
y_{10}	.3921	x_{10}	.7351
y_{11}	.4592	x_{11}	.8661
y_{12}	.4974	x_{12}	.8549
y_{13}	.3714		
y_{14}	.4575		
y_{15}	.3189		

Edward G. Carmines is an associate professor of political science at Indiana University, Bloomington. His primary research interests are in American politics and methodology, and he has published articles in these areas in a variety of academic journals. He is the coauthor of Statistical Analysis of Social Data *(Rand McNally, 1978),* Realiability and Validity Assessment *(Sage, 1979), and* Measurement in the Social Sciences: The Link Between Theory and Data *(Cambridge University Press, 1980). His current research focuses of the emergence and development of political issues.*

John P. McIver is a graduate student in political science at Indiana University. In addition to statistical issues, his research interests include intergovernmental relations, public policy analysis, and political attitudes and participation.

CHAPTER FOUR

Latent Trait Modeling
of Attitude Items

MARK REISER
Indiana University

Over the past few decades, there has been considerable effort within the field of educational measurement devoted to the theoretical development of a unidimensional scaling model for discrete variables. This measurement model is known variously as the latent trait model, the item characteristic curve model, the item-response curve model, the item-response model, and, in a special case, the Rasch model. It originates with Lawley (1943), Lord (1952, 1953a, 1953b), Rasch (1960), and Birnbaum (1968). We will make use of the term "latent trait model" here, and we will refer to the scores produced for each individual in the sample to which the model is fit as "scale scores." These terms serve to bridge the gap in terminology used by those interested in attitude measurement as opposed to those interested in educational measurement. For example, in educational research, item-response models

AUTHOR'S NOTE: *The author would like to thank George Bohrnstedt and Neil Henry for comments that improved the chapter significantly. Art Stinchcombe and Otis Dudley Duncan also made valuable comments on an* are used to measure ability, a term that clearly does not apply for attitude measurement.

Despite the fact that the latent trait model is closely related to latent structure analysis (Lazarsfeld 1950, 1954, 1960; Lazarsfeld and Henry, 1968), there has been little use of the model in attitude measurement research. In this chapter we will first present the model and then show how it can be used as a tool for the statistical analysis of a set of item responses.

For clear and comprehensive introduction to the latent trait model, the reader is referred to Torgerson (1958). Torgerson offers not only an introduction to the scaling model, but also discusses how the item-response model relates to both the latent class model and to the Thurstonian models for item scaling. There has been a great deal of progress in methods for parameter estimation in the latent trait model since Torgerson completed his monograph in 1958; therefore interested readers need to go elsewhere for discussions of this work (see Bock and Wood, 1971; Lumsden, 1976).

MODEL

The basis of the latent trait model is that responses to dichotomous or polytomous items are stochastically related to a continuous latent variable. In discussing the model, we will be speaking of an "agree" response as though it is the one of the two possible responses to a dichotomous item associated with a higher trait value on the part of the respondent. Of course, some items can be worded so that the "not agree" response actually indicates a higher trait value, or so that the respondent has to answer the item with a "yes" or a "no." For purposes of discussion, we will be referring to the response associated with

earlier version. Partial support for this research came from an NIMH—supported training grant in measurement, PHS T32 MH 15789-02. Computer funds were provided by the University of Indiana Wrubel Computing Center.

a higher trait value as the agree response, regardless of how the item may be worded.

If the probability of a response to an item was a linear function of the latent variable, a method not too different from a linear regression could be used to fit a model to some data. But the function is not linear; instead it is represented by an ogive or S-shaped curve, called an item characteristic or item-response curve. The choice for the function that gives this curve is usually between the normal ogive and the logistic curve. The logistic item characteristic curve takes the following form:

$$P(k_{ij} = 1 \mid \theta_j, c_i, a_i) = \frac{1}{1 + \exp(-z_{ij})} \qquad [1]$$

where

$$k_{ij} = \begin{cases} 1 \text{ if respondent } j \text{ agrees with item } i \\ \\ 0 \text{ otherwise,} \end{cases}$$

a_i and c_i are item parameters discussed below,

θ_j is the respondent trait value on the latent variable, and

$$z_{ij} = a_i\theta_j + c_i, \qquad [2]$$

The item intercept, c_i, gives an indication of item "difficulty" in the sense that an item would be difficult if fewer than 50% of a sample gave the agree response. The item slope, a_i, is the parameter associated with item discriminating power. It is analogous to a factor loading for a one-factor model of the items.

The logistic curve is used by Rasch (1960, 1966), Birnbaum (1968), Wood et al. (1976), Bock (1972), and Anderson (1972, 1980), and it is implicit in the model that follows from Luce's choice axiom (1959). The latent trait model with this function has many similarities to Berkson's (1944) logit analysis.

The normal ogive item characteristic curve is the cumulative frequency function of the normal distribution:

$$P(k_{ij} = 1 \mid \theta_j, a_i, c_i) = \frac{1}{\sqrt{2\pi}} \int_{-\infty}^{z_{ij}} \exp\left(-\frac{1}{2} z^2\right) \, dz \qquad [3]$$

where all symbols have the same meaning as in equation 1. The normal ogive is used by Lawley (1943), Lord (1952), and Bock and Liebermann (1970). Birnbaum (1968) and Samejina (1969) discuss both the logistic and normal curves, and Yellott (1977) gives an in-depth study of their interrelationship in scaling models. The normal ogive is in the tradition of Thurstonian scaling, and a latent trait model based on it is closely associated with Finney's probit analysis model. Indeed, if the underlying continuous variable that we are considering was observable, we could estimate the item parameters, a_i and c_i, with a probit analysis. Figures 1 and 2 show some normal ogive item characteristic curves.

Since for purposes of discussion we are considering only dichotomous items, the probability that respondent j does not agree with item i is simply the complement of the probability of the agree response:

$$P(k_{ij} = 0 \mid \theta_j, a_i, c_i) = 1 - P(k_{ij} = 1 \mid \theta_j, a_i, c_i) \qquad [4]$$

The logistic curve is used more frequently than the normal because it is simpler mathematically, and the parameter estimates obtained with the two functions differ for all practical purposes only by a constant (see Haberman, 1974: 34). On the other hand, the connection between the normal ogive curve and scaling models can be developed to provide a conceptualization of the parameters of the latent trait model as scaling parameters. This development will be presented here to provide a geometrical interpretation of the item parameters for the benefit of those who are being introduced to latent trait theory. The inclusion of the development is not intended as a promotion of the scaling model, since the probabilistic relationship between item responses and a continuous latent variable

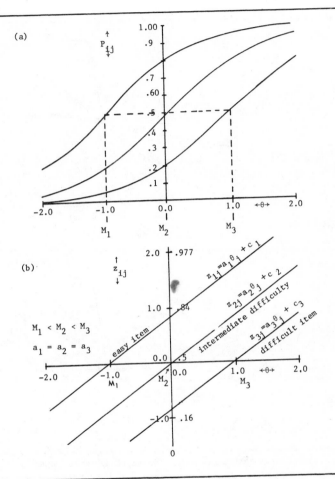

Figure 1: Item Characteristic Curves: Equal Slopes, Different Thresholds

NOTE: The item threshold, M_i, falls at the point where 50% of the respondents with that trait value agree with the item. The plot shows the curves in (a) with the probabilities on the x axis transformed to standard normal deviates. Probabilities are shown on the right side of the y axis.

can be posited without it. Some readers may prefer to skip directly to the discussion following expression 15. The following presentation is based on Torgerson (1958) and Bock and Jones (1968), the latter giving a rigorous statistical presentation of Thurstonian scaling.

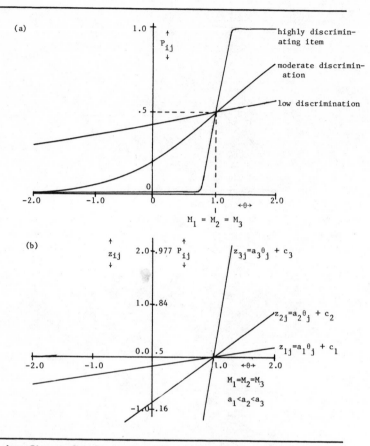

Figure 2: Item Characteristic Curves: Equal Thresholds, Different Slopes

NOTE: Items with higher discriminating power have steeper slopes. The curves in (a) with the probabilities on the x axis transformed to standard normal deviates.

THE SCALING MODEL

The probability that a respondent agrees with an item can be obtained as a function of the item parameters and the re-sponent's trait value by considering the positions of the item and respondent on the scale that underlies all of the items. Respondent j has position θ_j and item i has position M_i. The positions for item and respondents may vary across occasions

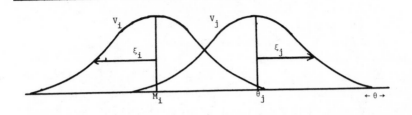

Figure 3: Discriminal Variables V_i and V_j

NOTE: The random variable V_j exceeds V_i with a probability that can be expressed in terms of their distributions.

because of random influences; hence the positions are represented by probability distributions. The distributions have mean θ_j and M_i for respondent j and item i respectively (see Figure 3).

The distributions in Figure 3 are usually taken to be normal distributions with standard deviations ξ_j and ξ_i. This is a reasonable assumption if the influences that disturb the positions over occasions are entirely random. The situation in Figure 3 is very closely related to models for Thurstonian scaling (see Bock and Jones, 1968). Mosteller (1958) has found that the type of distributions assumed around the scale positions has little effect on the final parameter estimates in the Thurston models.

When a respondent answers an item, his response is a function of the distance between the position of the item and his own position, and the variability of the positions. We may represent the respondent's perception of the position of the item by the discriminal variable V_i, where

$$V_i = M_i + \epsilon_i, \qquad [5]$$

and his perception of his own position by the discriminal variable V_j, with

$$V_j = \theta_j + \epsilon_j \qquad [6]$$

The ϵ_i and ϵ_j terms, error components representing random influences on positions, are assumed to be uncorrelated. This important assumption means that conditional on the means θ_j and M_i, the discriminal responses are independent; no other variables influence V_i and V_j.

Respondent j, then, agrees with item i whenever $V_j > V_i$, and we can write this relationship as a function of the variable $V_{ij} = V_i - V_j$. The respondent agrees whenever

$$V_{ij} = M_i + \epsilon_i - \theta_j - \epsilon_j < 0. \qquad [7]$$

V_{ij}, representing the difference between two normally distributed variables, is also distributed normally with mean $M_i - \theta_j$ and variance $\sigma^2 = \xi_i^2 + \xi_j^2$ (ϵ_i and ϵ_j are uncorrelated).

Since the probability that the respondent agrees with item i is equal to the probability that $V_{ij} < 0$, and since V_{ij} has a normal distribution, we can represent the probability of the agree response as area under the normal density curve (see Figure 4).

This probability is given by the cumulative frequency function for the normal distribution:

$$P(k_{ij} = 1 \mid \theta_j, M_i, \sigma_i) = \frac{1}{\sqrt{2\pi}\sigma_i} \int_{-\infty}^{0} \exp - \frac{1}{2} \frac{\left[y - (M_i - \theta_j) \right]^2}{\sigma_i^2} \, dy \qquad [8]$$

where

$$k_{ij} = \begin{cases} 1 \text{ if respondent j agrees with item 1} \\ 0 \text{ otherwise} \end{cases}$$

Two transformations of expression 8 will give the probability of an agree response as it is usually written. First, a fairly standard procedure with normal distributions is to change the variable of integration:

$$\text{If } z = \frac{y - (M_i - \theta_j)}{\sigma_i}, \qquad [9]$$

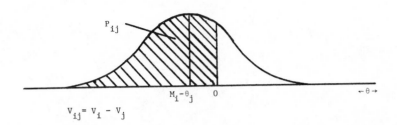

Figure 4: Variable V_{ij}

NOTE: The location of the zero point depends on the distance between M_i and θ_j. If M_i equals θ_j, the zero point falls at the mean, $M_i - \theta_j$. In that case, 50% of the respondents would agree with the item.

then

$$dz = \frac{1}{\sigma_i} \, dy, \qquad [10]$$

and at $y = 0$,

$$z = \frac{-(M_i - \theta_j)}{\sigma_i}. \qquad [11]$$

With this change of variable,

$$P(k_{ij} = 1 \mid \theta_j, M_i, \sigma_i) = \frac{1}{\sqrt{2\pi}} \int_{-\infty}^{-\frac{(M_i - \theta_j)}{\sigma_i}} \exp\left(-\frac{1}{2} z^2\right) dz \qquad [12]$$

Letting

$$-\frac{(M_i - \theta_j)}{\sigma_i} = \frac{\theta_j - M_i}{\sigma_i} = z_{ij}, \qquad [13]$$

$$P(k_{ij} = 1 | \theta_j, M_i, \sigma_i) = \frac{1}{\sqrt{2\pi}} \int_{-\infty}^{z_{ij}} \exp\left(-\frac{1}{2} z^2\right) dz \qquad [14]$$

The second transformation involves only the item parameters. If

$$a_i = \frac{1}{\sigma_i}, \quad \text{and} \quad c_i = -M_i a_i$$

then

$$z_{ij} = a_i \theta_j + c_i. \qquad [15]$$

This expression for z_{ij} originates with Tucker (1952). We now have the same expression for the item characteristic curve as we had in expression 2, and a new item parameter, M_i. M_i is the item threshold, and it represents the θ value on the underlying continuum at which a respondent with $\theta_j = M_i$ would have a probability of .5 for responding positively to the item. Both c_i and M_i are indicators of item difficulty, and as can be seen above, the threshold is equal to the negative of the intercept divided by the slope.[1]

PROBABILITY MODEL FOR SAMPLED DATA

Expressions 1 through 4 give the probabilities of responses to only one item. In order to write the probability of a respondent's entire response pattern, the principle of local independence is invoked. This principle embodies the assumption that there are two components to the variability of responses to an item. One component represents systematic variance that can be accounted for by the underlying latent variable, and the other component, which may consist of systematic and error variance, represents variance that is specific to the item alone. The important assumption is that

there is no combination of items that have any common
variance that cannot be accounted for by the single latent
variable. The principle of local independence is expressed
mathematically by writing the probability of a response
pattern with the binomial distribution function:

$$P(k_j = k|\theta_j, a, c) = \prod_{i=1}^{n} P(k_{ij} = 1|\theta_j)^{k_{ij}} \left[1 - P(k_{ij} = 1|\theta_j)\right]^{1-k_{ij}} \quad [16]$$

where a and b are vectors containing parameters for the n
items, k_j is the response pattern of the jth respondent, and k is
any one of the 2^n possible response patterns.

Expression 11 gives the probability of a response pattern
conditional on the respondent parameter θ_j. In terms of estimating the item parameters, a and c, the respondent parameter
θ appears as a nuisance parameter. It is a frequent practice in
estimation to eliminate a nuisance parameter from an equation
by integrating it out. The unconditional probability of response
pattern k, then, is

$$P(k_j = k|a, c) = \int_{-\infty}^{\infty} P(k_j = k|\theta_j, a, c)\ \phi(\theta)d\theta \quad [17]$$

where $\phi(\theta)$ represents the distribution of the latent variable,
θ, in population of interest.

Equations 11 and 12 look similar to the expressions that
Lazarsfeld called his accounting equations. However, there
are four differences between 11 and 12 and the accounting
equations (cf. Lazarsfeld, 1960):

(1) Latent structure analysis (LSA) uses any polynomial function
for the traceline between the latent variable and the probability of the response, with the simplest function being the most
preferred. The latent trait model (LTM) uses the normal (or
the nearly equivalent logistic) ogive in expressions 1 and 3.

(2) LTM usually (although not always) assumes normality for $\phi(\theta)$, while LSA makes no assumption about the distribution.
(3) LTM scales the items by specifying the item characteristic curve as a function of item parameters in 1 or 3. LSA provides no scaling of the items. For practical applications, this is the biggest difference between the models.
(4) In both theories, the latent variable is represented by a continuous one-dimensional space. LSA usually represents the resulting distribution of people over the space in classes that are as few in number as possible. LTM gives a point estimate on the latent space of the value most likely to produce each response pattern. There are 2^n response patterns for binary items.

PARAMETER ESTIMATION

With the ready availability of modern computers, estimates of the item parameters are now universally obtained by the method of maximum likelihood. If the latent trait model holds, the 2^n response patterns will have a multinominal distribution, with the probability of each response pattern given by expression 12. This relationship, when interpreted as a function of the unknown item parameters, gives the likelihood of the data, L. First derivatives of log L with respect to the unknown parameters are called the likelihood equations. They can be solved for the unknown parameters by a method such as Newton-Raphson (see Bock and Liebermann, 1970). This method of estimation is particularly appropriate when the number of items is small, as is usually the case in attitude scales. Bock and Aitken (forthcoming) have recently developed an especially efficient method for estimating the item parameters by reformulating the likelihood equations to make use of the EM-algorithm (Dempster et al., 1977). Other methods of estimation also exist (see Anderson, 1972, 1980; Bock and Kolakowski, 1973a, 1973b; Wood et al., 1976; and Wright and Panchapakesan, 1969).

When working with data, the model can be made somewhat more restrictive by constraining all of the item slopes in expression 11 to be equal. Such a model has become known as the one-parameter model (Birnbaum, 1968), and along with a logistic response curve, it is equivalent to the model developed by Rasch (1960). In the one-parameter model, if $M_i < M_h$ for items i and h, then $P_{jh} > P_{ij}$ for all values of θ. This is a very desirable feature, but it does not always hold when items are free to have different slopes. The two-parameter model, as it is known when the slopes are free to vary, and the one-parameter model are hierarchically nested in the sense that has become familiar with log-linear models (Goodman, 1974) and with structural equation models (Jöreskog, 1978). The fit of each model can be assessed with a likelihood ratio chi-square calculated over observed and expected frequencies for response patterns:

$$G^2 = -2N \sum_{\ell}^{2^n} P_\ell \log \frac{\hat{P}_\ell}{P_\ell} \qquad [18]$$

where

P_ℓ = observed proportion

$\hat{P}_\ell$ = expected proportion

n = number of items

N = the number of respondents

Since there are $2^n - 1$ free cells in the set of response patterns, the degrees of freedom are given by

$df_2 = 2^n - 2n - 1$ for the model where 2n parameters   [19]
                          are estimated

$df_1 = 2^n - n - 2$ for the model where n + 1 parameters   [20]
                          are estimated

If a chi-square is calculated for both models, the difference between the chi-squares also has a chi-square sampling distribution, on $df_1 - df_2$ degrees of freedom. Thus it is possible to test if there is an improvement in the fit of the model if item slopes are allowed to vary.

If the one parameter model fits the data, the respondent raw score is a sufficient statistic for the data in a response pattern (Anderson, 1977), and it can be used for particularly economical estimation. Anderson (1972) and Wright and Panchapakesan (1969) use this sufficient statistic in their methods of estimation. However, if the one-parameter model does not fit the data, it is not possible to estimate the two-parameter model with their methods.

When there is a large number of items in a scale, obtaining the parameter estimates can be quite expensive because of the numerical procedures required to calculate the integral in expression 12. Bock and Kolakowski (1973a, 1973b), Wood et al. (1976), and Wright and Panchapakesan (1969) circumvent this problem by making assumptions that allow them to group respondents to get estimates of P_{ij} for different values of θ. Their methods appear to be superseded by the solution given in Bock and Aitken (forthcoming), which avoids the integration by reformulating the likelihood equation.

Once the item parameter estimates have been obtained, maximum likelihood estimates of respondent scores can be calculated from expression 11 in a fairly straightforward manner. See the references cited above for giving methods of item parameter estimation. One problem exists with the maximum likelihood estimates for scores, in that the estimate for patterns with all-disagree or all-agree responses are negative and positive infinity. These are not really useful values, and they reflect more on the measurement properties of the items than on the respondent scores. If the item set contained more items with discriminating power in the tails of the distribution of the latent variables, there would be few respondents agreeing with all of the items, and few disagreeing with all of them. Since attitude scales usually have a small number of items, the frequencies for the all-agree and all-disagree response patterns may be large. In this situation, Bayes estimates can be used to hold the estimates away from infinity by incorporating information into the estimation process from a specified prior distribution of the latent variable (see Samejima, 1969; Muthen, 1977; Bock and Aitken, forthcoming). Since we are concentrating here on modeling items, we will not go farther with the topic of scoring respondents.

The theoretical development has now progressed to the point that the model can be applied to some data. In the next section we will use the model to examine some race-relations items for which data were collected from two different samples. With two samples, we will be able to address the topics of item parameter invariance and scale linking.

A RACIAL TOLERANCE SCALE

The model as described in the previous section was fit to the five most homogeneous items dealing with racial tolerance on the 1972 General Social Survey (Davis, 1978). When there is doubt, the homogeneity of items can be assessed beforehand by, for example, an exploratory factor analysis. See Christoffersson (1975) and Muthen (1978, 1979) for factor analysis of dichotomous items.

Parameters were estimated with the method of Bock and Aitken (forthcoming), using both the normal and logistic response curves.[2] Since the results with the normal differed from those with the logistic by only a constant, only the results from the logistic will be reported.

The data consisted of the responses of 1339 white adults, between the ages of 18 and 88, to the following five items:

JOB: Do you think Negroes should have as good a chance as white people to get any kind of job, or do you think white people should have the first chance at any kind of job? [As good a chance.]

SCHOOL: Do you think white students and Negro students should go to the same schools or to separate schools? [Same schools.]

TABLE 1
Parameters for 5 Racial Tolerance Items

Item	Threshold	(S.E.)	Intercept	(S.E.)	Slope	(S.E.)
JOB	-2.0583	(.1809)	5.4270	(.0397)	2.6366	(.1275)
SCHOOL	-1.2225	(.1223)	3.2564	(.2681)	2.6637	(.0935)
MAR	- .3168	(.1709)	.5498	(.0704)	1.7353	(.0590)
DIN	- .6573	(.3083)	1.4333	(.0994)	2.1808	(.0905)
PRES	- .6501	(.4048)	1.3653	(.0602)	2.1002	(.1226)

NOTE: Estimates are converged in solution to four decimal places, and are for the logistic curve. If the intercepts and slopes are divided by 1.7, the estimates correspond to the normal ogive model.

DIN: How strongly would you object if a member of your family wanted to bring a Black friend home to dinner? [Not at all.]

PRES: If your party nominated a Black for President, would you vote for him if he were qualified for the job? [Yes.]

MAR: Do you think there should be laws against marriages between Blacks and Whites? [No.]

Responses for each item were recoded to form a dichotomy. The response showing racial tolerance is listed inside brackets with the item in the list above. All other responses were recoded into one category that was used as showing racial intolerance.

The estimated slopes in Table 1 show that the items are fairly similar, with MAR having a somewhat weaker relationship to the scale than the other items. All of the thresholds are negative, which means that for each item more than 50% of the respondents gave the response associated with higher racial tolerance.

For the five items in Table 1, G^2 = 29.24 on 21 df (p = .1) for the two-parameter model, and G^2 = 306.39 on 25 df for the one-parameter model. The difference between the two chi-squares is also distributed as a chi-square on 4 df (p < .01). Thus, the two-parameter model provides a much better fit to the data than does the one-parameter model. Although the two-parameter model is acceptable, the fit is even better than indicated for two reasons. First, the expected proportion was quite low for some patterns, and the low values will tend to inflate the statistic as well as the degrees of freedom. If one could define some patterns as neighboring others, patterns with low expected proportions could be collapsed into others. Strictly speaking, however, the chi-square approximation does not hold for the collapsed set of patterns (see Koehler and Larntz, 1980). Second, the 1972 General Social Survey was carried out on a modified probability sample, not a simple random sample as assumed in the multinomial model. In the modified sample, there is a clustering of households at the last stage, an aspect that will tend artificially to increase goodness-of-fit statistics (see Kish and Frankel, 1974; Fellegi, 1980). Thus, the model appears to fit the data well.

ITEM PARAMETER INVARIANCE

When the parameters for an item are estimated from samples with different mean levels of the latent variable, it amounts to estimating different portions of the same ogive curve. If the sample has a lower mean on the underlying variable, estimation will be based on a slightly different portion of the curve than if the sample had a higher mean. The parameters from the two estimations will be invariant, of course, only up to a linear transformation, since the mean of the sample represents the zero point within a set of items. Choosing samples with different means on the underlying variable merely moves the zero point around among the items, *if* the models hold in all parts of the population. If the samples differ in dispersion of the latent variable, the parameters may be moved closer together or further apart by a constant distance. Figure 5 shows item parameters that are invariant across two samples.

If the item invariance does not hold across samples, that is, if item parameters move relative to one another, then local independence does not hold in the population. This situation

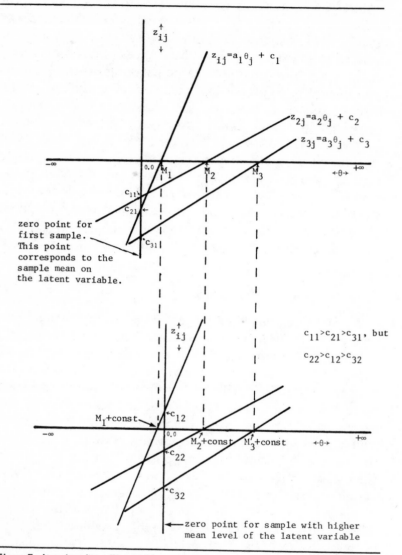

Figure 5: Invariant Item Thresholds

NOTE: The item thresholds are the x-axis intercepts. Their relative distances do not change across the samples. The y-axis intercepts are not invariant.

would indicate that some exogenous variable related to the selection of the samples was also influencing the latent variable. For example, a set of items designed to measure social adjustment could be calibrated on two different ethnic groups and ordered by difficulty. If the order of the items differs across the groups, we would have to look for some aspect of the ethnic differences that would be causing the items to measure different variables in the two samples. The differences might be present for only one or two items, or they might be present for all of the items.

If the latent trait model holds for a set of data, the invariance of the item parameters is a powerful feature. Whether or not the invariance holds can be assessed by checking to see that the relative positions of the parameters change by no more than a linear transformation. For a rigorous check, one could perform an item-by-sample analysis of variance with item *parameters* as the dependent variable. There would, of course, be main effects for items and main effects for samples, but there should be no item-by-sample interactions. We have already looked at some race-relations items from the 1972 General Social Survey. Since some of these items were administered to independent samples at yearly intervals, we can check for invariance of the item parameters by estimating new parameters based on a sample at one of the other time points.

Table 2 shows parameter estimates for six racial tolerance items from the 1977 General Social Survey. Four of the items also appeared in Table 1 for the 1972 sample, and two of the items were new in 1977. The new items, SUB and DIF4, asked the following:

SUB: Some religious and business groups have set up programs to encourage Black people to buy houses in white suburbs. Do you favor or oppose these voluntary programs to integrate white suburbs? [Favor.]

DIF4:   On the average Blacks have worse jobs, income, and housing than white people. Do you think

TABLE 2
Parameters of 1977 Racial Tolerance Items

Item	Threshold	(S.E.)	Change in threshold 1972 to 1977	Inter-cept	(S.E.)	Slope	(S.E.)	Change in slope 1972 to 1977
SCHOOL	-1.2208	(.1418)	+.002	3.1515	(.1671)	2.5815	(.0989)	-.082
MAR	- .6597	(.0630)	-.343	1.5726	(.1209)	2.3838	(.0501)	+.649
DIN	- .7297	(.1009)	-.072	1.4128	(.1737)	1.9360	(.0748)	-.245
PRES	- .8746	(.0636)	-.225	1.7761	(.0758)	2.0307	(.0587)	-.070
SUB	.5521	(.0899)	---	-.9168	(.1022)	1.6605	(.0696)	---
DIF4	.8229	(.1161)	---	-.9544	(.1243)	1.1598	(.0806)	---

NOTE: Estimates are for the logistic curve.

these differences are because most Blacks just don't have the motivation or willpower to pull themselves up out of poverty? [No.]

The model fit to the 1977 data has a G^2 of 63.5 on 51 df ($p = .11$), indicating an acceptable fit. Again, the 1977 GSS was conducted on a modified random sample, and a few of the elements in the set of response patterns showed low expected values. The sampling design for 1977 was different from the 1972 design, but it is not clear what difference the change in design makes.

Tables 1 and 2 can be investigated for changes in parameters for the items that appear in both tables. What we are looking for in examining these parameters is a change over time in the relative positions of the items. There seems to be no overall constant shift in the slopes, but DIN shows a slight decrease and MAR shows a relatively large increase. The change for item DIN will not be interpreted, since it is on the borderline of significance, given the standard errors. The thresholds remain constant for items SCHOOL and DIN, but decrease for items MAR and PRES. Clearly, the change for PRES should not be interpreted, given the standard error for 1972. With no evidence of an overall shift due to differences in mean level or dispersion between the samples, we must explain the relative shifts for the one item, MAR. In 1977, MAR shows a stronger relationship to the scale (higher slope), and it has shifted, relatively, to a position indicating that it was easier to give the answer associated with racial tolerance. The next step is to look for aspects of this item distinguishing it from the other items.

There are two aspects of the item MAR which could account for the change over time. First, it is the only item that asks if there should be a law governing certain behaviors. Since the past few years have seen some fairly strong feelings about laws dealing with essentially private behaviors, it is possible that less support for a law could have caused the shift of the item.

The other aspect of MAR that could account for the shift involves the social distances depicted in the items. Of the four items common to Tables 1 and 2, this item clearly involves feelings about the greatest social distance between the respondent and Blacks. Social distances can be maintained at schools and even at a dinner, but marriage requires a lowering of all social barriers. Tables 1 and 2 indicate that by 1977 attitudes about marriage between Blacks and whites became more like the other attitudes by virtue of the increase in the slope of the item. For this reason, the second explanation seems more likely. If the aspect of a law was related to the change, the item should show a weaker relationship to the scale by a lower slope.

SCALE LINKING

Table 2 also contains two items new to the General Social Survey in 1977. Both of these items show positive thresholds, indicating that fewer than 50% of the sample gave the response associated with racial tolerance. These items serve to demonstrate the possibility of scoring respondents on different sets of items, another powerful feature of the latent trait model. In models of measurement based on true score theory, comparisons between scores can be made only if respondents are administered the same items or parallel forms. Thus, for purposes of comparing 1972 respondents to 1977 respondents, scores would be based only on items SCHOOL, MAR, DIN, and PRES. In the latent trait model, on the other hand, scores based on different sets of items are comparable as long as the sets contain some common "anchor" items. The anchor items are used to establish a common metric for parameters from one sample or time point and parameters from another sample or time point. The difference here between the true score and latent trait models comes down to definitions of measurement. In the classical model the respondent score is defined as an expected value over some set of items. If the set of items is changed, the expected value changes unless the items match in difficulty. In the latent trait model, the respondent score is the value of θ that maximizes the likelihood from expression 11, given the item parameters. If the set of items is changed, the continuous product in expression 11 is just taken over different items. The likelihood of response patterns taken over different items is maximized by the same value of θ, provided all items are calibrated to the same metric of the same scale, as established with the anchor items. Scores based on different item sets will, however, differ in precision of measurement as a function of how well the entire scale is represented in the two sets. These topics can be explained better by returning to the examples.

For the 1972 and 1977 data, there are four anchor items—the four common items SCHOOL, MAR, DIN, and PRES. By looking at the parameters for the anchor items over the two time points, we found no overall shift in either slopes or thresholds. We did find that item MAR shifted relative to the other items, so we would probably want to exclude it for comparisons across time. If we assume that the nonanchor items would show the same behavior as the anchor items we can achieve a stronger model for measurement across time. That is, we must assume that JOB, SUB, and DIF4 would behave like SCHOOL, PRES, and DIN across time, not showing any relative shifts as occurred for item MAR. If we make this assumption, we can obtain a common metric as shown in Figure 6.

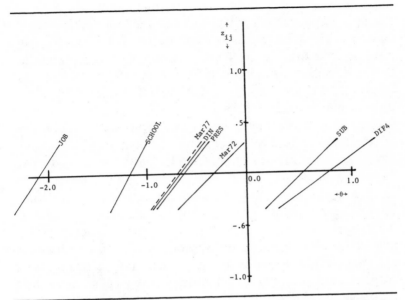

Figure 6: Thresholds and Slopes for 1972 and 1977 Racial Tolerance items on a Common Metric

NOTE: The vertical scale is in units of standardized normal deviates. The lines for SCHOOL, DIN, and PRES represent averages for the 1972 and 1977 parameter estimates weighted by their precision.

If there had been an overall shift of the item parameters between 1972 and 1977, the situation would be only slightly more complicated. We would have to adjust the parameters from one of the years (chosen arbitrarily) to the metric of the other year, using effects estimated by, for example, the analysis of variance mentioned previously. We can adjust for overall effects because they only represent differences between samples (different mean level or different dispersion of the latent variable). We cannot, however, adjust for item-by-sample interactions, because they indicate that the items are measuring different variables in the different samples.

It is interesting to note that the slopes for the two more difficult items, SUB and DIF4, are relatively lower, indicating a weaker relationship to the underlying variable. We have seen that the latent trait model can be used for powerful comparisons over time points. It can also be used for comparisons of the functioning of scale items within time points across, for example, demographic groups. The General Social Survey contains several items that are like SUB and DIF4 in that they have positive thresholds. Work now in progress indicates that none of the other difficult items fits the scale for the sample as a whole. There are, however, differential results for various demographic groups. There tend to be more items that can be formed into a consistent scale for those who have higher levels of education, a finding that would be consistent with the well-known results of Converse (1964, 1970, 1975; see also Stinchcombe, 1976). Region of the country and rural versus urban residence also seem to be related to relative shifts for some items. One implication of this finding would be, of course, that the scales may not be appropriate for making comparisons across the demographic groups. More interesting implications are that people in the different groups may be basing their responses on different values, or they may be generating their responses by different processes.

SUMMARY

For simplicity of exposition, this discussion was restricted to a model for dichotomous items. While most items can be recoded to accommodate the dichotomous restriction, the latent trait model has been generalized for polytomous items. With more than two response categories, the categories can be considered to form a set of graded (Samejima, 1969) or nominal (Bock, 1972) alternatives. The graded case is a direct generalization of the model presented here, with the boundary between each successive pair of categories having an associated threshold in terms of the underlying latent variable. For the nominal case, no ordering of the categories is specified, of course, although for each item one category is specified as preferred.

The model for dichotomous items has also been generalized, in the factor analytic tradition, to allow a multidimensional latent space (Christoffersson, 1975; Muthen, 1977, 1978, 1979). If the factor model is cast so that the binary response variable is a function of an underlying continuous variable, then the one factor model is identical to the latent trait model. With multiple dimensions, or factors, an item has a loading on each factor, but thresholds are collapsed into one difficulty parameter per item.

Latent trait theory provides a statistical model for items that are intended to form a one-dimensional scale. Here the model was applied to some race-relations items from two national surveys separated in time by five years. For the items common to the two surveys, parameters remained constant over time, except for an item that asked about a law against marriages between Blacks and whites. Explanations for the shift in this item were given in terms of the item content. The procedure for linking new items was also discussed.

NOTES

1. The sign of an item difficulty parameter is completely arbitrary. In the psychometric literature, c_i is by far a more common parameter then M_i. Hence, it is a frequent convention to use negative values of c_i on items for which fewer than 50% of the sample give the agree response. This convention would mean that the scale of thresholds on the X axes in Figures 1 and 2 would go from positive to negative in the left to right direction. Since we are focusing more attention here on the item thresholds, we will use the opposite convention so that positive to negative proceeds right to left, and a difficult item has a positive threshold.

2. The BILOG computer program can be used for this analysis. It is available from International Educational Services, P.O. Box A3650, Chicago, IL 60637.

REFERENCES

ANDERSON, E. B. (1980) Discrete Statistical Models with Social Science Applications. New York: Elsevier North Holland.
_____(1977) "Sufficient statistics and latent trait models." Psychometrika, 42: 69-82.
_____(1972) "The numerical solution of a set of conditional estimation equations." J. of the Royal Stat. Society Series B, 34: 42-45.

BERKSON, J. (1944) "Application of the logistic function to bioassay." J. of the Amer. Stat. Assn. 39: 357-365.

BIRNBAUM, A. (1968) "Some latent trait models and their use in inferring an examinee's ability," in F. M. Lord and M. R. Novick, Statistical Theories of Mental Test Scores, Reading, MA: Addison-Wesley.

BOCK, R. D. (1972) "Estimating item parameters and latent ability when responses are scored in two or more nominal categories." Psychometrika 35: 179-197.

———and M. AITKEN (forthcoming) "Marginal maximum likelihood estimation of item parameters: an application of the EM algorithm." Psychometrika.

BOCK, R. D. and L. JONES (1968) The Measurement and Prediction of Judgment and Choice. San Francisco: Holden-Day.

BOCK, R. D and D. KOLAKOWSKI (1973a) "LOGOG maximum likelihood item analysis and test scoring: logistic model for multiple responses, a Fortran IV program." Chicago: National Educational Services.

———(1973b) "NORMOG maximum likelihood item analysis and test scoring—Normal Ogive Model, a Fortran IV program." Chicago: National Educational Services.

BOCK, R. D. and M. LIEBERMANN (1970) "Fitting a response model for n dichotomously scored items." Psychometrika 35: 179-197.

BOCK, R. D. and R. WOOD (1971) "Test theory." Annual Rev. of Psychology 22: 193-244.

CHRISTOFFERSSON, A. (1975) "Factor analysis of dichotomized variables." Psychometrika 40: 5-32.

CONVERSE, P. E. (1975) "Public opinion and voting behavior," in F. I. Greenstein and N. W. Polsby (eds.) Nongovernmental Politics, Vol. 4 of the Handbook of Political Science. Reading, Mass: Addison-Wesley.

———(1970) "Attitudes and non-attitudes: continuation of a dialogue," in E. R. Tufte (ed.) The Quantitative Analysis of Social Problems. Reading, MA: Addison-Wesley.

———(1964) "The nature of belief systems in mass publics," in D. E. Apter, (ed.) Ideology and Discontent. New York: Free Press.

DAVIS, J. A. (1978) General Social Surveys, 1972-1978 (machine-readable data file): Cumulative Data. Principal Investigator, James A. Davis; Associate Study Director, Tom W. Smith; Research Assistant, C. Bruce Stephenson. Chicago: National Opinion Research Center. (New Haven, CT: Roper Public Opinion Research Center, Yale University, distributor)

DEMPSTER, A. P., N. M. LAIRD, and D. B. RUBIN (1977) "Maximum likelihood from incomplete data via the EM algorithm." J. of the Royal Stat. Society Series B, 39: 1-38.

FELLEGI, I. P. (1980) "Approximate tests of independence and goodness of fit based on stratified multistage samples." J. of the Amer. Stat. Assn. 75, 370: 261-268.

GOODMAN, L. (1974) "The relationship between modified and usual multiple-regression approaches to the analysis of dichotomous variables." Soc. Methodology: 83-110.

HABERMAN, S. (1974) The Analysis of Frequency Data. Chicago: Univ. of Chicago Press.

JÖRESKOG, K. G. (1978) "Structural analysis of covariance and correlation matrices." Psychometrika 43: 443-477.

KISH, L. and M. R. FRANKEL (1974) "Inference from complex samples." J. of the Royal Stat. Society Series B, 36: 1-37.

KOEHLER, K. J. and K. LARNTZ (1980) "An empirical investigation of goodness-of-fit statistics for sparse multinomials." J. of the Amer. Stat. Assn. 75, 370: 336-344.

LAWLEY, D. N. (1943) "On problems connected with item selection and test construction." Proceedings of the Royal Society of Edinburgh 61: 273-287.

LAZARSFELD, P. F. (1960) "Latent structure analysis and test theory," in H. Gulliksen and S. Messick, Psychological Scaling. New York: John Wiley.

———(1954) "A conceptual introduction to latent structure analysis," in P. F. Lazarsfeld (ed.) Mathematical Thinking in the Social Sciences. New York: Free Press.

———(1950) "The logical and mathematical foundation of latent structure analysis," in S. A. Stouffer et al., Measurement and Prediction. Princeton, NJ: Princeton Univ. Press.

LAZARSFELD, P. F. and N. W. HENRY (1968) Latent Structure Analysis. Boston: Houghton Mifflin.

LORD, F. M. (1953a) "An application of confidence intervals and of maximum likelihood to the estimation of an examinee's ability." Psychometrika, 18: 57-75.

———(1953b) "The relation of test score to the trait underlying the test." Educ. and Psych. Measurement 13: 517-548.

———(1952) "A theory of test scores." Psychometric Monograph 7.

LUMSDEN, J. (1976) "Test theory." Annual Rev. of Psychology 27: 251-280.

LUCE, R. D. (1959) Individual Choice Behavior. New York: John Wiley.

MOSTELLER, F. (1958) "The mystery of the missing corpus." Psychometrika 23, 4.

MUTHEN, B. (1979) "A structural probit model with latent variables." J. of the Amer. Stat. Assn. 74: 807-811.

———(1978) "Contributions to factor analysis of dichotomous variables." Psychometrika 43: 551-560.

———(1977) "Statistical methodology for structural equation models involving latent variables with dichotomous indicators." Research Report 77-7, Department of Statistics, University of Uppsala.

RASCH, G. (1966) "An item analysis which takes individual differences into account." British J. of Mathematical and Stat. Psych. 19: 49-57.

———(1960) Probabilistic Models for Some Intelligence and Attainment Tests. Copenhagen: Danish Institute of Educational Research.

SAMEJIMA, F. (1969) "Estimation of latent ability using a response pattern of graded scores." Psychometric Monograph 17.

STINCHCOMBE, A. (1976) "Why has the correlation between abortion liberalism and education gone down between 1972 and 1975?" Chicago: NORC Xeroxed.

TORGERSON, W. (1958) Theory and Methods of Scaling. New York: John Wiley.

TUCKER, L. R. (1952) "A level of proficiency scale for a unidimensional skill." Amer. Psychologist 7.

WOOD, R. L., M. W. WINJERSKY, and F. M. LORD (1976) "LOGIST: a computer program for estimating examinee ability and item characteristic curve parameters." Research Memorandum 76-6. Princeton, NJ: Educational Testing Service.

WRIGHT, B. D. and N. PANCHAPAKESAN (1969) "A procedure for sample-free item analysis." Educ. and Psych. Measurement 29: 23-48.

YELLOTT, Jr., J. I. (1977) "The relationship between Luce's choice axiom, Thurston's theory of comparative judgment, and the double exponential distribution." J. of Mathematical Psychology 15: 109-144.

Mark Reiser is a Post Doctoral Fellow in the Program in Measurement and an assistant professor in the Department of Education, both at Indiana University–Bloomington. His research interests include quantitative models for dichotomous variables, and models for attitude change.

CHAPTER FIVE

The Factor Analysis
of Ipsative Measures

DAVID J. JACKSON
National Institute of Mental Health
DUANE F. ALWIN
University of Michigan

INTRODUCTION

Cattell (1944) initiated the use of the term "ipsative" (from the Latin *ipse*: he, himself) to refer to raw score transformations that center scores about the individual's mean. Ipsative scores were contrasted to the more common 'normative' scores, which are centered about the variable means. The ipsative transformation produces a set of scores with the property that the sum of the variables for each individual equals a constant.[1] Perhaps the most common use of scores produced by the ipsative transformation occurs in situations where it is desirable to remove mean differences in scores among individual cases or groups of

AUTHORS' NOTE: *The authors wish to thank George W. Bohrnstedt and John R. Nessleroade for helpful suggestions on an early draft of this article and Cynthia L. Sipe for computational assistance.*

cases (e.g., Cunningham et al., 1977). Although, in the classical statement of the ipsative transformation, the constant is zero (because the individual's ipsative scores are deviations from his mean on the set of variables) it is now common to use the term "ipsative" to refer to any set of variables that sum to a constant for individual cases, regardless of the value of the constant (Horst, 1965: 290-291). The particular value of the constant is largely irrelevant.

It is important to note, as well, that sets of variables may occur which have the ipsative property, but not as a result of an ipsative transformation of nonipsative scores. For example, sets of variables produced from rankings and some Q-sorts have the ipsative property. The issues discussed in this article are particularly relevant to such sets of variables.

Numerous warnings exist in the psychometric literature against the application of factor analysis to sets of variables with the ipsative property (e.g. Cattell, 1952; Guilford, 1954; Tucker, 1956; Horst, 1965), but these warnings are not always heeded. In this paper we will underscore the basis for such warnings by showing that the assumptions of the common factor model, as usually stated, are inappropriate for sets of variables with ipsative properties. This is demonstrated within the framework of the development of a common factor model that can be applied to any set of variables with the ipsative property. We will show that a common factor model is defined for a set of variables that have undergone an ipsative transformation if a common factor model holds for the preipsative set, and we will show that for sets of ipsative variables that do not result from an ipsative transformation, the same model may be used under a set of assumptions regarding the response process. Finally, we will illustrate the usefulness of the model for the latter case by applying it to sample data on a set of ipsative measures of parental values.

THE IPSATIVE TRANSFORMATION

Let y be a $(p \times 1)$ vector of random variables observable in some known population. The only constraints on y are that the variables have a common metric and that the y covariance structure is positive-definite. The general form of the ipsative transformation of y is as follows:

$$x = y - 1w \qquad [1]$$

where x is a $(p \times 1)$ vector of variables with the ipsative property, 1 is a $(p \times 1)$ unit vector and w is a scalar. In the general case, w equals $p^{-1}(1'y - c)$, where c is the constant to which the scores of each individual sum. This transformation, then, produces a set of variables that sum to c for each individual; however, the value of the constant is irrelevant.[2] As a matter of convenience we may set c equal to zero, so that $w = p^{-1}1'y$.

Equation 1 may be rewritten as

$$x = y - 1p^{-1}1'y \qquad [2a]$$

$$= y - p^{-1}11'y \qquad [2b]$$

$$= (I - p^{-1}U)y \qquad [2c]$$

where $U = 11'$ (a $p \times p$ matrix of unities). The ipsative transformation matrix in equation 2c, $(I - p^{-1}U)$, is a symmetric idempotent matrix with a rank of $p - 1$ (see Horst, 1965: 288-289; Harris, 1953: 54).

Let the ipsative transformation be represented by $A = (I - p^{-1}U)$, so that $x = Ay$. The covariance matrix for x may be expressed using this notation as

$$\Sigma_x = A \, \Sigma_y A \qquad [3]$$

where Σ_y is the covariance matrix of the preipsative variables. As noted, A has a rank of $p - 1$, so this constitutes a singular transformation of Σ_y. Consequently, Σ_x is singular and cannot be analyzed in the same manner that is possible for Σ_y.

The ipsative covariance matrix, Σ_x, has a number of interesting properties (see Clemans, 1956):

(1) The rows (or columns) of Σ_x sum to zero.
(2) The sum of the covariances of a set of ipsative variables with a criterion variable is zero.
(3) As p increases, Σ_x approaches Σ_y.[3]

Because the ipsative covariance matrix is not positive-definite, it may not be feasible to subject Σ_x to routine factor analysis.[4] It is possible, however, to delete one row and column associated with an arbitrarily selected variable in order to obtain a non-singular matrix, but the routine factor analysis of this submatrix does not provide a solution to the ipsative problem.

A COMMON FACTOR MODEL FOR IPSATIVE MEASURES

In this section of the article we will develop a common factor model that can be applied to ipsative measures. As we pointed out earlier, our primary interest here is in data that have not been "ipsatized" by an ipsative transformation, but which have the ipsative property as a result of the measurement method. In order to develop a factor model that can be applied in this situation, we first must develop a factor model for variables that have undergone an ipsative transformation. To do this we assume that a factor model exists for the set of preipsative variables. Then, by transforming the coefficient matrices of this model, we may obtain the coefficient matrices of the ipsative factor model. We turn now to the development of this model.

Let

$$y = \wedge_y \; \xi + \epsilon \qquad\qquad\qquad [4]$$

be the population common factor model for the set of measured nonipsative variables, y, where $\wedge_y$ is the factor pattern coefficient matrix, ξ is a $(k \times 1)$ vector of common factors, and ϵ is a $(p \times 1)$ vector of disturbances (see Lawley and Maxwell, 1971). For our purposes the properties of this model are as follows:

(1) $E(y) = 0$
(2) $E(\xi) = 0$
(3) $E(\epsilon) = 0$
(4) $E(\xi\epsilon') = 0$
(5) $E(\xi\xi') = \Phi_y$
(6) $E(\epsilon\epsilon') = \Psi^2_y$

For convenience we have treated all variables, latent and manifest, as centered, and we assume that ξ and ϵ are statistically independent. The matrices Φ_y and Ψ_y^2 are the covariance matrices for the factors and disturbances respectively. Here we assume that Ψ_y^2 is a positive-definite diagonal matrix, but in general the assumption that Ψ_y^2 is diagonal is not necessary. The covariance structure of y may be written in terms of the model as:

$$E(yy') = \Sigma_y = \wedge_y \Phi_y \wedge'_y + \Psi_y^2 \qquad [5]$$

Given the above model and knowledge of the properties of the ipsative transformation, we may obtain the ipsative common factor model by substituting equation 4 for y in equation 2b, as follows:

$$x = (\wedge_y\xi + \epsilon) - 1p^{-1}1'(\wedge_y\xi + \epsilon) \qquad [6a]$$

$$= (\wedge_y\xi + \epsilon) - 1(\bar{\lambda}'\xi + \bar{\epsilon}) \qquad [6b]$$

where $\bar{\lambda}$ is a $(k \times 1)$ vector of the average values of the coefficients in the columns of Λ_y, and $\bar{\epsilon}$ is the average value of the residual disturbances on the model for y (see equation 4). We may rearrange equation 6b as follows:

$$x = (\wedge_y - 1\bar{\lambda}')\,\xi + \epsilon - 1\bar{\epsilon} \qquad [6c]$$

and because $(\epsilon - 1\bar{\epsilon}) = A\epsilon$, equation 6c may be rewritten as

$$x = (\wedge_y - 1\bar{\lambda}')\,\xi + A\epsilon \qquad [6d]$$

This is the common factor representation for a set of ipsative variables which have the ipsative property as a result of an ipsative transformation, given knowledge that a common factor model for the preipsative variables exists.

Note that the primary differences in the factor models for the ipsative and preipsative variables are their coefficient matrices. The factor pattern coefficient matrix for y is Λ_y, while the factor pattern matrix for x is $(\Lambda_y - 1\bar{\lambda}')$. As a result of the ipsative transformation, then, the factor pattern coefficients in the model for x are deviations of the factor pattern coefficients in $\wedge_y$ from the average factor pattern coefficients in the columns of $\wedge_y$. The coefficient matrix relating the disturbances to the x vector is A rather than I, as is implicitly the case for y. Since A is nondiagonal, the ipsative transformation affects the disturbances by correlating them in a systematic fashion.

The common factor model for x, then, can be written as follows:

$$x = [\Lambda_x \mid A] \begin{bmatrix} \xi \\ \epsilon \end{bmatrix} \qquad [7]$$

where $\Lambda_x = (\Lambda_y - 1\bar{\lambda}')$ and $A = (I - p^{-1}U)$. In addition to the ipsative property of x, the properties of this model are as follows:

(1) $E(x) = 0$
(2) $E(\xi) = 0$
(3) $E(\epsilon) = 0$
(4) $E(\xi\epsilon') = 0$
(5) $E(\xi\xi') = \Phi_y$
(6) $E(A\epsilon\epsilon'A) = A\Psi_y^2 A = \Psi_x^2$

The covariance structure for x may then be written as:

$$E(xx') = \Sigma_x = \Lambda_x \Phi_y \Lambda_x' + A\Psi_y^2 A \qquad [8]$$

The above factor model for x follows from the assumptions posed from the beginning, that (a) $x = Ay$ and (b) $y = \Lambda_y \xi + \epsilon$. Note that by the transformation of y into x, the disturbances on the factor model for x become correlated. As indicated above, the covariance structure of the disturbances in the model for x is $\Psi_x^2 = A\Psi_y^2 A$. The diagonal elements of this matrix are $\psi_{x_i}^2 = (1 - 2p^{-1})\psi_{y_i}^2 + p^{-1}\bar{\psi}_y^2$ and the off-diagonal elements are $\psi_{x_{ij}} = -p^{-1}(\psi_{y_i}^2 + \psi_{y_j}^2 - \bar{\psi}_y^2)$, where $\psi_{y_i}^2$ and $\psi_{y_j}^2$ are the ith and j^{th} elements in the diagonal of Ψ_y^2 and $\bar{\psi}_y^2$ is the average of the diagonal elements of Ψ_y^2.

AN ILLUSTRATION

Consider the following $p = 5$, $k = 1$ factor model for some known population:

$$y = \begin{bmatrix} 1.0 \\ 1.1 \\ 1.2 \\ 1.3 \\ 1.4 \end{bmatrix} \xi + \epsilon$$

$$\Phi_y = [2.0]$$

Diag. $\Psi_y^2 = [.90 \quad 1.2 \quad 1.0 \quad .80 \quad .60]$

The population covariance structure for y given this model is:

$$\Sigma_y = \begin{bmatrix} 2.90 & 2.20 & 2.40 & 2.60 & 2.80 \\ 2.20 & 3.62 & 2.64 & 2.86 & 3.08 \\ 2.40 & 2.64 & 3.88 & 3.12 & 3.36 \\ 2.60 & 2.86 & 3.12 & 4.18 & 3.64 \\ 2.80 & 3.08 & 3.36 & 3.64 & 4.52 \end{bmatrix}$$

For $p = 5$ the ipsative transformation matrix, as defined in equation 2c, is:

$$A = \begin{bmatrix} .80 & -.20 & -.20 & -.20 & -.20 \\ -.20 & .80 & -.20 & -.20 & -.20 \\ -.20 & -.20 & .80 & -.20 & -.20 \\ -.20 & -.20 & -.20 & .80 & -.20 \\ -.20 & -.20 & -.20 & -.20 & .80 \end{bmatrix}$$

The ipsative transformation of Σ_y into Σ_x is as follows:

$$\Sigma_x = \begin{bmatrix} .80 & -.20 & -.20 & -.20 & -.20 \\ -.20 & .92 & -.26 & -.24 & -.22 \\ -.20 & -.26 & .78 & -.18 & -.14 \\ -.20 & -.24 & -.18 & .68 & -.06 \\ -.20 & -.22 & -.14 & -.06 & .62 \end{bmatrix}$$

Finally, the ipsative factor coefficent matrix is:

$$\Lambda_x = (\Lambda_y - 1\bar{\lambda}') = \begin{bmatrix} -.20 \\ -.10 \\ .00 \\ .10 \\ .20 \end{bmatrix}$$

It can be shown that $\Lambda_x \, \Phi_y \, \Lambda_x' + A \, \Psi_y^2 \, A$ exactly reproduces Σ_x.

ESTIMATION OF THE
IPSATIVE COMMON FACTOR MODEL

The common factor model defined above for a set of ipsative variables bears an interesting relationship to the common factor model for the corresponding set of preipsative variables. First, it should be pointed out that the factors of the model remain the same after an ipsative transformation, and the factor covariance matrix remains unchanged. Second, under the ipsative transformation, the factor pattern coefficient matrix contains deviations from the average factor pattern coefficients in the columns of the original factor pattern matrix. Third, the ipsative transformation causes the disturbances to be correlated. These observations have implications for the factor analysis of sets of ipsative variables, and on this basis we suggest that the naive exploratory factor analysis of ipsative variables is inappropriate. Such an analysis would assume that $A = I$, and would therefore represent some type of an approximation. The estimated factor pattern in such an analysis would approximate $(\Lambda_y - 1\bar{\lambda}')$, however, not Λ_y, although the rank-ordering of the magnitudes of the coefficients in the two coefficient matrices would be identical. In any event, there exists a problem with the interpretation of the ipsative factor pattern coefficient matrix since the values in $\bar{\lambda}$ are unknown.

As we indicated above, Σ_x is singular, and it is not feasible to analyze this matrix without deleting a row and column associated with an arbitrarily selected variable in x. Let x* be this set of p − 1 variables. For present purposes, suppose we have deleted the pth variable, although the deletion of any variable in this vector will suffice. In fact, the parameters of the ipsative common factor model are invariant regardless of the variable deleted.

We may now write a common factor model for x* as follows:

$$x^* = [B_1 \mid B_2] \begin{bmatrix} \xi \\ \epsilon \end{bmatrix} \qquad [9]$$

where B_1 contains the first $p - 1$ rows of the matrix $(\Lambda_y - 1\bar{\lambda}')$ and B_2 contains the first $p - 1$ rows of A. Note that B_1 is a $(p - 1) \times k$ submatrix of Λ_x^* and B_2 is a $(p - 1) \times p$ submatrix. In other words $\Lambda_x^* = [B_1 \mid B_2]$ is a $(p - 1) \times (k + p)$ coefficient matrix. The covariance matrix for $\begin{bmatrix} \xi \\ \epsilon \end{bmatrix}$ in this case is as follows:

$$\Phi_{x^*} = \begin{bmatrix} \Phi_y & 0 \\ \hline 0 & \Psi_y^2 \end{bmatrix} \qquad [10]$$

Recall that Ψ_y^2 is diagonal, but Φ_y may be nondiagonal.

Note that the coefficients in in B_2 are known, so they are to be constrained in the estimation of the model. Our objective, then, is to estimate the parameters in B_1, Φ_y, and Ψ_y^2, and they may be estimated if the model is identified. A necessary condition for the identification of the model is a minimum of k^2 independent constraints on B_1 and Φ_y (see Jöreskog, 1978; Sörbom and Joreskog, 1976). Finally, we should note that the factor pattern coefficients for the pth variable may be obtained by taking the negative of the sum of the first $(p - 1)$ values in each column of B_1.

Using the above illustration to demonstrate the manner by which the coefficients of the ipsative common factor model may be estimated, we present the $k = 6$ factor model that would be estimated for x in the above 5 variable cases. The model is as follows:

$$\Lambda_{x*} = \begin{bmatrix} -.20 & .80^f & -.20^f & -.20^f & -.20^f & -.20^f \\ -.10 & -.20^f & .80^f & -.20^f & -.20^f & -.20^f \\ .00 & -.20^f & -.20^f & .80^f & -.20^f & -.20^f \\ .10 & -.20^f & -.20^f & -.20^f & .80^f & -.20^f \end{bmatrix}$$

$$\Phi_{x*} = \begin{bmatrix} 2.0 & 0.0^f & 0.0^f & 0.0^f & 0.0^f & 0.0^f \\ 0.0^f & .90 & 0.0^f & 0.0^f & 0.0^f & 0.0^f \\ 0.0^f & 0.0^f & 1.2 & 0.0^f & 0.0^f & 0.0^f \\ 0.0^f & 0.0^f & 0.0^f & 1.0 & 0.0^f & 0.0^f \\ 0.0^f & 0.0^f & 0.0^f & 0.0^f & .80 & 0.0^f \\ 0.0^f & 0.0^f & 0.0^f & 0.0^f & 0.0^f & .60 \end{bmatrix}$$

Note that the coefficients in the first column of $\wedge_{x*}$ represent deviations of the λ_i values from the average λ_i value in the common factor model given above ($\bar{\lambda} = 1.2$). The factor pattern coefficient for the pth variable is the negative of the sum of the $p - 1$ values in the first column of $\wedge_{x*}$, or .20. The remainder of the Λ_{x*} matrix is constrained equal to the values there (as indicated by the "f" superscript). Note that the ϕ_{11} in the Φ_{x*} matrix equals Φ_y, and ϕ_{22}, ϕ_{33}, ϕ_{44}, ϕ_{55}, and ϕ_{66} in Φ_{x*} are the values of the residual variances for the y vector in Ψ_y^2.

We began this illustration by defining a common factor model for y. Since the common factor model for the ipsative set of variables, x, is defined, given knowledge of the common factor model for y, the above model for x* exactly reproduces the first $(p - 1)$ rows and columns of Σ_{x*}.

AN APPLICATION OF THE IPSATIVE COMMON FACTOR MODEL

Here we will develop a set of assumptions that permit the application of the above ipsative common factor model to other sets of variables that have the ipsative property. We make three critical assumptions: (1) that for a given set of variables with the ipsative property, e.g. a set of rankings, there exists a corresponding set of hypothetical nonipsative variables in the population; (2) that the set of ipsative variables observed in the population of interest is an ipsative transformation of the hypothetical set of nonipsative variables; and (3) that a common factor model holds in the population of interest for the hypothetical set of nonipsative variables.

Given these assumptions, we may estimate the parameters of an ipsative common factor model for any set of variables with the ipsative property. Unfortunately, there is no direct way of determining the veracity of these assumptions for the types of ipsative variables of interest, e.g. rankings, because they have not explicitly undergone an ipsative transformation. We can indirectly assess the adequacy of these assumptions using sample data from sufficiently large samples where the sample moments differ trivially from the population moments. In such cases the failure of our estimated model to reproduce the sample covariance matrix would provide some suggestion about the adequacy of the model. There is a degree of ambiguity here, however, as the failure of the model to reproduce the sample covariances may result from at least two sources: (1) the misspecification of the factor model for the hypothetical y, especially the number of factors, and (2) the misspecification of the response process; in other words, errors in the assumptions indicated above for applying the ipsative common factor model. Because there is no known exploratory factor analysis method that can be used to determine an adequate number of factors in the ipsative factor model in this case, there may be some difficulty in specifying the number of factors appropriate for the model.

In determining the goodness-of-fit of a particular application of the ipsative common factor model, the model should be compared with a baseline model that posits no common factors, as in assessing the relative fit of factor models generally. In the present case one would compare a particular model with the following model:

$$\Sigma_x = \Psi_x^2 = A \ \Psi_y^2 \ A \qquad [11]$$

The χ^2 goodness-of-fit statistic for this model can be used in the computation of a Tucker-Lewis coefficient of relative fit as a baseline model against which the fit of other models may be judged (Tucker and Lewis, 1973).

There are additional approaches to determining the adequacy of the above assumptions for modeling the latent content of sets of variables with the ipsative property which have not explicitly undergone an ipsative transformation. The first of these involves a systematic study of the response process involved in the production of such variables. What is the relation between the response process involved in ranking p objects and the response process involved in obtaining nonipsative measurements—for example, ratings of p objects along some dimension? Can the relation be described by a mathematical function such $x = Ay$? We will not pursue this set of issues here except to note that little is known about the relationship. A second approach to assessing the above assumptions for such ipsative measures involves Monte Carlo simulation. Here it is possible to compare the factors that result from making different sets of assumptions regarding the response process.

AN ANALYSIS OF
KOHN'S MEASURES OF PARENTAL VALUES

In this section of the article we apply the ipsative common factor model to Kohn's measures of parental desires for children's behavior (Kohn, 1969: 257). Kohn developed the following set of questions for measuring parental child-rearing values:

(a) Which three qualities listed on this card would you say are the most desirable for a (boy, girl) of (child's) age to have?
(b) Which one of these three is the most desirable of all?
(c) All of these may be desirable, but could you tell me which three you consider least important?
(d) And which one of these three is least important of all?
    (1) that he has good manners
    (2) that he tries hard to succeed
    (3) that he is honest
    (4) that he is neat and clean

(5) that he has good sense and sound judgment
(6) that he has self-control
(7) that he acts like a boy (she acts like a girl) should
(8) that he gets along well with other children
(9) that he obeys his parents well
(10) that he is responsible
(11) that he is considerate of others
(12) that he is interested in how and why things happen
(13) that he is a good student.

Using this information Kohn (1969: 48) coded the responses according to the following scheme:

5 = The most valued of all.
4 = One of the three most valued, but not the most valued.
3 = Neither one of the three most nor one of the three least valued.
2 = One of the three least valued, but not the least valued.
1 = The least valued of all.

This measurement strategy represents a reduced-ranking procedure. Instead of ranking the 13 characteristics from most to least important, respondents are essentially asked to sort the characteristics into 5 ranked categories with a requisite number in each category. In either case, such a ranking procedure produces a set of scores with the ipsative property.

In order to use these data to relate parental values to social class, Kohn (1969: 56-58) employed the methods of exploratory factor analysis to form a weighted composite from these items. Some weighting of the item scores was obviously necessary, as the unweighted sum of the items has no variability over individuals. He reported some difficulty in inverting the correlation matrix among his measures for the purpose of computing factor scores, which would be predicted given knowledge of the ipsative property of the measures. In any event, according to Kohn (1969: 57), the exploratory factor analysis of these measures "yields one factor easily identified as self-direction versus conformity to external standards" and two additional factors. He focused his primary attention, however, on the self-direction/conformity factor.

For our purposes, we will use sample data on Kohn's measures from the General Social Surveys (GSS) of 1973, 1975, 1976 and 1978 (see Alwin and Jackson, 1980, for a complete description of the population of interest and the precise nature of the measures used in the GSS). Table 1 presents the sample covariance matrices for the subpopulations of mothers (N = 1,069) and fathers (N = 721) from the NORC-GSS surveys. The sample data from the subpopulations of mothers and fathers are analyzed separately because of the expectation of substantive differences in the coefficients of the factor model. As noted above, the rows (or columns) of the full symmetric covariance matrices for these variables sum to zero, a property of ipsative covariance matrices.

In this analysis we obtain maximum-likelihood estimates of the unconstrained parameters of the ipsative common factor model developed above (see equations 6 and 7) using confirmatory factor analysis (Sörbom and Jöreskog, 1976). The results for this model where k = 1 are given in Tables 2 and 3. We have identified the model by setting Φ_y (or ϕ_ξ) equal to unity, and because A and Φ_y contain only fixed parameters, we have estimated the 26 parameters in Λ_x and Ψ_y^2. The estimated coefficients of Λ_x are deviations of the factor pattern coefficients of Λ_y from their average, $\bar{\lambda}$. The value of $\bar{\lambda}$ is, however, unknown, but this is irrelevant, since whatever its value, the coefficients in Λ_x maintain the same relative magnitude.

The relative rankings of the pattern coefficients in the estimated Λ_x in Tables 2 and 3 conform to our substantive expectations, and these results show considerable similarity for mothers and fathers. The measures indicating a preference for self-directed behavior in children (items 12, 5, 10, 11, 6) covary in one direction with the factor, while the measures indicating conformity to external authority (items 9, 1, 4, 3, 7) covary in the opposite direction with the factor. Because the coefficients in $\wedge_x$ are identified up to a change in sign, the direction of the latent factor is dependent on the starting values.

The pattern of coefficients reported in Tables 2 and 3 are similar, although not identical, to the results reported by Kohn for his original data and his reanalysis of the 1973 GSS data (Kohn, 1976: 540). In terms of the pattern of coefficients ob-

(continued on page 162)

TABLE 1

Sample Covariance Matrices for Kohn's Measures of Parental Values from the 1973, 1975, 1976, and 1978 General Social Surveys: mothers (N = 1069) above the diagonal and fathers (N = 721) below the diagonal

Variable	1	2	3	4	5	6	7	8	9	10	11	12	13
1. Manners	.665 / .704	-.038	-.007	.061	-.189	-.051	-.082	-.021	.049	-.134	-.074	-.183	.004
2. Success	-.070	.556 / .619	-.054	-.087	-.040	-.034	-.101	-.059	-.026	-.039	-.052	-.017	-.011
3. Honest	-.023	-.107	.739 / .777	.005	-.237	-.024	-.066	-.051	-.071	-.037	-.034	-.166	.003
4. Clean	.062	-.121	.039	.665 / .687	-.130	-.034	-.094	-.026	.059	-.105	-.053	-.212	-.049
5. Judgement	-.134	-.020	-.240	-.043	.858 / .847	-.012	-.114	-.015	-.169	.025	-.035	.118	-.061
6. Control	-.084	-.030	-.019	-.058	-.007	.444 / .473	-.078	-.012	-.060	.011	-.024	-.058	-.070
7. Role	-.097	-.075	.005	-.118	-.130	-.071	.902 / .927	-.035	.069	-.074	-.059	-.186	-.083
8. Gets along	-.058	-.076	-.040	-.033	-.029	-.037	-.035	.388 / .504	-.033	-.038	-.009	-.034	-.056
9. Obeys	.041	-.062	-.096	-.007	-.218	-.070	.043	.006	.600 / .693	-.177	-.085	-.181	.024
10. Responsible	-.124	.039	-.052	-.037	-.010	.007	-.091	-.091	-.167	.583 / .632	-.010	.038	-.044
11. Considerate	-.058	-.084	-.045	-.084	.000	-.011	-.092	.011	-.128	-.017	.489 / .587	.011	-.065
12. Interested	-.199	-.034	-.170	-.193	.056	-.031	-.174	-.031	-.114	-.003	.013	.943 / .968	-.074
13. Studious	.041	.022	-.029	-.093	-.073	-.061	-.092	-.091	.080	-.087	-.091	-.089	.479 / .563

NOTE: A more complete description of the variables may be found in the text.

159

TABLE 2

Sample Estimates of the Ipsative Common Factor Model for Kohn's Measures of Parental Values from the 1973, 1975, 1976, and 1978 General Social Surveys: mothers (N = 1069)

Parameter estimates

Λ

Λ_x

	ξ	ε_1	ε_2	ε_3	ε_4	ε_5	ε_6	ε_7	ε_8	ε_9	ε_{10}	ε_{11}	ε_{12}	ε_{13}
x_1	.308	$.923^a$	$-.077^a$	$-.077^a$	$-.077^a$	$-.077^a$	$-.077^a$	$-.077^a$	$-.077^a$	$-.077^a$	$-.077^a$	$-.077^a$	$-.077^a$	$-.077^a$
x_2	-.029	$-.077^a$	$.923^a$	$-.077^a$	$-.077^a$	$-.077^a$	$-.077^a$	$-.077^a$	$-.077^a$	$-.077^a$	$-.077^a$	$-.077^a$	$-.077^a$	$-.077^a$
x_3	.151	$-.077^a$	$-.077^a$	$.923^a$	$-.077^a$	$-.077^a$	$-.077^a$	$-.077^a$	$-.077^a$	$-.077^a$	$-.077^a$	$-.077^a$	$-.077^a$	$-.077^a$
x_4	.271	$-.077^a$	$-.077^a$	$-.077^a$	$.923^a$	$-.077^a$	$-.077^a$	$-.077^a$	$-.077^a$	$-.077^a$	$-.077^a$	$-.077^a$	$-.077^a$	$-.077^a$
x_5	-.382	$-.077^a$	$-.077^a$	$-.077^a$	$-.077^a$	$.923^a$	$-.077^a$	$-.077^a$	$-.077^a$	$-.077^a$	$-.077^a$	$-.077^a$	$-.077^a$	$-.077^a$
x_6	-.060	$-.077^a$	$-.077^a$	$-.077^a$	$-.077^a$	$-.077^a$	$.923^a$	$-.077^a$	$-.077^a$	$-.077^a$	$-.077^a$	$-.077^a$	$-.077^a$	$-.077^a$
x_7	.132	$-.077^a$	$-.077^a$	$-.077^a$	$-.077^a$	$-.077^a$	$-.077^a$	$.923^a$	$-.077^a$	$-.077^a$	$-.077^a$	$-.077^a$	$-.077^a$	$-.077^a$
x_8	-.018	$-.077^a$	$-.077^a$	$-.077^a$	$-.077^a$	$-.077^a$	$-.077^a$	$-.077^a$	$.923^a$	$-.077^a$	$-.077^a$	$-.077^a$	$-.077^a$	$-.077^a$
x_9	.346	$-.077^a$	$-.077^a$	$-.077^a$	$-.077^a$	$-.077^a$	$-.077^a$	$-.077^a$	$-.077^a$	$.923^a$	$-.077^a$	$-.077^a$	$-.077^a$	$-.077^a$
x_{10}	-.261	$-.077^a$	$-.077^a$	$-.077^a$	$-.077^a$	$-.077^a$	$-.077^a$	$-.077^a$	$-.077^a$	$-.077^a$	$.923^a$	$-.077^a$	$-.077^a$	$-.077^a$
x_{11}	-.103	$-.077^a$	$-.077^a$	$-.077^a$	$-.077^a$	$-.077^a$	$-.077^a$	$-.077^a$	$-.077^a$	$-.077^a$	$-.077^a$	$.923^a$	$-.077^a$	$-.077^a$
x_{12}	-.441	$-.077^a$	$-.077^a$	$-.077^a$	$-.077^a$	$-.077^a$	$-.077^a$	$-.077^a$	$-.077^a$	$-.077^a$	$-.077^a$	$-.077^a$	$.923^a$	$-.077^a$
x_{13}	.085	$-.077^a$	$-.077^a$	$-.077^a$	$-.077^a$	$-.077^a$	$-.077^a$	$-.077^a$	$-.077^a$	$-.077^a$	$-.077^a$	$-.077^a$	$-.077^a$	$.923^a$

Φ_y [1.000^a]

(Diag.) Ψ_y^2 [.613 .600 .781 .637 .780 .464 .983 .404 .516 .555 .511 .824 .506]

a. Fixed parameters

χ^2 (53 df) = 174.62

TABLE 3
Sample Estimates of the Ipsative Common Factor Model for Kohn's Measures of Parental Values from the 1973, 1975, 1976, and 1978 General Social Surveys: fathers (N = 721)

Parameter estimates

	Λ_x	ε_1	ε_2	ε_3	ε_4	ε_5	ε_6	ε_7	ε_8	ε_9	ε_{10}	ε_{11}	ε_{12}	ε_{13}
x_1	.280	.923[a]	-.077[a]	-.077[a]	-.077[a]	-.077[a]	-.077[a]	-.077[a]	-.077[a]	-.077[a]	-.077[a]	-.077[a]	-.077[a]	-.077[a]
x_2	-.080	-.077[a]	.923[a]	-.077[a]	-.077[a]	-.077[a]	-.077[a]	-.077[a]	-.077[a]	-.077[a]	-.077[a]	-.077[a]	-.077[a]	-.077[a]
x_3	.132	-.077[a]	-.077[a]	.923[a]	-.077[a]	-.077[a]	-.077[a]	-.077[a]	-.077[a]	-.077[a]	-.077[a]	-.077[a]	-.077[a]	-.077[a]
x_4	.129	-.077[a]	-.077[a]	-.077[a]	.923[a]	-.077[a]	-.077[a]	-.077[a]	-.077[a]	-.077[a]	-.077[a]	-.077[a]	-.077[a]	-.077[a]
x_5	-.349	-.077[a]	-.077[a]	-.077[a]	-.077[a]	.923[a]	-.077[a]	-.077[a]	-.077[a]	-.077[a]	-.077[a]	-.077[a]	-.077[a]	-.077[a]
x_6	-.115	-.077[a]	-.077[a]	-.077[a]	-.077[a]	-.077[a]	.923[a]	-.077[a]	-.077[a]	-.077[a]	-.077[a]	-.077[a]	-.077[a]	-.077[a]
x_7	.141	-.077[a]	-.077[a]	-.077[a]	-.077[a]	-.077[a]	-.077[a]	.923[a]	-.077[a]	-.077[a]	-.077[a]	-.077[a]	-.077[a]	-.077[a]
x_8	.006	-.077[a]	-.077[a]	-.077[a]	-.077[a]	-.077[a]	-.077[a]	-.077[a]	.923[a]	-.077[a]	-.077[a]	-.077[a]	-.077[a]	-.077[a]
x_9	.397	-.077[a]	-.077[a]	-.077[a]	-.077[a]	-.077[a]	-.077[a]	-.077[a]	-.077[a]	.923[a]	-.077[a]	-.077[a]	-.077[a]	-.077[a]
x_{10}	-.238	-.077[a]	-.077[a]	-.077[a]	-.077[a]	-.077[a]	-.077[a]	-.077[a]	-.077[a]	-.077[a]	.923[a]	-.077[a]	-.077[a]	-.077[a]
x_{11}	-.169	-.077[a]	-.077[a]	-.077[a]	-.077[a]	-.077[a]	-.077[a]	-.077[a]	-.077[a]	-.077[a]	-.077[a]	.923[a]	-.077[a]	-.077[a]
x_{12}	-.311	-.077[a]	-.077[a]	-.077[a]	-.077[a]	-.077[a]	-.077[a]	-.077[a]	-.077[a]	-.077[a]	-.077[a]	-.077[a]	.923[a]	-.077[a]
x_{13}	.178	-.077[a]	-.077[a]	-.077[a]	-.077[a]	-.077[a]	-.077[a]	-.077[a]	-.077[a]	-.077[a]	-.077[a]	-.077[a]	-.077[a]	.923[a]

Φ_y [1.000[a]]

(Diag.) Ψ_y^2 [.673] .659 .833 .728 .792 .482 1.007 .538 .570 .621 .599 .959 .566

a. Fixed parameters

χ^2 (53 df) = 204.996

161

tained, the approximation to the ipsative common factor model using the methods of exploratory factor analysis in this case appears to be relatively good, although the extent to which these results can be generalized is unclear. As we pointed out in the above discussion, as p increases, the ipsative transformation matrix approaches an identity. The consequence of this is to reduce the effects of the ipsative transformation on the covariance structure. In any event, it is not clear to us how large p must be to safely ignore the effects of the ipsative property of the measures. We are reluctant to conclude from the present findings that the ipsative property of these parental values indicators may safely be ignored.

As we indicated in the preceding discussion, it is necessary to consider the overall fit of the ipsative common factor model in order to evaluate its utility. In Tables 2 and 3 we have reported the likelihood-ratio χ^2 values for evaluating the goodness-of-fit of the model presented there. Under the assumption of multi-variate normality in the y vector, these χ^2 values may be used as measures of fit in large samples (see Jöreskog, 1978: 447). The χ^2 values obtained both for mothers (χ^2 = 174.62) and fathers (χ^2 = 204.99) with 53 degrees of freedom are statistically significant at extremely low levels of Type I error, and provide a statistical basis for the rejection of the model. It is important, however, to evaluate the goodness-of-fit of this model in light of the fit of alternative models. This is partly due to the fact that the above likelihood-ratio χ^2 statistics are partially a function of sample size and cannot therefore be interpreted un-ambiguously in large samples (Jöreskog, 1978: 447).

In addition, statistical measures of fit generally have meaning only within a comparative framework, and it is useful therefore propose meaningful alternatives to the present model (Jöreskog, 1978: 448). Therefore, as suggested above, we compare the results of the model presented in Tables 2 and 3 with the results of a model that posits no latent common factors for the variables; i.e., $\Sigma_x = \Psi_x^2 = A \Psi_y^2 A$. In addition, we examine a model that posits two latent factors for the observed indicators.

The model suggested here as a baseline against which to compare the present model provides a poorer fit to the sample

JACKSON, ALWIN   163

data for both mothers (χ^2 = 475.05) and fathers (χ^2 = 356.59), as would be expected. Using the Tucker-Lewis coefficient (TLC) to assess the relative fit of our model over this zero-factor model, a slight improvement is revealed for fathers (TLC = .361) and a moderate improvement is revealed for mothers (TLC = .636). In other words, within the set of assumptions we have made here in order to apply the ipsative common factor model to this particular set of ipsative variables, there is evidence that a self-direction/conformity factor, originally identified by Kohn (1969: 57), exists for these measures. At the same time, the evidence for this is not strong, in the sense that the model allowing for this latent factor provides only a modest improvement in fit to the sample data over a model that posits no such factor.

As noted in the above discussion, there is no direct way within the present context to evaluate the adequacy of the set of assumptions we have made in order to apply the ipsative common factor model in the present case. The relatively poor fit of our model to the sample data used here may indicate problems with this particular set of assumptions or with the complexity of the factor model assumed to hold for the y vector. In order to examine this second possibility we have estimated a 2-factor ipsative common factor model. The results for this model reflect an improved fit to the data for both mothers (χ^2 = 99.33, TLC = .792) and fathers (χ^2 = 133.89, TLC = .529), but the overall fit to the data in either case, as reflected in the Tucker-Lewis coefficients, is not entirely satisfactory. We suspect that the addition of factors to the model will improve the overall fit to the sample data, but it is unclear whether this would add substantially to our understanding of the applicability of the ipsative common factor model to these measures.

SUMMARY AND CONCLUSIONS

In the above presentation we have developed a common factor model for variables that have undergone an ipsative transformation, given knowledge of the factor model for the pre-ipsative variables. The ipsative common factor model has been defined, given the existence of two facts: (1) x = Ay and (2) y = $\wedge_y\xi$ + ϵ. In the remainder of the article we have addressed the question of the applicability of the ipsative common factor model to sets of variables with ipsative properties which result from the measurement procedure rather than an ipsative transformation of nonipsative variables. We argued that if one is willing to assume that there exists a hypothetical nonipsative set of measures (y) corresponding to the ipsative set (x), that x = Ay, and that y = $\wedge_y\xi$ + ϵ, then it is possible to apply the ipsative common factor model to such measures. Unfortunately, there is no direct way to evaluate the measures' validity within this set of assumptions.

The evaluation of the applicability of the ipsative common factor model in these cases requires (1) an examination of the differences in the response processes involved in producing data with ipsative and nonipsative properties, e.g. rankings vs. ratings, and (2) the specification of plausible alternative models for sets of ipsative variables that represent both the latent content of the variables and their ipsative properties. Finally, there is also some utility in applying the ipsative common factor model to sets of ipsative variables, such as Kohn's measures of parental values, in order to obtain greater experience regarding the descriptive usefulness of the ipsative common factor model.

NOTES

1. Horst (1965: 287-288) refers to the ipsative transformation as the "minor transformation" or "right centering," while the normative transformation is called the "major transformation" or "left centering." When both transformations are performed, the scores are said to be "double-centered." See also Harris (1953),Tucker (1956), and Hicks (1970).

2. Horst (1965: 292) shows that ipsative measures that sum to the constant c for each individual will sum to zero when the x's are left-centered.

3. This is a function of the fact that as p increases, the ipsative transformation matrix, A, approaches an identity.

4. This observation may not apply to all methods of factor analysis, but methods that utilize generalized least squares (GLS) and maximum likelihood (ML) procedures to fit the model require a positive-definite sample covariance matrix (Jöreskog, 1978: 446).

REFERENCES

ALWIN, D. F. and D. J. JACKSON (1980) "The statistical analysis of Kohn's measures of parental values." In H.O.A. Wold and K. G. Jöreskog (eds.) Systems Under Indirect Observation: Causality, Structure and Prediction. New York: Elsevier North-Holland.

CATTELL, R. B. (1952) Factor Analysis. New York: Harper & Row.

——— (1944) "Psychological measurement: ipsative, normative and interactive." Psych. Rev. 51: 292-303.

CLEMANS, W. V. (1956) "An analytical and empirical examination of some properties of ipsative measures." Ph.D. dissertation, University of Washington.

CUNNINGHAM, W. H., I.C.M. CUNNINGHAM, and R. T. GREEN (1977) "The ipsative process to reduce response set bias." Public Opinion Q. 41: 379-384.

GUILFORD, J. P. (1954) Psychometric Methods. New York: McGraw-Hill.

HARRIS, C. W. (1953) "Relations among factors of raw, deviation and double-centered score matrices." J. of Experimental Education 22: 53-58.

HICKS, L. E. (1970) "Some properties of ipsative, normative and forced choice normative measures." Psych. Bull. 74: 167-184.

HORST, P. (1965) Factor Analysis of Data Matrices. New York: Holt, Rinehart & Winston.

JORESKOG, K. G. (1978) "Structural analysis of covariance and correlation matrices." Psychometrika 43: 443-477.

KOHN, M. L. (1976) "Social class and parental values: another confirmation of the relationship." Amer. Soc. Rev. 41: 538-545.

——— (1969) Class and Conformity: A Study in Values. Homewood, IL: Irwin.

LAWLEY, D. N. and A. E. MAXWELL (1971) Factor Analysis as a Statistical Method. New York: Elsevier North-Holland.

SORBOM, D. and K. G. JORESKOG (1976) COFAMM—Confirmatory Factor Analysis with Model Modification. Chicago: National Educational Resources.

TUCKER, L. R. (1956) "Factor analysis of double-centered score matrices." Research Memorandum (RM-56-3). Princeton, NJ: Educational Testing Service.

——— and C. LEWIS (1973) "A reliability coefficient for maximum-likelihood factor analysis." Psychometrika 38: 1-10.

David J. Jackson is a research sociologist for the Population Research Section of the Mental Health Study Center, National Institute of Mental Health. His research interests are factorial ecology, use of census data in mental health-related research, and measurement.

Duane F. Alwin is Associate Research Scientist in the Survey Research Center and Associate Professor in Sociology at The University of Michigan. In addition to the quantitative analysis of measurement issues, his research interests include the sociology of education and the social psychology of inequality.

PART III

Empirical Examples

CHAPTER SIX

Response Errors in Self-Reported
Number of Arrests

GORDON A. WYNER
National Analysts

RESPONSE ERROR RESEARCH

Over the years, a great many studies have been conducted to assess the problem of measurement error in survey data (for an overview of the literature see Phillips, 1971; Deutscher, 1973; Bradburn and Sudman, 1974; Wyner, 1976). While the extent of error and the nature of the errors (random or systematic) depend upon the specific survey question being investigated, it is safe to say that response error is widespread. Survey estimates of means and relationships between variables may be substantially biased due to response errors, yet the magnitude of the bias is usually unexplored and therefore unknown.

Attempts to overcome the problem have originated from two different directions. One approach, that of the survey researcher, has been to refine the interviewing process in the hope of reducing the amount of error in the data-collection phase of research. For example, the literature is replete with studies of the effects of the interviewer on survey responses (Hyman, 1974; Phillips, 1971; Deutscher, 1973; Bradburn and Sudman, 1974; Wyner, 1976;).

The results of these studies can, in some cases, be used in the selection and training of interviewers to minimize their impact on the data. One limitation of this approach is that it has focused on isolated factors that influence response—e.g., interviewer style, social desirability, recall—without evaluating their joint influences.

The second approach is that of the data analyst, for whom the problem is one of statistically controlling the impact of response error or parameter estimates. In recent years, a number of methods have been developed to increase this level of control. In essence, these methods employ measured variables (such as self-reports of behavior) as indicators of an unobservable structure of true variables and measurement (or response) errors. Various estimation techniques allow for the specification and testing of alternative assumptions about the system of relationships between observable and unobservable variables (Jöreskog, 1970; Lawley and Maxwell, 1971).

AN ALTERNATIVE APPROACH

This study will explore the problem of response error in a different way, one which should inform both the data collection and data analysis approaches. A specific survey measure—a question about how many times one has been arrested—will be examined in detail to answer these questions:

(1) What is the extent of response error in the measure?
(2) Are the response errors random, or do they follow a systematic pattern?
(3) Why do response errors occur? Can they be explained by memory loss or motivational factors, or both?
   —Does the length of time since the arrests occurred lead to underreporting?
   —Does the seriousness of an arrest record lead to underreporting?
   —Do personal attitudes about the desirablilty or undesirability of being arrested lead to overreporting or underreporting?
(4) To what extent is the survey response an adequate proxy for the actual number of arrests?

The answers to these questions should be of interest to practitioners of the unobservable variables approach, as they provide
an alternative way of obtaining empirical estimates of error
structure parameters. The results of this direct estimation approach may prove useful for specifying the error structure to be
tested in an unobservable variable model.

The approach used in this study is basically to test empirically
the assumptions which are often made about errors of measurement. In particular, these random error assumptions are called
into question:

(1) The expected value of error is zero.
(2) Errors are uncorrelated with actual values.
(3) Errors are uncorrelated with each other.

In classical test theory, these assumptions are often viewed as a
necessary part of the theory, not to be subjected to testing (Lord
and Novick, 1968). This is appropriate when there is no
absolutely true score for each person, but when a true score is only
a construct that has the desired random error properties.
However, there is another entire class of measurement problems,
involving the measurement of variables that have absolute true
scores on natural quantitative scales, for which it is appropriate to
test these assumptions.

It is this latter class of problems—common in social and
economic surveys—that is relevant here. There is significant
doubt as to whether the random error properties which are often
invoked in errors in variables models (Johnston, 1972: 282) are in
fact true. If they are not true, various kinds of biases in estimates
can seriously distort inferences drawn from self-report data
(Cochran, 1963, 1968, 1970; Chai, 1969, 1971; Chai and Frankfurter, 1974).

The questions addressed in this study that should be of most
interest to survey researchers relate to the reasons for response
error. An explanatory model of response error provides insights
into how the data-collection process might be controlled to
reduce errors. It focuses attention on those factors that cause
response error, rather than emphasizing factors that are merely
easy to manipulate (e.g., interviewer assignments).

The quality of self-reported measures of arrests in particular has long been a concern of researchers in the areas of crime and delinquency (Ball, 1966; Clark and Tifft, 1966; Gould, 1969; Walsh, 1967). Even though the concept of arrests has obvious limitations (for example, arrests do not necessarily correlate with the true incidence of crime), the concept has some legitimate uses in research (as in experimental rehabilitation studies). It is important, then, to understand the error structure of self-reports and to determine the reports' adequacy as a proxy for actual arrests.

DATA AND METHODS

SAMPLE SELECTION

The sample for this investigation was drawn from the ex-addict group in the Vera Institute of Justice Supported Employment Experiment. The program was designed to give ex-heroin addicts living in Manhattan an opportunity to gain experience in jobs requiring a minimum of stress and strict supervision so that they could gradually acquire work habits that would enable them to compete in the private labor market.

Virtually all of the program participants had some criminal record. The average number of arrests was about 8, the average number of convictions was more than 4, and two-thirds of the sample had been incarcerated (an average of 4.6 times).

From the total research sample, a subsample of 79 who had a complete arrest record on file with the New York Police Department was selected for this study. The subsample is representative of the total sample, having very similar distributions on all demographic variables: 92% male, 75% black, 22% Spanish-speaking, with an average age of 30 and an average education of 10 years.

As a part of regular quarterly interviews, respondents were asked about their arrest histories. After the brief interview, they were asked to answer a 20-item, self-administered questionnaire with an interviewer on hand in case of questions. Respondents were all given $5.00 for their participation.

Data from interviews were combined with arrest record data coded from New York Police Department arrest sheets. At no time did the researcher have access to names of respondents. These two sets of data were merged by matching identification numbers.

OPERATIONAL DEFINITIONS OF VARIABLES

Self-reported Measures of Arrests. The self-report measure was designed to be comparable to the criterion measure derived from New York Police Department arrest records. The question asked was: "How many times were you arrested as an adult by the New York City Police up through February, 1975?" The end date was chosen to coincide with the dates of available records. The interviews were conducted during October and November of 1975. Interviewers were told to instruct respondents to exclude arrests outside New York City, as well as juvenile arrests.

Actual Arrests. For each person in the sample for whom there was a complete arrest record (N = 79) the total number of arrests was computed. This count, based on police records, serves as the "true" value for each person in the analyses.

It is possible that the arrest data themselves contain errors. However, most of the large sources of error are irrelevant to the purposes of this study. For example, it is of no consequence to this study that police enforcement policies affect the number of arrests made or that the social class background or residence of a criminal partly determines the probability of being arrested.

The only errors that are of consequence are of these types: a person is apprehended and formally charged by the police with committing a crime and that arrest does not appear on his record, or one or more additional arrests that never occurred do appear on his record. These could result from influence being exercised on behalf of some individuals or from clerical errors. Because neither possibility is amenable to study, it has to be assumed for our purposes that the effects of these errors do not seriously distort the conclusions. In particular, this means assuming that the true arrest distribution is not substantially different in character from the police record arrest distribution and that the correlates of error in this study would not be substantially different.

Response Error in Self-Reports of Arrests. The response error variable is constructed by subtracting the actual number of arrests from the self-reported number for each person. Thus a positive response error denotes an overstatement of the number of arrests, and a negative response error denotes underreporting.

Predictors of Response Error. The independent variables are of three kinds: (1) the potential of the question to motivate response errors (as in the generally perceived seriousness or undesirability of crimes); (2) question difficulty (or recall difficulty inherent in question); and (3) personal motivation (personal beliefs about undesirability or desirability of an arrest record).

Variables in the first two categories were derived from police records. As an indicator of the potential for motivation in the question, the number of arrests which carried multiple charges was selected. In general, more charges indicate that a more serious accusation is being made, one with greater potential punishment. The more undesirable the arrests, the greater the likelihood that a respondent would understate the actual number.

Question difficulty was measured by the number of arrests occurring before 1960 (15 years prior to the interviews). Clearly, recall error is a function of the time since the events being asked about took place (Bradburn and Sudman, 1974).[1]

Personal motivation was tapped by a scale of perceived desirability/undesirability of arrests. The items comprising the scale were murder, disturbing the peace, possession of heroin, assault and battery, numbers running, robbery, reckless driving, and burglary. Respondents rated each item on a nine-point scale from extremely undesirable to extremely desirable. Responses to each item were grouped into three categories—extremely undesirable (1), undesirable (2-4), and neutral or desirable (5-9)—and averaged for each person. This concept of "trait desirability" has been shown in a variety of contexts to predict self-reporting of behavioral traits (Phillips and Clancy, 1970, 1972).

RESULTS

RESPONSE ERRORS, ACTUAL ARRESTS, AND SELF-REPORTS

A comparison of the distributions of these three variables is instructive (Figure 1). The mean of the actual number of arrests (from arrest records) is 9.25, almost identical to the mean self-report, 8.96. This implies that the mean response error is small (−.29) and that errors essentially cancel out for this sample. The tendency of some people to substantially understate is almost entirely compensated for by others who overstate.

The variances of the distributions of self-reports and actual values are also quite similar. However, visual inspection shows that these distributions do not coincide. Although they have some general similarity in shape, there are some obvious peaks on the self-report distribution that do not appear on the true value distribution. In particular there are high frequencies of self-reports at X_0 = 5, 10, 20, which might be the result of a response tendency to pick convenient numbers (i.e., responses with 0 or 5 in the last digit). Of the 8 responses of X_0 = 20, 5 are substantial over statements of the true number of arrests. Overstatements account for 4 of the 6 responses of X_0 = 10. The peak at X_0 = 5 is due primarily to understatements. Of the 9 people who gave that response, 6 underreported. Because the low peaks represent underreports and the high peaks represent overreports, the variance of self-reports is increased. These peaks also contribute to a positive relationship (r = .44) between response errors and self-reports.

The response error distribution shows wide variation in errors. Only 10 of 79 people in the sample gave completely accurate responses. Almost half of the people gave responses that were within plus or minus 2 arrests of their true value. However, more than 20% of the people made errors of plus or minus 5 or more arrests, and five respondents made errors of overstatement or understatement greater than 10, including a plus 15 and a minus 14 response error. The distribution of errors is unimodal, with frequencies falling off fairly rapidly in both tails, suggesting that it might be approximately normal. However, a goodness-of-fit test did not support this conjecture.

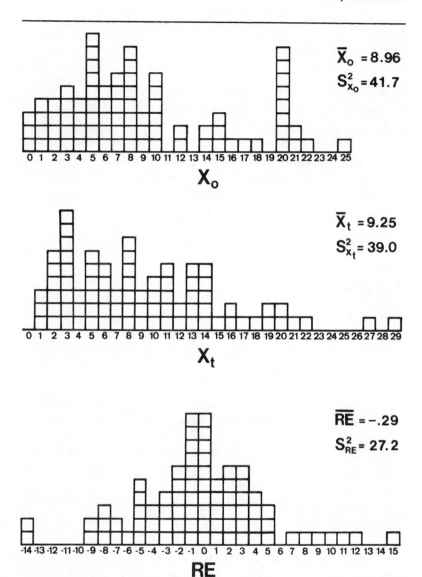

Figure 1: Frequency distributions: self-reports, actual values, and response errors in arrests.

Another way of conceptualizing response error is as a fraction of actual values. The distribution of percentage response errors shows respondents as accurate or inaccurate relative to their position on the true value distribution. Looked at in this manner, there is still wide variation in the errors. Among the respondents, one-sixth underreported their arrests by more than 50%, while another one-sixth overreported their true number of arrests by more than 50%. Less than a third of the sample (28%) gave responses that were within plus or minus 20% of their actual value.

A direct crosstabulation of response errors by actual values indicates that there is a fairly strong negative relationship (Table 1). The likelihood of an understatement increases as the number of arrests increases. Complete accuracy, on the other hand, decreases as the number of arrests gets larger. The correlation between response errors and actual arrests is –.38. Clearly, the second random error assumption—which postulates no correlation—is violated in these data.

PREDICTORS OF RESPONSE ERROR

In order to explain why response errors occur, response error was regressed on the three predictor variables: number of multiple charge arrests, number of arrests before 1960, and arrest trait desirability. The ordinary least squares estimates of regression coefficients and summary statistics are presented in Table 2. All three predictors are significant at the .05 level for one-tailed tests. The coefficient of determination, R^2, is significant also, indicating that the overall model is supported. Approximately 18% of the response error variance (corrected R^2) is accounted for by the predictors. The negative coefficient on "number of multiple charge arrests" indicates that underreporting is partially due to the general social undesirability of a serious arrest record. For each additional arrest with multiple charges, the model predicts that there is about a 50% chance that it will not be reported.

TABLE 1
Response Error (Positive, Zero, or Negative)
by Actual Number of Arrests*

		Actual No. of Arrests				
		1-5	6-11	12-29		
	Negative	37 (10)	44 (12)	64 (16)	48 (38)	
Response Error	0	26 (7)	11 (3)	0 (0)	13 (10)	
	Positive	37 (10)	44 (12)	36 (9)	39 (31)	
		34 (27)	34 (27)	32 (25)	100 (79)	

$x^2 = 9.33$, P - .05

= -.177

*Cell sizes in parentheses.

Apart from what is generally viewed as undesirable, the significant coefficient on arrest trait desirability indicates that individual attitudes about what is desirable have an independent effect on response accuracy. If the scale is viewed as a 3-point continuum (the average of items scored on a 3-point scale), the magnitude of the coefficient indicates that the difference in response errors for the extreme categories is about 4. Those who rated having an arerst record as neutral or desirable overreport 4 more arrests (according to the model) than those who rate having an arrest record as extremely undesirable.

The fact that these first 2 predictor variables are unrelated (r = -.015) and have independent effects on response error supports the conceptual distinction between the motivation to misreport inherent in the question and motivation particular to individuals.

TABLE 2
Regression of Response Error on Multiple Charge Arrests,
Arrest Trait Desirability, and Arrests before 1960*

Independent Variable	Full Sample
Number of Multiple Charge Arrests	- .518 (.182)
Arrest Trait Desirability	1.840 (.956)
Number of Arrests Before 1960	- .431 (.181)
Constant	-1.696
R^2	.20
R^2 corrected	.18
F Ratio	6.33

*Standard errors in parentheses.

*Standard errors in parentheses.

Together these factors explain about 13% of the response error variance.

The significance of "number of arrests before 1960" is a clear indication that something other than motivation is also producing errors. The question's difficulty for each respondent is captured by this measure, which takes account of the differing recall periods required for each person. For each arrest that occurred before 1960 (an arbitrary time period), the odds are almost even that it will be reported or that it will be omitted. Even if there were no motivational factors operating, there would still be systematic response errors due to the length of recall required by the question. In this sample, about 6% of the response error variance is due to the recall factor.

Acceptance of this explanatory model compels rejection of the third random error assumption—that errors are uncorrelated with each other.[2] Errors are likely to be correlated between people to the extent that they share the same attitudes towards being arrested and have arrest histories that are similar in terms of their distribution in time and seriousness.

SELF-REPORTS AND ACTUAL ARRESTS

After observing the extent and nature of response errors in the self-reports, it is useful to view the self-reports from the opposite perspective: to what extent does the self-report reflect the actual number of arrests?

The correlation of self-reports and actual values, which is a measure of validity, is .66. While this is low in absolute terms (only 44% of the variance in the measure can be attributed to the actual values), it is not extremely low when compared to measures frequently used in social science research (Robinson and Shaver, 1973). To make a precise determination of how high a validity coefficient is needed, the specfic goals of the study must be considered. Theoretical and simulation study results can be used to assess the effects of measurement error on statistical inferences (Chai and Frankfurter, 1974; Chai, 1971; Koch, 1969; Horvitz and Koch, 1969).

For practical purposes, it may not be extremely important that very few respondents give a completely accurate response. If a person has, say, 10 arrests, it may be unimportant if he says he has 8 or 12, as long as he does not report 2 or 20. In other words, it may be important to classify research subjects into discrete categories based on arrests, but not essential to know the precise number of arrests. Obviously, this is not true when it is necessary to know the number of arrests in a limited time period, a number which is apt to be small for all subjects. For example, in a rehabilitation program where respondents are asked whether or not they were arrested in the last year, the difference between 0 and 1 is crucial. However, when selecting people for a research program based on criminal histories or when matching an experimental and control group, several discrete categories may be adequate.

If the research does not require that information on specific values be retained, there may be a gain from giving up those individual values through grouping the data. It is possible to place people in less precise (i.e., wider) categories more accurately (i.e., with greater probability of correct classification).

In order to determine the impact of grouping on the accuracy of classifications, our sample was split into (approximate) fifths, fourths, thirds, and halves based on the distribution of self-reports. Each of these grouped variables was then crosstabulated with actual arrests, grouped in the same manner. For example, to obtain 4 approximately equal groups, self-reports were grouped as 0-4, 5-7, 8-12, and 13-29. With no grouping, only 13% would be correctly classified. When grouped in 5 categories, 43% are correctly classified; 4 categories, 53%; 3 categories, 63%, 2 categories, 76%.

Another measure of the effect of grouping is the coefficient gamma relating self-reports and actual arrests. Gamma is a measure of association for ordinal variables, varying from minus 1 to plus 1, measuring the consistency of ordered pairs of observations with the category ranking. When the data are grouped into 5 categories, $\Gamma = .72$; 4 categories, $\Gamma = .75$; 3 categories, $\Gamma = .80$; 2 categories, $\Gamma = .83$. The ordinal relationship between self-reports and true values becomes stronger as the groups become larger.

These results still leave a large margin of error in the data; however, by giving up even more information, an increase in accuracy can be achieved. It is a common practice (particularly in social-psychological experiments) to trichotomize a sample on a classifying variable of substantive import and then select only those in the extreme categories for research purposes. It is assumed that misclassfications due to measurement errors are minimized, and adequate variation between categories remains.

The relationship of self-reports and actual arrests in three categories illustrates what is gained from that approach (see Table 3). Using all three categories, 63% would have been correctly classified. If only extreme categories are used, 38 of 49, or 78%, are correctly classified. This is somewhat better than the percentage that would be obtained from splitting the sample in half, but 30 observations (79 minus 49) must be thrown out.

There is an apparent advantage in taking extreme categories in maximizing the differences between groups. However, because

TABLE 3
Self-Reported Arrests by Actual Number of Arrests*

	0 to 5	76 (22)	14 (4)	4 (1)	34 (27)
Actual Number of Arrests	6 to 10	17 (5)	43 (12)	23 (5)	28 (22)
	11 to 29	7 (2)	43 (12)	73 (16)	38 (30)
		37 (29)	35 (28)	28 (22)	100 (79)

$x^2 = 41.8$, $P < .01$

$Y = .80$

*Cell sizes in parentheses.

the extreme groups really contain a number of people from the middle true group, the large variance would be partly due to overreporting and underreporting. The researcher might be misled by a nonsignificant difference between groups on some other (dependent) variable when, in fact, the two groups were not widely separated to begin with in true number of arrests (the independent variable). There is the advantage in this approach that only three people would be misclassified from one extreme category to another.

CONCLUSIONS AND IMPLICATIONS

The results presented here demonstrate the potential seriousness of the problem of response error. It would, of course, be wrong to draw sweeping conclusions from a study with such a limited scope in terms of sampling and data collection. However, results do have some implications for both the survey researcher and the data analyst.

If response error is to be reduced at the data-collection stage of research, all three causal factors investigated in this study should be considered. First, the recall period should be limited to the minimum time frame necessary. Questions that require respondents to recall numerous events that occurred decades ago should be avoided if possible. (The obvious exception to this is questions about extremely salient, individual events, such as wedding days, children's birthday, deaths, and the like.)

Second, the two types of motivational factors, personal and question-specific, should be considered simultaneously. Interviewers should be trained to provide an uncritical atmosphere in an interview, so that the tendency for respondents to understate on sensitive topics (such as arrests) will be minimized. Yet at the same time the interviewer should not be so positively approving of socially undesirable behaviors that the respondent is encouraged to overstate. In this study, the large number of positive response errors and their association with arrest trait desirability suggest that this can be a problem. More detailed studies under controlled interviewing conditions are required to assess the appropriate balance of these factors.

Data analysts should be wary of using self-report data containing substantial response errors. Frequently, small-scale investigations such as this study can be conducted to determine the extent of the problem. Another option is the use of the ad hoc grouping of observations under the assumption that, at best, only a small number of categories of response can be meaningfully distiguished. Although this does not provide a great deal of precision, this may represent a realistic use of the data.

Unobservable variable approaches can now be applied to a wide variety of possible correlated error structures (Bielby et al., 1978). The results of studies such as the present one can suggest which error structure parameters should be estimated and which can be ignored. If the gross amount of error is large (for example, if the variance of response errors approaches in magnitude the variance of self-reports), the use of other types of measures ought to be weighed. In the case of arrests, for example, the recorded arrests may have to be secured for the entire sample of interest.

No single approach is likely to be appropriate for all circumstances. However, the range of ways of attacking the problem should provide some assistance in minimizing the impact of response error in many research applications.

NOTES

1. These two predictors of response error were selected from a set of variables derived from arrest records. Other measures of question motivation included number of arrests for felonies, crimes against persons, and drug offenses. Other measures of question difficulty included average number of months between arrests and interview and variance of number of months between arrests and interview. Factor analysis of these variables revealed two independent dimensions of question difficulty and motivation. Multiple-charge arrests and number of arrests before 1960 were selected because they tap the relevant dimensions and are uncorrelated with each other, which facilitates the estimation of their separate effects on response error.

2. Other analyses were conducted to determine whether nonlinear or nonadditive relationships could add any explanatory power to the model. The results of those analyses indicated that the 3-variable linear model was an adequate representation of the structure generating response error.

REFERENCES

BALL, J. (1966) "The reliability and validity of interview data obtained form 59 narcotic drug addicts." Amer. J. of Sociology 72: 640-654.

BIELBY, W., R. HAUSER, and D. FEATHERMAN (1977) "Response errors of nonblack males in models of intergenerational transmission of socioeconomic status." Amer. J. of Sociology 83: 1242-1288.

BRADBURN, N. and S. SUDMAN (1974) Response Effects in Surveys. Chicago: Aldine.

CHAI, J. (1971) "Correlated measurement errors and the least squares estimator of the regression coefficient." J. of Amer. Stat. Assn. 66: 478-483.

——— (1969) "The bias of the ordinary least squares estimator of the regression coefficient for a bivariate population when both variables are subject to correlated measurement errors." Proceedings of the Social Statistics Section, American Statistical Association: 433-453.

——— and G. FRANKFURTER (1974) "Errors in variables for the simple linear model: the effects of correlated errors of measurement on interval estimation and hypothesis testing." Proceedings of the Social Statistics Section, American Statistical Association.

CLARK, J. and L. TIFFT (1966) "Polygraph and interview validation of self-reported deviant behavior." Amer. Soc. Rev. 31: 516-523.

COCHRAN, W. G. (1970) "Some effects of errors of measurement on multiple correlation." J. of the Amer. Stat. Assn. 65: 22-34.

——— (1968) "Errors of measurement in statistics." Technometrics 10: 637-666.

——— (1963) Sampling Techniques. New York: John Wiley.

DEUTSCHER, I. (1973) What We Say What We Do: Sentiments and Acts. Glenview, IL: Scott, Foresman.

GOULD, L. (1969) "Who defines delinquency: a comparison of self-reported and officially-reported indices of delinqueny for three racial groups." Social Problems 17: 325-336.

HORVITZ, D. AND G. KOCH (1969) "The effect of response errors on measures of association," pp. 247-282 in N. L. Johnson and H. Smith (eds.) New Developments in Survey Sampling. New York: John Wiley.

HYMAN, H. (1954) Interviewing in Social Research. Chicago: Univ. of Chicago Press.

JOHNSTON, J. (1972) Econometric Methods. New York: McGraw-Hill.

JORESKOG, K. (1970) "A general method for analysis of covariance structures." Biometrika 57: 239-251.

KOCH, G. (1969) "The effect of non-sampling errors on measures of association in 2x2 contingency tables." J. of Amer. Stat. Assn. 64: 851-854.

LAWLEY, D. and A. MAXWELL (1971) Factor Analysis as a Statistical Method. London: Butterworths.

LORD, F. and M. NOVICK (1968) Statistical Theories of Mental Test Scores. Reading, MA: Addison-Wesley.

PHILLIPS, D. (1971) Knowledge from What. Chicago: Rand McNally.

——— and K. CLANCY (1972) "Some effects of social desirability in survey studies." Amer. J. of Sociology 77: 921-940.

——— (1970) "Response bias in field studies of mental illness." Amer. Soc. Rev. 35: 503-515.

ROBINSON, J. and P. SHAVER (1973) Measures of Social-Psychological Attitudes. Ann Arbor: University of Michigan Survey Research Center.

WALSH, W. B. (1967) "Validity of self-report." J. of Consulting Psychology 14: 18-23.

WYNER, G. A. (1976) "Sources of response error in self-reports of behavior." Ph.D. dissertation, University of Pennsylvania.

Gordon A. Wyner is a Research Group Manager with National Analysts, a division of Booz-Allen & Hamilton, Inc. He specializes in survey research applications for industry and government. He received his Ph.D. in sociology from the University of Pennsylvania.

CHAPTER SEVEN

Children's Reports of
Parental Socioeconomic Status
A Multiple Group Measurement Model

ROBERT D. MARE
University of Wisconsin—Madison

WILLIAM M. MASON
University of Michigan

Much recent research has been concerned with measurement error and its implications for linear models of sociological phenomena. The literature is now rich with attempts to model and estimate measurement error and to use the resulting models to construct more sophisticated structural equation models (Goldberger and Duncan, 1973; Bielby and Hauser, 1977b). Within this framework, an important class of applications consists of intergroup comparisons of measurement or constrained factor analytic models relating observable indicators to unobservable latent variables. This may consist of estimating a

---

AUTHORS' NOTE: *We are indebted to Alan C. Kerckhoff for making available to us the data used in this article. This research was supported in part by funds granted to the Institute for Research on Poverty at the University of Wisconsin— Madison by the Department of Health, Education, and Welfare pursuant to the provisions of the Economic Opportunity Act of 1964.*

measurement or factor model for the same population at two points in time, or of comparing the models for several populations at a point in time. For example, K. O. Mason et al. (1976) examine change in sex-role attitude factor models between the early 1960s and the mid-1970s. Bielby et al. (1977a) estimate response error models for measures of socioeconomic attainment in black and nonblack populations. And W. M. Mason et al. (1976) compare the accuracy of children's reports of parental socioeconomic statuses among age-race groups. In each case separate models of the relationships between unobserved and observed variables and among the unobserved variables themselves are specified for the groups of interest. The pattern and the strength of these relationships, both within and across populations, are central substantive concerns.

Thus far, most comparisons of measurement error and factor analytic models for two or more groups have been deficient because they estimated models independently for each group. That is, they have lacked a common framework within which to estimate the models for all groups simultaneously. For example, in contrasting the response error patterns of children of different age groups, W. M. Mason et al. (1976) estimate separate models for each group, allowing all group differences to be reflected in the parameter estimates. In general, this procedure has two important limitations. First, it precludes statistical tests of group differences in the measurement models. A test for group differences requires a comparison of two models: (1) a model in which the specifications (or parts of them) for the several groups are constrained to be the same; and (2) an unconstrained model in which the specifications (or parts of them) vary across groups. The second model always fits the data better than the first because it has more parameters. The test consists of assessing the statistical significance of the improvement in fit in going from the first model to the second. The test requires a framework for, first, obtaining pooled (constrained) estimates for the several groups and, second, estimating the unconstrained model for all groups simultaneously. Estimating separate models for each group does not permit the explicit comparison required by the test.

A second limitation of estimating the models of each group independently from the others is that it fails to exploit intergroup similarity in measurement models, resulting in less reliable parameter estimates than would otherwise be possible. Groups may differ in part of their measurement error pattern but be invariant in others. For example, the correlations between attitude constructs may change over time, but the relationships between attitude constructs and specific response items may not. A reasonable strategy, then, is to hold constant some elements of the models and allow variation where substantive reasoning indicates that it may occur. This affords better parameter estimates because they are based on more observations (a result of pooling groups) and use fewer degrees of freedom (a result of between-group equality constraints).

There is a statistical framework for the simultaneous estimation of measurement models in several populations (Jöreskog, 1971a).[1] To date, however, it has received little use in social research, despite the common task of comparing measurement or restricted factor analytic models across groups. We intend, in this article, to illustrate the use of Jöreskog's framework through a substantive example; namely, age variation in the reliability of children's reports of parental socioeconomic characteristics. We will analyze the data drawing upon the substantive arguments of W. M. Mason et al. (1976) and refining that earlier work. Our article will, first, review the problem of response unreliability in children's reports of parental characteristics and, second, will present a measurement model for children's and parents' reports for a single population, discussing its weaknesses. Third, it will outline a multiple-group approach to measurement error estimation and apply Jöreskog's (1971a) framework to the substantive problem at hand. Fourth, it will discuss alternative specifications of the measurement model in connection with specific hypotheses. Finally, it will present empirical results.

ERRORS IN CHILDREN'S REPORTS
OF PARENTAL SOCIOECONOMIC STATUS

The measurement reliability of socioeconomic characteristics is important in understanding the socioeconomic attainment process. Survey respondents make errors in reporting their own and others' socioeconomic statuses, reporting errors may be non-random, and groups may differ in the extent and pattern of their errors. Therefore, inferences based on attainment models depend on whether such models explicitly take account of measurement error (Bielby and Hauser, 1977a; Bielby et al., 1977a, 1977b; Broom et al., 1978).

Problems of measurement error in achievement process studies are more serious when children are the survey respondents who supply information on parental socioeconomic character-istics. This is typically the case in studies of the early achievement process. Because knowledge of social statuses is acquired through socialization, young persons may have a seriously incomplete picture of their parents' social standing and, therefore, make considerable errors in reporting their parents' characteristics (W. M. Mason et al., 1976, and references cited therein). The reliability of children's responses about parental characteristics varies with age. For whites, W. M. Mason et al. (1976) show that elementary school children are noticeably less reliable than their parents themselves, while high school youths approach their parents in reporting accuracy. Children's reporting errors may be nonrandom and the incidence of nonrandomness may depend on the particular parental socioeconomic characteristic for which information is elicited. The same authors also show that white elementary school children's response errors for fathers' and mothers' grades of school completed are positively correlated, while reporting errors for other pairs of parental statuses for elementary school children and for all pairs of statuses for older children are essentially random.

These findings on the quality of children's reports by grade level are based on measurement models estimated separately for each of three grades. As a result, the between-grade findings are not supported by statistical tests. In addition, separate estimation for each group results in less than optimal estimates of measurement model parameters. As will be discussed below, some parameters of the measurement models should not vary across grade levels. Estimating a separate model for each group, therefore, requires estimating more parameters than are needed, reducing the reliability of parameter estimates.

In the following discussion, we outline a measurement model for a single grade level, point out where between-group constraints can produce a parsimonious multiple group model, and discuss the simultaneous measurement model.

A SINGLE GROUP MEASUREMENT MODEL

Our data consist of parents' and children's reports on three parental socioeconomic characteristics—father's occupation, father's grades of schooling, and mother's grades of schooling—involving children in the sixth, ninth, and twelfth grades.[2] A strategy for modeling children's response errors is to specify linear covariance structure models of parental and child reports. Parents' and children's reports of the same parental characteristics are viewed as linear functions of a common, unobservable true parental status. For each grade level, for the ith individual, the model can be written as follows:

$$FAFED_i = TRFED_i + \epsilon_{1i} \tag{1}$$

$$MOMED_i = TRMED_i + \epsilon_{2i} \tag{2}$$

$$FAFOC_i = TRFOC_i + \epsilon_{3i} \tag{3}$$

$$SOFED_i = \lambda_4 TRFED_i + \epsilon_{4i} \tag{4}$$

$$SOMED_i = \lambda_5 TRMED_i + \epsilon_{5i} \tag{5}$$

$$SOFOC_i = \lambda_6 TRFOC_i + \epsilon_{6i}. \tag{6}$$

TRFED is father's true (unobservable) grades of schooling completed, and FAFED and SOFED are father's and son's reports of father's schooling respectively. Similarly, TRMED is mother's true grades of schooling completed, and MOMED and SOMED are mother's and son's reports of mother's schooling respectively. TRFOC is father's true occupational status score, and FAFOC and SOFOC are the status scores of father's and son's reports of father's occupation. The λ's are parameters to be estimated from the data. The parameters λ_1, λ_2, and λ_3 have been set equal to unity in equations 1, 2, and 3 to identify the model. The ϵ's are stochastic disturbances. All variables are expressed as deviations from their respective means.

To complete the model, we specify the pattern of covariances among the true parental characteristics and among the errors in the six equations. True scores are allowed to covary freely, providing estimates of the covariances among parental characteristics corrected for measurement error. Error covariances are specified as free or zero, depending upon the extent to which respondents use information on one status characteristic in reporting another.

Thus we have a six-equation measurement model for each grade level. The three coefficients relating sons' reports to their respective true parental statuses, the six elements of the covariance matrix of the true parental statuses, and the variable number of elements of the covariance matrix of the errors are estimated by the method of maximum likelihood. The model's adequacy in reproducing the observed covariance matrix of parents' and children's reports is evaluated by a goodness-of-fit statistic (Jöreskog, 1969). The extent of nonrandom measurement error is given by the model itself (that is, by the between-equation covariances of ϵ's). The reliabilities of the reports are calculated from the parameter estimates. For example, consider fathers' and sons' reports of fathers' schooling (FAFED and SOFED). Let $\hat{\phi}_{11}$ be the estimated variance of TRFED, $\hat{\psi}_{11}$ be the estimated variance of the disturbance ϵ_1, and $\hat{\psi}_{44}$ be the estimated variance of the disturbance ϵ_4. Then the estimated reliability of FAFED is

$$\frac{\hat{\phi}_{11}}{\hat{\phi}_{11} + \hat{\psi}_{11}} \qquad [7]$$

and the estimated reliability of SOFED is

$$\frac{\hat{\lambda}_4^2 \hat{\phi}_{11}}{\hat{\lambda}_4^2 \hat{\phi}_{11} + \hat{\psi}_{44}} \qquad [8]$$

(Joreskog, 1971b). That is, an indicator's reliability is the fraction of its expected variance due to the variance of its corresponding true score.

Following our earlier discussion, this model has several limitations. First, comparisons across grade levels can be casual at best, as estimating the models independently affords no formal way of testing between-grade differences. Second, between-grade comparisons of children's reporting reliabilities are affected by extraneous sources of grade-to-grade variation. The reliability of children's reports cannot be assessed independently of the true parental status distributions and parents' reports of their statuses. Both the true characteristics and parents' reports of them, however, vary across grades due to sampling variability. Therefore, parameter estimates describing the relationship between true parental statuses and children's reports of them— and thus the estimated child report reliabilities—may vary independently of the effects of maturation. Fluctuations in the quality of parental reports need not induce systematic biases in the reliability estimates for children, but they do reduce the precision of the reliability estimates.

Finally, estimating separate models for each group, results in unnecessary complexity. As discussed below, one can combine the information for all grades to estimate a single set of true parental status covariances and parental report reliabilities. This relatively parsimonious formulation fits the data at hand. Estimating a separate model for each group, therefore, requires many more parameters than are needed to describe the data.

A MULTIPLE GROUP MEASUREMENT MODEL

Superior reliability estimates of parents' and children's reports and explicit statistical tests of between-grade measurement model differences can be obtained using a framework which simultaneously estimates the measurement parameters for all grade levels. In the model described above, separate sets of parameters for covariances among true parental characteristics and for the error variances of parental reports are estimated for each group. In general, therefore, the estimated reliabilities of parental reports will vary over children's grade levels. But while children's reporting performance can be expected to vary with their ages (as a result of the learning process), parents' performances should not depend upon children's ages. Nor should the joint distribution of true parental characteristics vary by children's ages.[3] Accordingly, we seek a model which allows the parameters reflecting children's reporting to vary by age, but which constrains the parental performances and status distributions to be stable over children's ages. In particular, we wish to modify the model described above by constraining the true status covariance matrix and the disturbance variances for parental reports to be invariant across grade levels. Such models may be estimated in Jöreskog's (1971a) general framework for the simultaneous covariance structure analysis of multiple populations. Within this framework it is possible to specify both group-invariant and group-specific parameters and to assess the adequacy of inter- and intragroup parameter restrictions through goodness-of-fit statistics.

Jöreskog's model is applied to our measurement error problem as follows: We estimate equations 1 through 6 above for each of three populations. Suppressing the individual level subscript i, we can express these equations in the matrix form

$$X_j = \Lambda_j F_j + \epsilon_j \qquad [9]$$

where X_j is a 6×1 vector of observed parental and child reports expressed as deviations from their means, Λ_j is a 6×3 matrix of coefficients, F_j is a 3×1 vector of true parental status variables, ϵ_j is a 6×1 vector of disturbances, and $j = 1, 2, 3$. The covariance matrix for the status reports implied by the model is then

$$\mathcal{E}(X_j X_j') = \Lambda_j \Phi_j \Lambda_j' + \Psi_j, \qquad [10]$$

where $\Phi_j = \mathcal{E}(F_j F_j')$, $\Psi_j = \mathcal{E}(\epsilon_j \epsilon_j')$, and $\mathcal{E}$ denotes the expectation operator. When we stipulate that the joint distribution of true parental statuses and the reliability of parents' reports are invariant, we require that $\Phi_1 = \Phi_2 = \Phi_3$, and

$$\psi_{(ii)1} = \psi_{(ii)2} = \psi_{(ii)3} \qquad (i = 1, 2, 3), \qquad [11]$$

where the last subscript of ψ refers to grade level and the (ii) denotes the first three diagonal elements of Ψ_j, that is, the error variances of the equations for parents' reports of the three parental status characteristics. Equating the true score variances and the disturbance variances for parents' reports across groups guarantees, by the definition of reliability (equation 7), that parental report reliabilities are group invariant.[4] To complete the model, the form of the off-diagonal elements of Ψ_j, the error covariance matrix for each grade level, must be specified. We consider the form of Ψ_j below.

SPECIFICATIONS AND HYPOTHESES

This section discusses the range of measurement model specifications possible within the framework outlined above and presents hypotheses to guide the interpretation of the empirical results. Equations 1 through 6 show parents' and sons' reports as linear functions of unmeasured true parental statuses. Equation 10 expresses the covariances of the status reports implied by the model as functions of true status and disturbance covariances. Equation 11 states the between-group equality restrictions on the true parental characteristics and the error variances of parents' reports. It remains to specify the pattern of parents' and sons' measurement errors. We must determine whether the model implies that reports of parental status characteristics are independent or whether some of the reports depend upon one another.

To specify whether reports depend only upon the true status they represent or upon reports of other status characteristics as well is to set the form of the disturbance covariance matrix Ψ_j. The general form for the jth grade group is given in Figure 1. Because Ψ_j is symmetric, it can be partitioned into three distinct 3×3 submatrices of disturbance covariances: Ψ_{11} for parents'

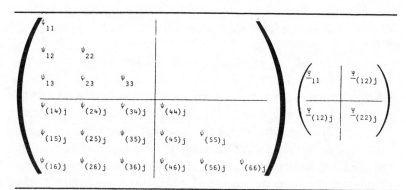

Figure 1: **General form of the disturbance covariance matrix for the jth grade level** (ψ_j).

reports, $\Psi_{(22)j}$ for sons' reports, and $\Psi_{(12)j}$ between parents' and sons' reports. The j subscript is not used with Ψ_{11}, as the covariances among parents' reports do not vary across grade levels of their sons. The elements of $\Psi_{(22)j}$ and $\Psi_{(12)j}$, on the other hand, are indexed by sons' grades, to indicate that the pattern of error covariances may be age-dependent.

For each group there are a number of possible error patterns. The simplest is random error. In this case, Ψ_j is diagonal for each grade level, where the diagonal elements are the error variances of sons' and parents' reports. If errors are not random, then it is necessary to consider several forms of nonrandomness. One form is nonrandomness among sons' reports, implying nonzero covariances among the errors in sons' reports; that is, nonzero off-diagonal elements in submatrix $\Psi_{(22)j}$. In general, $\Psi_{(22)j}$ is not the same for all j, as patterns of nonrandomness among sons' reports will vary by grade level. A second form is nonrandomness among parents' own status reports. This implies nonzero off-diagonal elements in submatrix Ψ_{11} of Figure 1. In contrast to the error covariances for sons' reports, those for parents' reports should not vary across sons' grade levels. The third type of non-random disturbance is between parents' and sons' reports. Nonzero covariances between the disturbances of parents' and sons' reports imply nonzero elements in submatrix $\Psi_{(12)j}$ in Figure 1. This class of disturbance covariances, while logically possible, is of minimal substantive interest here. It is difficult to conceive of mechanisms generating covariances between parents' and sons' reporting errors.

A second range of possibilities reflects alternative assumptions about children's changing report reliability across grade levels. Although parental reporting reliability and status distributions are assumed constant across grade levels from the outset, sons' report reliabilities are initially assumed to vary. In some cases, however, estimates of sons' reliabilities may turn out to be essentially unchanging across grades, even though we have not assumed this in advance. In addition, for some grade levels, sons' report reliabilities may turn out not to differ from those of their parents (W. M. Mason et al., 1976). In such cases it is desirable to reestimate models which explicitly incorporate these findings.

To do so requires constraints on the elements of Λ_j and Ψ_j. Consider the covariance matrix Ψ_j in Figure 1, along with the coefficient matrix of the jth group:

$$\Lambda_j = \begin{pmatrix} 1 & 0 & 0 \\ 0 & 1 & 0 \\ 0 & 0 & 1 \\ \lambda_{4j} & 0 & 0 \\ 0 & \lambda_{5j} & 0 \\ 0 & 0 & \lambda_{6j} \end{pmatrix}$$

Insofar as we wish to allow the reliability of sons' reports to vary across grade levels, we place no restrictions on the elements of Λ_j and Ψ_j. But if, for example, we want to specify a priori that the reliability of sons' reports of fathers' occupations for ninth- and twelfth-grade sons are equal, we impose the constraints $\lambda_{62} = \lambda_{63}$ and $\psi_{(66)2} = \psi_{(66)3}$. If we want to specify a priori that twelfth-grade sons report mothers' schooling as reliably as their mothers, then we impose the constraints $\lambda_{53} = 1.0$ and $\psi_{(55)3} = \psi_{22}$.

There are many possible specifications, and substantive reasoning is required to select a reasonable class of models from which to seek a model that fits the data. Such reasoning is developed at length by W. M. Mason et al. (1976) and is briefly summarized below. The discussion is organized around the hypothesis that reporting reliability and the incidence of non-random reporting errors vary by sons' ages and the parental status being reported.

VARIATIONS IN RELIABILITY BY AGE

Boys in lower grades are more likely than boys in higher grades to report their parents' statuses with error. As boys grow older their sensitivity to dimensions of social stratification increases. Older boys, moreover, will simply have heard more often what their parents' educational attainments and occupations are. At some point, therefore, sons' and parents' reporting reliability can be expected to converge.

VARIATIONS IN RELIABILITY
BY PARENTAL CHARACTERISTICS

We seek reliability estimates for reports of three parental statuses: mother's and father's grades of school completed, and father's occupation. Children may not learn these three characteristics at the same rate, implying that their report reliability will vary by the characteristics that they are asked about. In contrast with father's occupation, which is current and tangible, parental education is remote and relatively abstract. Children may frequently hear about the kind of work their fathers do, but possibly less often about how far their parents went in school. Therefore, sons may be better reporters of their father's occupation than of the educational attainment of either parent, and may approach their parents' report reliability for father's occupation at a lower grade level than for their parents' educational attainments.

VARIATIONS IN NONRANDOM ERROR BY AGE

Respondents uncertain about parental characteristics they are asked to report may use their knowledge of other statuses to help them. Operationally, this implies nonzero covariances between the errors in respondents' reports. If nonrandom reporting errors result from uncertainty, then the least knowledgeable respondents—boys in the lowest grades—will be most likely to have nonzero error covariances.

VARIATIONS IN NONRANDOMNESS BY PARENTAL CHARACTERISTICS

Not all reporting errors, however, are equally likely to be nonrandomly distributed. Mother's and father's grades of schooling are reported in response to a common stimulus, that is, a request for the highest grade of school completed by each parent, and sons therefore may resolve their uncertainty by making these two measures agree. Such agreement results, then, from a common basis of measurement for the variables, rather than from a sophisticated appreciation of assortative mating. Conversely, other types of nonrandom error are less common because they presuppose too sophisticated an understanding of social stratification. A boy uncertain of his father's schooling might guess it from his father's occupation. But the sons most likely to be uncertain of their parent's statuses—the youngest—are least likely to have the understanding to make informed guesses. Such sophisticated forms of nonrandom error therefore are unlikely to occur.

EMPIRICAL RESULTS

This section presents the results of our measurement error model estimation for young white males. We will first present summary goodness-of-fit statistics for a number of specifications. Then we will discuss the parameter and reliability estimates for the model we deem best, interpreting these results in light of the arguments presented above.

Several criteria, in addition to goodness-of-fit, are used to select a "best" model. First, parameter estimates should imply that both parents and sons report parental status with at least some error. Although equations 1 through 6 of the model require this, some empirical versions of the model may imply zero or negative error variances, suggesting that the model is misspecified. Second, the parameter estimates should imply reliability estimates for sons' reports which are stable or increasing with grade level. If estimates imply that sons' reporting performances deteriorate with age, this suggests either an incorrectly specified pattern of error covariances or implausible estimates resulting from sampling variability. In the latter case, a specification which equates sons' report reliabilities over grade levels is in order. Third, parents' own status reports should be at least as reliable as their sons' reports. And finally, the error covariance pattern must be substantively interpretable.

In selecting a measurement model we sought a plausible pattern of error covariances which fits the data, and then, given

TABLE 1
Goodness-of-Fit Statistics for Measurement Models for Sixth, Ninth, and Twelfth Grade White Males

Model[a]	x^2	Degrees of Freedom	Probability
A. Random errors	67.7	36	.001
B. Covariances among all sons' errors for all grades	36.1	27	.113
C. Covariances between errors in sons' reports of fathers' and mothers' schooling for 6th graders	50.9	35	.040
D. Covariances between errors in sons' reports of fathers' and mothers' schooling for 6th and 9th graders	44.2	34	.112
E. Model D with reliabilities of 12th grade sons' reports of fathers' occupation and schooling equated to reliabilities of fathers' reports	47.5	38	.140
F. Model D with reliabilities of all 12th grade sons' reports equated to parents' report reliabilities	49.2	40	.151
G. Model D with reliabilities of all 12th grade sons' reports and 9th grade sons' reports of mothers' schooling and fathers' occupation equated to parents' report reliabilities	50.5	44	.233
H. Model D with reliabilities of all 9th and 12th grade sons' reports equated to parents' report reliabilities	59.0	46	.098

a. In all models the covariance matrix of true parental characteristics and the error variances of parents' reports are held constant across grades.

TABLE 2
Estimated Reliabilities of Sons' and Parents' Reports of
Parental Socioeconomic Characteristics, by Grade

Characteristic	Reporter	Grade of Son 6	9	12
Father's Schooling	Father	.853	.853	.853
	Son	.611	.760	.944
Mother's Schooling	Mother	.890	.890	.890
	Son	.498	.862	.870
Father's Occupation	Father	.915	.915	.915
	Son	.710	.908	.937

NOTE: The model includes error covariances between sons' reports of father's and mother's schooling for sixth and ninth grade white males (Model D in Table 1).

this pattern, considered alternative sets of between-grade reliability constraints to find the point at which the boys' responses are as reliable as their parents'.

Table 1 presents goodness-of-fit statistics for eight distinct specifications.[5] Each of these specifications requires the estimation of equations 1 through 6 simultaneously for sixth-, ninth-, and twelfth-grade boys. In addition, each specification incorporates the intergrade equality restrictions for parents discussed above: to wit, the covariance matrix of the unobservable true parental status reports and the error variances of parental reports of their socioeconomic characteristics are held constant across sons' grade levels.

Model A of Table 1 assumes that all reporting errors are random. The likelihood ratio chi-square value for this model is 67.7 with 36 degrees of freedom, indicating that random reporting errors are very unlikely to have generated the observed covariance matrices. In addition, this specification implies implausible reliability estimates (not shown here). All reliabilities for twelfth-grade sons' reports and one reliability for ninth-grade sons' reports exceed the corresponding parents' reliabilities. Evidently a more complex model is required.

TABLE 3
Model G Parameter Estimates

Characteristic	Reporter	True Score Variances ϕ	Error Variances θ	Slope λ_{ij}	Reliability $\dfrac{\lambda_{ij}^2\phi_{jj}}{\lambda_{ij}^2\phi_{jj}+\theta_{ij}}$
Father's Schooling	6th Grade Son		2.19	0.74	.592
	9th Grade Son		1.73	0.90	.732
	12th Grade Son	5.82	0.69	1.00	.894
	Father		0.69	1.00	.894
Mother's Schooling	6th Grade Son		2.34	0.89	.505
	9th Grade Son		0.44	1.00	.873
	12th Grade Son	3.00	0.44	1.00	.873
	Mother		0.44	1.00	.873
Father's Occupation	6th Grade Son		182.64	0.94	.711
	9th Grade Son		45.78	1.00	.918
	12th Grade Son	514.68	45.78	1.00	.918
	Father		45.78	1.00	.918

True Score Covariances (ϕ) and Correlations[*]

		1	2	3
1.	Father's Schooling	5.82	.641	.744
2.	Mother's Schooling	2.68	3.000	.525
3.	Father's Occupation	40.70	20.610	514.680

[*]Covariances are below the diagonal; variances are on the diagonal; and correlations are above the diagonal.

Error Covariances ($\Psi_{(12)j}$) and Correlations between Son's Reports of Mother's and Father's Schooling

	Covariance	Correlation
6th Grade	1.11	.57
9th Grade	.40	.39

Previous analysis of these data indicates that the only significant correlation in the errors of sons' reports is for the reports of mothers' and fathers' schooling for sixth-graders (W. M. Mason et al., 1976). To see if a similar finding results from the present estimation framework, we first consider a less parsimonious model in which all sons' errors are mutually correlated (Model B in Table 1). Both the sizes of the error correlations implied by the estimated error covariances and their standard errors will suggest which error covariances should be retained in the model. With a loss of nine degrees of freedom

TABLE 4

Covariance Matrices for White Sixth, Ninth, and Twelfth Grade
Sons' and Parents' Reports of Parental Socioeconomic Characteristics

		1.	2.	3.	4.	5.	6.
Sixth Grade							
1.	SOFED	5.86					
2.	SOMED	3.12	3.32				
3.	SOFOC	35.28	23.85	622.09			
4.	FAFED	4.02	2.14	29.42	5.33		
5.	MOMED	2.99	2.55	19.20	3.17	4.64	
6.	FAFOC	35.30	26.91	465.62	31.22	23.38	546.01
Ninth Grade							
1.	SOFED	8.20					
2.	SOMED	3.47	4.36				
3.	SOFOC	45.65	22.58	611.63			
4.	FAFED	6.39	3.16	44.62	7.32		
5.	MOMED	3.22	3.77	23.47	3.33	4.02	
6.	FAFOC	45.58	22.01	548.00	40.99	21.43	585.14
Twelfth Grade							
1.	SOFED	5.74					
2.	SOMED	1.35	2.49				
3.	SOFOC	39.24	12.73	535.30			
4.	FAFED	4.94	1.65	37.36	5.39		
5.	MOMED	1.67	2.32	15.71	1.85	3.06	
6.	FOFOC	40.11	12.94	496.86	38.09	14.91	538.76

NOTE: SOFED = son's report of father's schooling, SOMED = son's report of
mother's schooling, SOFOC = son's report of father's occupation, FAFED = father's
report of his schooling, MOMED = mother's report of her schooling, FAFOC =
father's report of his occupation. The number of observations is 80 for each group.

(one for each error covariance in each of the three grade levels),
the chi-square statistic drops by more than thirty, a highly
significant improvement in fit. The standard errors of the error
covariances (not shown here), however, indicate that all but
two of the nine covariances are not significantly different from
zero. These are the covariances between the sons' errors in
reporting fathers' and mothers' schooling for both sixth- and
ninth-graders.

Models C and D in Table 1 are suggested by the above findings.
The first assumes a single error covariance between sons' reports
of parents' educational attainments for sixth-graders, the model
implied by the earlier analysis. The second assumes that the
error covariances between sons' reports of parents' schooling
occur for both sixth- and ninth-grade sons. Plainly, the latter

has a superior fit. Model C is a clear improvement upon the purely random error model, but, for the additional degree of freedom required to estimate Model D, the chi-square statistic drops by more than six points. The descriptive levels of significance in the last column of the table show, moreover, that Model D is as likely to have generated the sample covariances as Model B, in which all sons' disturbances are correlated.

We next consider whether Model D implies reasonable estimates of sons' and parents' report reliabilities. Table 2 presents reliabilities calculated from the parameter estimates of the model. For each of the three parental socioeconomic characteristics, sons' reporting reliabilities increase monotonically with grade level. These estimates imply, however, that for both fathers' characteristics, twelfth-grade sons are more reliable respondents than their fathers. To see if these anomalies result from sampling fluctuations, we can estimate a more constrained model which retains the present pattern of disturbance covariances, but equates the reliabilities for sons' and parents' reports. If these constraints do not make the model fit significantly worse than Model D, then we have adequately characterized the data.

In addition to rectifying the anomalously high sons' reliabilities in Table 2, we also want to see the point at which sons' and parents' reports are equally accurate. Table 2 suggests that not only twelfth-grade sons' reports of fathers' statuses, but also their reports of mothers' schooling and at least some of the ninth-graders' reports may be as reliable as the corresponding parents' reports. Hence we estimate a variety of models, making differing assumptions about the point at which sons' and parents' reports are equally reliable.

Goodness-of-fit measures for alternative between-grade equality specifications appear in Table 1 (Models E, F, G, and H). Model E, which has equal parent and son reliabilities for twelfth-graders' reports of fathers' characteristics, preserves the satisfactory fit of Model D. Models F and G further improve the specification through additional equality constraints between sons' and parents' report reliabilities. The excellent fit of Model G suggests that twelfth-graders report all three parental statuses as reliably as parents, and that ninth-graders report both mothers' schooling and fathers' occupation as well as the parents. If we go on to Model H, however, and equate ninth-grade sons' and their fathers' reliabilities for fathers' schooling, the fit of the model deteriorates markedly.

The analysis suggests that children do not approach their parents' level of reporting accuracy at the same rate for all characteristics, but by the twelfth grade, sons and parents are equally reliable for all characteristics we consider. Parameter and reliability estimates for Model G, which embodies these findings, appear in Table 3. The reliability estimates for parents' and sons' reports given in the final column of the table confirm several of the arguments made above. First, they show that sixth-graders are only one-half to two-thirds as reliable respondents as twelfth-graders and their parents. Second, the estimates show that boys report father's occupation more accurately than the schooling of either parent. These differences occur at every grade level, though they are generally weaker at the higher grade levels. Finally, white boys do not favor either parent in reporting grades of schooling. Father's schooling is reported somewhat more reliably than mother's by sixth- and twelfth-graders, but the opposite is true for ninth-graders.

The final panel of Table 3 presents the estimated covariances and correlations between errors in reports of mothers' and fathers' schooling by sixth- and ninth-grade sons. These correlations are substantial, suggesting that sons may resolve their uncertainty about parental schooling by reconciling their parents' schooling levels, two variables which are measured in the same metric.

CONCLUSION

This article has illustrated the use of the simultaneous factor analytic methods developed by Jöreskog (1971a) in estimating measurement models for children's reports of parental socioeconomic characteristics at various grade levels. By estimating models for all grade levels simultaneously, we have used the structure of the data to obtain estimates superior to those obtainable from estimating separate models for each group. In particular, we have held equal those parameters which should be naturally stable across groups (except due to sampling variability). This produces a more parsimonious and reliable model for the several groups taken together. In addition, the simultaneous estimation permits explicit statistical tests of group differences in measurement error patterns, permitting further model simplification.

NOTES

1. Since this article was written, software has become available for estimating simultaneous equation models with both observed and unobserved variables in multiple populations (Jöreskog and Sörbom, 1978). Although these models are more complex than the ones discussed in this article, their logic and rationale are similar.

2. For a full description of the sample design and the complete data set, see Kerckhoff (1974). The data derive from a 1969 sample of approximately 500 Fort Wayne, Indiana black and white sixth-, ninth-, and twelfth-grade boys and their parents; however, the present analysis is based on the white sample. The boys and their parents reported parental statuses in independent interviews. Parents' schooling is measured in grades completed, and father's occupation is measured by the Duncan socioeconomic index. Table 4 presents the covariance matrices of children's and parents' reports for the 3 grade levels used in the analysis. Covariances are pairwise present, that is, calculated over all nonmissing observations on each pair of variables. Variances are based on the maximum numbers of nonmissing univariate observations.

3. In principle, there may be slight nonsampling variability among parents by children's ages in cross-sectional data. On average, parents of older children are older than parents of younger children and may therefore have somewhat different status distributions insofar as socioeconomic characteristics are related to age. Such variations, however, should be very small. In these data the most extreme age difference between groups of children averages six years. A corresponding six-year age difference for their parents implies trivial differences in their status distributions. Moreover, neither in the raw data nor in the earlier analyses of W. M. Mason et al. (1976) is there evidence of systematic variation in parental status distributions or parental report reliability by children's grade level.

4. The converse, however, is not true. Equal reliability requires only that the *ratio* of the true score variance to the sum of the true score variance and the report error variance be equal, rather than the variances themselves. The restrictions given by equation 11, then, are stronger than a strict equal-reliability condition requires. We impose these restrictions for two reasons. First, they are not unreasonable. Neither the distributions of true parental characteristics nor the parental reports' error variances should vary significantly by children's grade level. Second, the equal-reliability restriction per se is nonlinear (see equation 7), and therefore difficult to impose in practice.

5. All models were estimated using the program SIFASP (van Thillo and Jöreskog, 1970).

REFERENCES

BIELBY, W. T. and R. M. HAUSER (1977a) "Response error in earnings functions for nonblack males." Soc. Methods and Research 6 (November): 241-280.
——— (1977b) "Structural equation models." Annual Rev. of Sociology 3: 137-161.
BIELBY, W. T., R. M. HAUSER, and D. L. FEATHERMAN (1977a) "Response errors of black and nonblack males in models of the intergenerational transmission of socio-economic status." Amer. J. of Sociology 82 (May): 1242-1288.
——— (1977b) "Response errors of nonblack males in models of the stratification process." J. of Amer. Stat. Assn. 72 (December): 723-735.
BROOM, L., F. L. JONES, P. McDONNELL, and P. DUNCAN-JONES (1978) "Is it true what they say about daddy?" Amer. J. of Sociology 84 (September): 417-426.
GOLDBERGER, A. S. and O. D. DUNCAN (1973) Structural Equation Models in the Social Sciences. New York: Seminar.
JORESKOG, K. G. (1971a) "Simultaneous factor analysis in several populations." Psychometrika 36 (December): 409-426.
——— (1971b) "Statistical analysis of sets of congeneric tests." Psychometrika 36 (June): 109-133.
——— (1969) "A general approach to confirmatory maximum likelihood factor analysis." Psychometrika 34 (June): 183-202.
——— and D. SORBOM (1978) LISREL IV: Analysis of Linear Structural Relationships by the Method of Maximum Likelihood. Chicago: National Educational Resources.
KERCKHOFF, A. C. (1974) Ambition and Attainment. Washington, DC: American Sociological Association.
MASON, K. O., J. L. CZAJKA, and S. ARBER (1976) "Change in U.S. women's sex-role attitudes, 1964-1974." Amer. Soc. Rev. 41 (August): 573-596.
MASON, W. M., R. M. HAUSER, A. C. KERCKHOFF, S. S. POSS, and K. MANTON (1976) "Models of response-error in student reports of parental socioeconomic characteristics," pp. 443-494 in W. H. Sewell et al. (eds.) Schooling and Achievement in American Society. New York: Academic.
van THILLO, M. and K. G. JORESKOG (1970) SIFASP—A General Computer Program for Simultaneous Factor Analysis in Several Populations. Research Bulletin 70-62. Princeton, NJ: Educational Testing Service.

Robert D. Mare is Assistant Professor of Sociology at University of Wisconsin—Madison. He is completing a monograph on changes in educational stratification in the United States and is conducting research on recent changes in the youth labor force and on socioeconomic influences on child mortality.

William M. Mason is Associate Professor of Sociology and Associate Research Scientist of the Population Studies Center at University of Michigan. His current research includes the study of political alienation, comparative analysis of human reproductive behavior, the statistics and methodology of multilevel analysis, and methodological and substantive issues involving cohort analysis.

CHAPTER EIGHT

Sex Differences
in Measurement Error
in Status Attainment Models

MARY CORCORAN
University of Michigan

INTRODUCTION

Empirical analyses of status attainment typically measure background by asking respondents to recollect their parents' or family's characteristics. If such retrospective reports are very unreliable, then this may bias parameter estimates (Bowles, 1972; Bowles and Nelson, 1974). A number of researchers have estimated response error models for men's retrospective reports of parental status (Bielby et al., 1977a, 1977b; Mason et al., 1976; Mare and Mason, in this issue) and several of these have estimated separate models of traits for different race or age-race groups. None examined measurement error patterns for women and only one study (Mare and Mason, this issue) has examined

AUTHOR'S NOTE: *The research reported in this article was supported by the U.S. Department of Health, Education and Welfare and by National Science Foundation Grant SOC 7818535. This article has benefited from comments by Duane Alwin, Robert Ferber, Robert Hauser, Kent Jennings, Otis Dudley Duncan, Robert Mare, and two anonymous reviewers. The analysis strategy was developed by Mare and William M. Mason (in this issue) in their investigation of age differences in quality of boys' reports of parental status. None of the above institutions or individuals is responsible for any opinions or errors in this article.*

the pattern and strength of such relationships across populations as well as within populations. As Mare and Mason point out, estimating models across groups has two advantages: one can explicitly test for intergroup differences, and, by constraining particular parameters to be the same across groups, one can obtain more reliable parameter estimates.

A number of researchers have proposed and estimated models of women's status attainment and/or of differences in status attainment between men and women (Alexander and Eckland, 1974; Chase, 1975; Featherman and Hauser, 1976; McClendon, 1976; Rosenfeld, 1978; Treiman and Terrell, 1975a, 1975b; Tyree and Treas, 1974). But few, if any, have explicitly considered the possibility of measurement error in women's retrospective reports of parental status and/or sex differences in such measurement error.

At first glance, it seems unlikely that the quality of retrospective reports of parental traits will vary by sex. Yet, there are at least three plausible reasons to expect some variation by sex: sex differences in verbal contacts with parents, sex differences in expectations about the ways in which status is attained, and sex-role identification with the same-sex parent.

Goldberg and Lewis (1969) report that by as early as 13 months girls talk to their mothers more often than boys do. Unpublished data from Kent Jennings' longitudinal study of adolescent political socialization suggest that sex differences in verbal contact still exist in adolescence. These sex differences in verbal interactions with parents might improve girls' later recall relative to that of boys.

Some have argued that men's and women's mobility occurs through different channels—men attain status through individual achievement, while women derive status from kinship patterns. This assumption is implicit in the relative dearth of work, until quite recently, on women's status attainment. Even this recent work considers mobility through marriage as well as through individual achievement (Tyree and Treas, 1974; Glenn et al., 1974). If boys and girls have different expectations about status attainment, with girls expecting to derive status from kinship relationships with men, then the father's status may be more salient for young women.

Third, children may take the same-sex parent as a role model (Rosenfeld, 1978). Thus, a father's characteristics may be more salient for boys and a mother's characteristics may be more salient for girls.

If the quality of retrospective reports of parental status varies by sex, this could systematically bias parameter estimates in structural equation models of sex differentials in the early status-attainment process. This could lead either to exaggerations or underestimations of the importance of sex differences in the status attainment process, depending on how the measurement error operates.

I will explore sex differences in retrospective reports of parental traits using a multiple group measurement model of young adults' reports of parental status similar to that employed by Mare and Mason. I will begin by estimating the extent and patterns of measurement error in women's and men's reports of their parents' status traits. As part of this estimate, I will test whether the structures of men's and women's measurement errors differ. Next, I will ask whether women's and men's retrospective reports of parental traits are less reliable than are their parents' contemporaneous reports of these traits. Finally, I will explore the extent to which corrections for measurement error alter estimates of sex differences in the educational attainment process.

DATA

SAMPLE

The Panel Study of Income Dynamics (PSID) is a nationally representative longitudinal survey of 5000 American families. The Panel Study is well suited for an exploration of measurement error in retrospective reports, as it follows families over time and takes separate interviews with children who leave home.

The sample used here includes white, noninstitutionalized male household heads, female household heads and wives aged 23-30 in 1976 who were living with both parents in 1968. I chose this age range because the majority of children leave home by age 23 (Hill, 1977). This sample provides reports of:

(1) father's completed education, father's occupation in 1968, and mother's completed education in 1968 as reported by father in 1968
(2) mother's completed education as reported by mother in 1976
(3) father's completed education, father's usual occupation while respondent was growing up, and mother's completed education as reported by the respondent *after* the respondent had moved out of the 1968 parental household.

Respondents were dropped if they were missing data on any of these reports. The original sample included 280 white women and 316 white men. Of these, 222 women and 264 men had fathers who reported on their own education and occupation and on their wives' education and had mothers who reported their schooling in 1976. Finally, 208 women and 217 men reported on all 3 parental characteristics.[1] Note that 6% (14 of 222) of the women compared to 18% (47 of 264) of the men failed to report on all three parental traits.

TIMING, WORDING AND CODING OF PARENTAL STATUS QUESTIONS[2]

The timing of questions about parents' traits differed by sex of offspring. Sons reported in the first interview year after they left home (or school). This means that sons could have left home any time from one day to eighteen months previously.[3] Daughters, if married, reported in 1976. Daughters who headed their own households reported in the year that they became household heads. This means that daughters reported any time from one day to seven and one-half years after they left home (or school). Therefore, daughters, on the average, will have been out of the parental home longer than have sons when they report on parental traits. If recall diminishes over time, this might lower the reliability of daughters' reports relative to those of sons.

Questions about parental schooling differed somewhat for parents and offspring. Detailed, multiple-item protocols were used when fathers and mothers reported their own schooling and when fathers reported their wives' schooling; offspring were asked only two questions. Parents were asked, "How many grades of school did you finish?" while offspring were asked, "How much education did your father (or mother) have?" Coding procedures were quite similar for offspring and parents.[4] It is unclear whether such differences in the number and wording of schooling questions would affect data quality, but I suspect that any such effects would operate to the parents' advantage.

The questions about father's occupation also differed slightly. Fathers were asked a question and a probe while offspring were asked a single question. Fathers were asked to report their "main occupation in 1968" (when offspring were 15 to 22 years old); offspring were asked, "What was your father's usual occupation while you were growing up?" Coding rules were the same for fathers and offspring. I used the Duncan score of father's occupation as a measure of the average occupational status of the father in the period during which children were growing up. Although the fathers' and children's questions do not apply to precisely the same time period, both questions give us a fix on the father's average occupational status. Indeed, one might argue that the offspring's question is more directly aimed at the desired characteristic.

SAMPLE ADVANTAGES AND DISADVANTAGES

The samples have advantages and disadvantages relative to other populations used in the analysis of measurement error. On the plus side, each has an extremely rich set of indicators of parental status. Both parents and children reported on parental characteristics. These reports were obtained at different times; the children were no longer living with their parents when they reported on parental traits; and the fathers described their own characteristics during a period when the children were still living at home. In addition, the sample sizes are large enough to estimate a fairly detailed model with some precision. Also, there are complete data on all the variables of interest.

On the other hand, the sample is restricted to young adults aged 15-22 in 1968 who were living in intact families in 1968 and who reported on their parents' traits within 8 years (1 day to 7-1/2 years) after leaving home. I suspect the quality of their retrospective reports should be as high or higher than that of adults in a wider age range or in a sample which includes children from broken homes. This sample should provide good upper-bound estimates of reliabilities for retrospective reports of parental status.

There is also the problem that eliminating cases with missing data reduced sample sizes by about 30%. This problem is compounded by the fact that sons were more likely than daughters to have missing data. If people with missing data on one question were more likely than other people to misreport on another question, then dropping missing data should raise the reliabilities of sons' reports relative to that of daughters' reports. However, most studies of measurement error have problems with missing data, and alternatives to excluding cases with missing data (e.g., use of pairwise correlations, assigning values) are equally limiting, as they often involve dubious assumptions and are likely to misrepresent the true structure (see Bielby et al., 1977a for an extensive discussion of this issue).

STATISTICAL MODELS

A SINGLE GROUP MEASUREMENT MODEL

For each sex, the basic measurement model can be described by the following seven algebraic equations:

$$ED_{f-f} = \lambda_{1f}ED_{f-t} + \epsilon_{1f} \tag{1}$$

$$ED_{f-o} = \lambda_{1o}ED_{f-t} + \epsilon_{1o} \tag{2}$$

$$OCC_{f-f} = \lambda_{2f}OCC_{f-t} + \epsilon_{2f} \tag{3}$$

$$OCC_{f-o} = \lambda_{2o}OCC_{f-t} + \epsilon_{2o} \tag{4}$$

$$ED_{m-f} = \lambda_{3f}ED_{m-t} + \epsilon_{3f} \tag{5}$$

$$ED_{m-o} = \lambda_{3o} ED_{m-t} + \epsilon_{3o} \qquad\qquad [6]$$

$$ED_{m-m} = \lambda_{3m} ED_{m-t} + \epsilon_{3m} \qquad\qquad [7]$$

where:

ED_{i-j} = j^{th} person's report of the ith person's education; OCC_{i-j} = the Duncan score of the jth person's report of the ith person's occupation; and i, j = f for father, o for offspring, m for mother, and t for true.

This specifies that the jth person's report of the ith parental characteristic is equal to the true score of that characteristic multiplied by λ_{ij} plus a response error (ϵ_{ij}) that is independent of the true score. To identify this model I set $\lambda_{1f} = \lambda_{2f} = \lambda_{3m} = 1$.

For each true parental status trait this is a congeneric model which allows for correlated errors (Jöreskog, 1969; Alwin and Jackson, forthcoming). In this model, true scores are allowed to covary; response errors are allowed to covary or are set at zero, depending upon hypotheses about measurement error. Parameter estimates can be used to calculate reliabilities (see Jöreskog, 1969).

One could examine sex differences in measurement error structures by estimating this model separately for sons and daughters, then comparing parameter estimates and reliabilities. However, this procedure does not permit a statistical test for sex differences in measurement error. Also, estimating models separately be sex produces two sets of parameter estimates for the covariances among true parental characteristics, as well as for the error variances of parental reports. This means that estimates of parental reliabilities will vary by sex of child. Because the accuracy of parents' reports probably does not vary with the sex of the child, it would be more efficient to combine information for both sexes to estimate a single set of true parental traits covariances and parental report reliabilities.

MULTIPLE GROUP MEASUREMENT MODEL

The shortcomings of the single group model approach can be handled by using Jöreskog's (1971) general framework for the simultaneous covariance structure analysis of multiple populations. In this framework, one can specify that the reliabilities of parents' reports and that the joint distribution of true parental characteristics are the same for sons and daughters, while allowing the measurement error structures and reliabilities of offspring's reports to vary by sex of offspring.[5]

Applying Jöreskog's model to equations 1 through 7 for young men and women gives a model of the form:

$$Y_k = \Lambda_k T_k + \epsilon_k$$

where:

$Y_k = 7 \times 1$ vector of observed parental and offspring reports

$T_k = 3 \times 1$ matrix of true scores

$\Lambda_k = 7 \times 3$ matrix of coefficients

$\epsilon_k = 7 \times 1$ vector of disturbance terms

and

$k = s$ for sons, d for daughters

This gives the following covariance matrix of observed reports:

$$\epsilon(Y_k Y'_k) = \Lambda_k \Phi_k \Lambda'_k + \Psi_k$$

where:

$\Phi_k = 3 \times 3$ covariance matrix of true scores

and

$\Psi_k = 7 \times 7$ covariance matrix of error terms

In order to specify that the joint distribution of true parental status and the reliabilities of parents' reports do not vary by sex of offspring, I equated the true score covariance matrices for sons and daughters ($\Phi_d = \Phi_s$) and equated error variances of the parents' reports of the parental characteristics for sons and daughters ($\Psi_{(11)s} = \Psi_{(11)d}$; $\Psi_{(33)s} = \Psi_{(33)d}$; $\Psi_{(55)s} = \Psi_{(55)d}$; and $\Psi_{(77)s} =$

$\Psi_{(77)d}$).[6] In addition the slopes of the regressions of true mother's schooling on father's report of mother's schooling were equated for sons and daughters ($\lambda_{3fd} = \lambda_{3fs}$).

SPECIFICATION OF ERROR COVARIANCES

I investigated four alternative error patterns, as listed in Table 1:

(1) All measurement errors are random (Model I). Here all error covariances are set at zero. Thus Ψ_s and Ψ_d are constrained to be diagonal.

(2) Offspring may guess at one parental status characteristic based on their knowledge of other parental status traits (Mason et al., 1976: 439-461). Offspring may overstate the consistency in parental status traits (Bielby et al.'s within-occasion, between-variable correlated error). This should result in correlations between the children's reporting errors. To test this, I allowed offspring's reporting errors to covary (Model II). The following covariances are estimated: $\Psi_{(24)d}$; $\Psi_{(26)d}$; $\Psi_{(46)d}$; $\Psi_{(24)s}$; $\Psi_{(26)s}$; $\Psi_{(46)s}$. Note this model might also pick up similarities in question sequences for 2 parental traits. For example, offspring's reports of mother's and father's schooling were elicited in response to similar sets of questions.[7]

(3) Fathers may overstate the consistency between their own and their wives' status traits. This should result in correlations between fathers' reporting errors of their own and of their wives' schooling. To test this I estimated $\Psi_{(15)d}$ and $\Psi_{(15)s}$ (Model III). Because fathers' measurement error structures are constrained not to vary by sex of offspring, these two covariances are equated.

(4) Finally, Models II and III are merged into a new model (Model IV) which allows offspring's reporting errors to covary and allows errors in fathers' reports of their own and of their wives' schooling to covary.

Other possible error patterns are less likely. Men might overstate the consistency in their own status characteristics so that the errors in fathers' reports of their schooling and education might covary. Bielby et al. (1977a, 1977b) investigated this type of nonrandom error in some detail and found no evidence of such error in their analysis of nonblacks. Offspring's and parents' reports of parental traits might covary but this seems unlikely, as reports are taken several years apart.

TEST FOR SEX DIFFERENCES IN MEASUREMENT ERROR

Models I to IV allow the offspring's measurement error structures to vary by sex. After choosing the best-fitting model from Models I to IV, I tested for sex differences in measurement error structures by comparing that model to a model which frees the same error covariances as the best-fitting model, but which constrains male and female offspring's measurement error structures to be equal. If the constrained model does not provide a significantly worse fit to the data, then one can conclude that any observed sex differences in the quality of retrospective reports could have arisen from sampling variability.

PROCEDURE FOR SELECTING A MODEL

In addition to using goodness-of-fit statistics, I selected models by substantive plausibility (Mare and Mason, this issue). In particular, I specified that children's retrospective reports of parental status should be no more reliable than parents' self-reports. If parameter estimates implied that this was not so, then it was likely to be due either to a misspecified model or to sampling variability, and I reestimated the models using a specification which equates parents' and offspring's reliabilities. Similarly, it seemed reasonable to specify that mothers' reports of their own schooling should be at least as reliable as are fathers' reports of their wives' schooling.

PROCEDURES FOR EXAMINING PARENT/CHILD AND MALE/FEMALE DIFFERENCES IN RELIABILITIES

Once I had chosen the best-fitting plausible model I investigated differences in estimated reliabilities between offspring and parents and between men and women. I did this by comparing models which equated slopes and error variances for particular groups (i.e., parallel measures models) to models which allowed these reliabilities to vary across groups. Whenever constraining reliabilities to be equal does not provide a significantly worse fit to the data, one cannot reject the hypothesis that the observed group differences in reliabilities could have arisen from sampling variability (see Mare and Mason, this issue).

RESULTS

CHOICE OF A BEST-FITTING MODEL

Table 1 reports the likelihood ratio-tests for Models I, II, III and IV when they are estimated using Jöreskog's general procedure for the simultaneous covariance structure analysis of multiple populations. These models are estimated with LISREL IV.

A comparison of Models I and II shows that allowing off-spring's reporting errors of different parental traits to covary results in a chi-square of 14.94 (38.43-23.49) with 6 (33-27) degrees of freedom. This improvement in fit is statistically significant and suggests that offspring tend to make reports of parental status consistent with one another. Further allowing errors in fathers' reports of their own and their wives' schooling to covary (Model IV) results in a significant chi-square of 7.04 (23.49-16.45) with 1 degree of freedom. Apparently, men make reports of their own and their wives' schooling consistent with one another.

Model V constrains Model IV so that sons and daughters have identical measurement error structures. This is done by equating error variances, error covariance and slopes across sexes. Thus, $\Psi_s = \Psi_d$ and $\Lambda_s = \Lambda_d$. Model V provides a significantly worse fit ($\chi^2 = 19.29$ with 9 degrees of freedom) to the data than does Model IV, suggesting that measurement error structures differ by sex.

Model IV provides the best fit among Models I through V. In Model IV, only 2 estimated covariances significantly differed from zero (using the .05 level): the covariances between errors in

sons' reports of father's and of mother's schooling, and the covariances between errors in fathers' reports of father's and of
mother's schooling. I simplified Model IV by setting all insignificant error covariances to zero. This new model (Model VI)
did not provide a significantly worse fit to the data than did
Model IV.

Under Model VI, the estimated reliabilities of daughters'
reports of father's education (.837) and of father's occupation
(.842) exceeded the estimated reliabilities of the fathers' own
reports (.815 and .832, respectively). Also, the estimated reliabilities of fathers' and mothers' reports of mother's schooling
were approximately equal (.902 vs. .892). I simplified Model VI
by equating the reliabilities of daughters' and fathers' reports
of father's schooling, of daughters' and fathers' reports of
father's occupation, and of fathers' and mothers' reports of
mothers' schooling (Model VII). Model VII did not provide a
significantly worse fit to the data than did Model VI ($\chi^2 = 5.55$
with 6 degrees of freedom). Thus, the apparently higher reliabilities of daughters' reports of father's schooling and occupation could be due to sampling error.

PARAMETER ESTIMATES

Table 2 lists the parameter estimates which obtain under
Model VII. The estimated reliabilities of sons' retrospective
reports of parental status were consistently lower than those
for daughters' retrospective reports or those for parents' self-
reports. This difference was largest for reports of mothers'
education. The estimated reliabilities of daughters' reports of
mothers' schooling were only slightly lower than those of parents'
reports.

TESTS OF PARENT/CHILD
AND MALE/FEMALE DIFFERENCES
IN REPORT RELIABILITIES

As a last step, I tested whether these differences in reliabilities
could be due to sampling variability. Model VIII constrains

TABLE 1
Goodness-of-Fit Statistics for Measurement Models
(for noninstitutionalized, white household heads and wives, aged 23-30 in 1976)

Model		x^2	Degrees of Freedom	Probability Level
I.	Random measurement errors	38.43	33	.237
II.	Covariances among all off-spring's errors	23.49	27	.658
III.	Covariances among errors in fathers' reports of their own and their wives' schooling	31.06	32	.514
IV.	Covariances among all off-spring's errors and among errors in fathers' reports of their own and their wives' schooling	16.45	26	.925
V.	Model IV with sons' and daughters' measurement error structures constrained to be equal	35.64	35	.438
VI.	Covariances between errors in reports of fathers' education and mothers' education for both sons and fathers	20.35	31	.928
VII.	Model VI with the reliabilities of daughters' reports of fathers' schooling, and fathers' occupation equated to the reliabilities of fathers' reports and with the reliabilities of fathers' and mothers' reports of mothers' schooling equated	26.80	37	.892
VIII.	Model VII with reliabilities of parents' and daughters' reports of mothers' education equated	28.68	39	.888
IX.	Model VIII with reliabilities of sons' reports of fathers' occupation and of fathers' education constrained to equal reliabilities of fathers' and of daughters' reports	36.62	43	.743
X.	Model IX with reliabilities of sons' reports of mothers' education constrained to equal reliabilities of daughters' and parents' reports	60.27	45	.064

TABLE 2
Parameter Estimates, Model VII

Characteristic	Reporter	True Score Variance	Error Variances	Slopes (Standard Errors are in Parentheses)	Reliability
Fathers' schooling	Father		2.005	1.000	.823
	Son	9.349	2.796	.933 (.050)	.744
	Daughter		2.005	1.000	.823
Fathers' occupation	Father		66.8	1.000	.837
	Son	343.8	88.4	.902 (.048)	.760
	Daughter		66.8	1.000	.837
Mothers' schooling	Father		.834	1.000	.894
	Son	7.015	1.778	.927 (.038)	.772
	Daughter		1.044	.980 (.033)	.866
	Mother		.834	1.000	.894

Error Covariances and Correlations Between Errors in
Reports of Mother's and Father's Schooling

	Covariance	Correlation
Sons	.544	.244
Fathers	.272	.210

parents and daughters to be equally reliable when reporting
mother's schooling. Model VIII does not provide a significantly
worse fit to the data than does Model VII. Young women's retrospective reports of parental status appear to be as reliable as are
parents' self-reports. When we further constrain our model so
that the reliabilities of reports of father's schooling are equated
for fathers and sons (and thus, for sons and daughters) the new

TABLE 3
Parameter Estimates, Model IX

Characteristic	Reporter	True Score Variance	Error Variances	Slopes (Standard Errors are in Parentheses)	Reliability
Fathers' schooling	Father		2.230	1.000	.801
	Son	9.004	2.230	1.000	.801
	Daughter		2.230	1.000	.801
Fathers' occupation	Father		73.2	1.000	.817
	Son	326.1	73.2	1.000	.817
	Daughter		73.2	1.000	.817
Mothers' schooling	Father		.884	1.000	.887
	Son		1.740	.939	.779
		6.946		(.038)	
	Daughter		.884	1.000	.887
	Mother		.884	1.000	.887

Error Covariances and Correlations Between Errors in
Reports of Mother's and Father's Schooling

	Covariance	Correlation
Sons	.453	.230
Fathers	.301	.215

model (Model IX) preserves a satisfactory fit to the data. Thus, the observed lower reliabilities of sons might be due to sampling variability. Finally, Model X equates the reliabilities of sons' and parents' reports of mother's schooling. Model X provides a significantly worse fit to the data than does Model IX. Sons' reports of mother's schooling are less reliable than are the reports of mothers, fathers, or daughters. Table 3 presents the parameter estimates which obtain under Model IX.

*EFFECTS OF MEASUREMENT ERROR ON
ESTIMATES OF SEX DIFFERENCES
IN THE EDUCATIONAL ATTAINMENT PROCESS*

Table 4 presents the regressions of the parental status measures on offspring's education. Estimates are derived given three dif-

TABLE 4
Regressions Uncorrected and Corrected for Measurement Error
(dependent variable = years of schooling)

Assumptions About Measurement Error	Male Equation			Female Equation		
	Coefficients (Standard error)			Coefficients (Standard error)		
	ED_{f-t}	OCC_{f-t}	ED_{m-t}	ED_{f-t}	OCC_{f-t}	ED_{m-t}
1) Sons' reports are without error	.207** (.065)	.019* (.010)	.140** (.069)	.153** (.068)	.009 (.010)	.230** (.065)
2) Model VII	.262** (.113)	.014 (.015)	.146* (.087)	.120 (.108)	.013 (.014)	.286** (.085)
3) Model IX	.276** (.117)	.014 (.015)	.152* (.088)	.125 (.116)	.013 (.015)	.283** (.087)

ferent assumptions about the measurement error structure: (1) offspring's reports are without error; (2) Model VII is correct; and (3) Model IX is correct. Corrected estimates are obtained by specifying the measurement structure of Model VII (or IX) and simultaneously estimating measurement and structural parameters (Bielby et al., 1977a, 1977b). Results obtained under the assumption that offspring's reports are without error are similar for men and women, but there is very weak evidence that the education of the same-sex parent has more effect than that of the other parent on young adults' level of schooling. Previous studies of status attainment (Treiman and Terrell, 1975a; Featherman and Hauser, 1976) have also reported weak evidence of modeling on the same-sex parent.

When corrections are made for measurement error, parameter estimates change slightly within equations, and the suggestive evidence of identification with the same-sex parent is strengthened. The impact of an additional year of parental schooling on offspring's schooling is larger by a factor of two when the parent and offspring are the same sex. Note, however, that corrections for measurement error have only modest effects within individual equations.

SUMMARY

Young women's retrospective reports of parental status seem as accurate as parents' own reports. In only one instance, mother's education, was the estimated reliability of women's reports lower than that of parents, and this was not significant. Also, there is no evidence to suggest that there are nonrandom errors in young women's retrospective reports.

The estimated reliabilities of young men's retrospective reports of father's education and father's occupation were consistently lower than the estimated reliabilities of parents' self-reports, but these differences were not significant. This is consistent with Bielby et al.'s (1977a, 1977b) result that contemporaneous reports of men's status were as reliable as were retrospective reports of father's education and father's occupation.

Young men's retrospective reports of mother's schooling were significantly less reliable than were fathers' reports or mothers' reports. This suggest that the quality of men's retrospective reports of maternal traits may be poor and that the mother's status has relatively low salience for sons. In addition, errors in sons' reports of mothers' and fathers' schooling were correlated ($r = .23$), suggesting that young men use one parent's schooling to guess about the schooling of the other parent. (Note that if this correlation were due to similarities in questions or coding, then it is surprising that it did not show up for daughters.)

Estimated reliabilities for reports of father's traits were always higher for young women than for young men, but these differences were not significant. Thus these data provide weak, if any, evidence to support the hypotheses that sex differences in verbal contacts and/or in the ways that status is attained improve women's relative ability to recollect paternal traits.

There is persuasive evidence that young women report maternal status more accurately than do young men. Sons' retrospective reports of a mother's schooling were considerably less reliable than were daughters' retrospective reports. Further, there was no evidence of nonrandom error in daughters' reports of parental traits, but the errors in sons' reports of their mothers' and fathers' schooling were correlated. This supports the hypothesis that maternal status is more salient for women than for men.

It may be useful to compare the magnitude of these sex differences in measurement error structure with other estimates of intergroup differences. For example, these differences are similar in magnitude to those reported by Mare and Mason for ninth- and twelfth-grade boys, but they are much smaller than the race differences reported by Bielby et al. (1977a).

Finally, there is suggestive but far from conclusive evidence that not correcting for measurement error may underestimate the extent of sex-role modeling on the same-sex parent in the schooling process. This suggests that it may be important that future researchers consider the possibility that failure to correct for measurement error may reduce estimates of sex differences in the status attainment process.

NOTES

1. These restrictions had trivial effects on the means and variances of these parental characteristics. Those interested can obtain tables from the author.

2. I am grateful to Professor R. Hauser (1979) for pointing out that these differences might affect reliabilities. The following discussion borrows heavily from points raised by Hauser. Those interested in the exact wording of questions or coding procedures can obtain these from the author.

3. There is one exception. Sons reported on their mothers' schooling in 1974 if they left home prior to 1974.

4. Again, there is an exception. "Don't know" responses were coded differently for parents and offspring. I dealt with this by looking up all such cases for offspring and recoding them using the parents' coding rules.

5. This is similar to the strategy employed by Mare and Mason (this issue).

6. This follows Mare and Mason's strategy.

7. Both Mare and Mason (this issue) and Hauser (1979) suggest this possibility.

REFERENCES

ALEXANDER, K. L. and B. K. ECKLAND (1974) "Sex differences in the educational attainment process." Amer. Soc. Rev. 39 (October): 668-682.

ALWIN, D. F. and D. J. JACKSON (forthcoming) "Applications of simultaneous factor analysis to issues of factor invariance," in D. J. Jackson and E. F. Borgatta (eds.) Factor Analysis and Measurement in Sociological Research. Beverly Hills, CA: Sage.

BIELBY, W. T., R. M. HAUSER, and D. L. FEATHERMAN (1977a) "Response errors of black and nonblack males in models of the intergenerational transmission of socio-economic status." Amer. J. of Sociology 82 (May): 1242-1288.

——— (1977b) "Response errors of nonblack males in models of the stratification process." J. of the Amer. Stat. Assn. 72 (December): 723-735.

BOWLES, S. (1972) "Schooling and inequality from generation to generation." J. of Pol. Economy (May/June): S219-S251.

——— and V. NELSON (1974) "The 'inheritance of IQ' and the intergenerational reproduction of economic inequality." Rev. of Economics and Statistics 56: 39-51.

CHASE, I. (1975) "A comparison of men's and women's intergenerational mobility in the United States." Amer. Soc. Rev. 40 (August): 483-505.

FEATHERMAN, D. L. and R. M. HAUSER (1976) "Sexual inequalities and socio-economic achievement in the U.S.: 1962-1973." Amer. Soc. Rev. 41 (June): 462-483.

GLENN, N. D., A. A. ROSS, and J. C. TULLY (1974) "Patterns of intergenerational mobility of women through marriage." Amer. Soc. Rev. 39 (October): 683-699.

GOLDBERG, S. and M. LEWIS (1969) "Play behavior in the year-old infant: early sex differences." Child Development 40 (March): 21-30.

HAUSER, R. M. (1979) Personal communication.

HILL, M. S. (1977) "The decision by young adults to split off from their parents' household." Ph.D. dissertation, University of Michigan.

JORESKOG, K. G. (1971) "Simultaneous factor analysis in several populations." Psychometrika 26 (September): 409-426.

——— (1969) "A general approach to confirmatory maximum likelihood factor analysis." Psychometrika 34 (June): 183-202.

——— and D. SORBOM (1978) LISREL IV: Analysis of Linear Structural Relationships by the Method of Maximum Likelihood. Chicago: National Educational Resources.

MASON, W. M., R. M. HAUSER, A. C. KERCKHOFF, S. S. POSS, and K. MANTON (1976) "Models of response error in student reports of parental socioeconmic characteristics," pp. 443-494 in W. H. Sewell et al. (eds.) Schooling and Achievement in American Society. New York: Academic.

McCLENDON, M. (1976) "The occupational status attainment processes of males and females." Amer. Soc. Rev. 41 (February): 52-64.

ROSENFELD, R. (1978) "Women's intergenerational occupational mobility." Amer. Soc. Rev. 43 (February): 36-46.

TREIMAN, D. J. and K. TERRELL (1975a) "Sex and the process of status attainment: a comparison of working women and men." Amer. Soc. Rev. 40 (April): 174-200.

——— (1975b) "Women, work, and wages—trends in the female occupational structure," in K. C. Land and S. Spilerman (eds.) Social Indicator Models. New York: Russell Sage.

TYREE, A. and J. TREAS (1974) "The occupational and marital mobility of women." Amer. Soc. Rev. 39 (June): 293-302.

Mary Corcoran is an assistant professor of political science and a study director at the Institute for Social Research at the University of Michigan. Her current work is in the areas of sex discrimination, social stratification and unemployment. She is a coauthor of Who Gets Ahead *(Basic Books, 1979).*

CHAPTER NINE

Occupational Characteristics and Classification Systems

New Uses of the
Dictionary of Occupational Titles
in Social Research

KENNETH I. SPENNER
Boys Town Center
for the Study of Youth Development

Detailed aspects of jobs have received increased attention in recent years. Witness the studies of job-person effects (Kohn and Schooler, 1978; Kohn, 1969), of alienation (Shepard, 1977) and job satisfaction (Kalleberg, 1977; Hackman and Lawler, 1971), of variations in prestige, status, and income (Goldthorpe and Hope, 1974; McLaughlin, 1978; Stolzenberg,

AUTHOR'S NOTE: *This research was supported by the Boys Town Center for the Study of Youth Development-Boys Town and by a grant from the Employment and Training Administration of the U.S. Department of Labor (91-55-76-45). Because grantees conducting research and development projects under government sponsorship are encouraged to express their own judgment freely, this research does not necessarily represent the official opinion of the Department of Labor or the Boys Town Center. I gratefully acknowledge various forms of assistance, comment and support provided by L. Otto, V. Call, S. Wendel, A. Haller, D. Featherman and the Center for Demography and Ecology at the University of Wisconsin—Madison. Finally, my thanks to R. Hauser, D. Featherman, L. Temme and M. Kohn for providing access to their data.*

1975), and of race and gender variations in discrimination (Snyder and Hudis, 1976; Lucas, 1974; Miller et al., 1979). These studies reflect two general approaches to the measurement of detailed job characteristics. One strategy takes measures from respondents for features of their current or past jobs. Kohn's (1969) 1964-1974 NORC data and the *1972-73 Quality of Employment Survey* (Quinn and Shepard, 1974) are landmark studies using this strategy. The alternate strategy uses job characteristics that are based upon an occupational classification system. Scores are assigned to jobs on the basis of the aggregate level of a characteristic for an extensive population, as in the census, or ratings of a characteristic are assigned to jobs in a classification system and then validated in actual job settings. The *Dictionary of Occupational Titles* (U.S. Department of Labor, 1965, 1977) is an example of the latter strategy.

This study reports on several characteristics that have been estimated for detailed 1960 and 1970 census occupations. Previously, they had only limited availability through the Dictionary of Occupational Titles (DOT) classification system. The report includes information on how the measures were generated, evidence on their validity as assessed against corresponding individual-level measures, and an assessment of the measurement slippage involved in moving between classification systems.

OCCUPATIONAL CHARACTERISTICS IN THE DOT AND CENSUS SYSTEMS

The two-volume third edition of the *Dictionary of Occupational Titles* (1965) contains an ostensible wealth of information for the student of occupations. The DOT is a functional occupational classification system. The designation of a job category primarily depends upon differences in the nature or function of the work task relative to competing categories. In contrast, the census classification system focuses upon socioeconomic differences between categories (Shartle, 1964; Edwards, 1933; Fine, 1968; Fine and Heinz, 1958).

The DOT makes reference to some 35,550 different job titles. Of these, 21,741 refer to "base," "defined related," and "undefined related" titles. There are about 13,800 base titles that have a unique definition and 6-digit code. In the 6-digit code, the first 3 digits refer to an occupation group and the latter 3 to the data, people, things score (see Appendix) for the job. Defined related titles (N = 1300) share a 6-digit code with a base title but have a separate definition in the DOT along with a 3-digit suffix code. Finally, an undefined related title shares the same 6-digit code, suffix code, and job definition with a base or defined related title, and differs only in being a nominal variation. For example, "coating-machine operator" is a base title; "saturator" and "roll-coating machine operator" are defined related titles; and "dull coat-mill operator" and "first-coat operator" are undefined related and alternate job titles. Each base title in the DOT, in addition to the data, people, and things code, has been scored on an additional set of characteristics (see Appendix).

The census classification systems of 1960 and 1970 embody an equally large number of job titles but summarize them with 296 detailed occupation titles and 149 industry titles in 1960, and 429 detailed occupational titles and 213 industry titles in 1970 (U.S. Bureau of the Census, 1960; 1971). Hauser and Featherman (1977: 51-80) provide a good summary of the use of the census classification systems in social surveys. Where job information in a social survey is coded in the census scheme, summary scores at the level of occupation or occupation-industry can be incorporated for analysis (as in Duncan Socioeconomic Status scores).

In social research, variants of the census systems are the most commonly used to code job information. A handful of studies, among them two Current Population Surveys and the 1972-1973 Quality of Employment Survey (Quinn and Shepard, 1974) use the census system and the DOT in coding the same job. Thus, lack of data bases with the requisite DOT in coding severely restricts application of the DOT information. In addition, no one-to-one mapping or correspondence exists between the lines of the census system and those of the DOT. Therefore, a major tactical problem confronting the analyst seeking to develop a set of scores

for census occupation-industry categories based on DOT information is the mapping and weighting of DOT jobs into census
categories. As part of a larger research program (Spenner, 1977;
Otto et al., 1979; also see Temme, 1975), we wanted the detailed
DOT variables for use with extant data bases with 1960 and 1970
census categories. The indicators of interest are:

INDICATOR	SOURCE
Median educational attainment	U.S. Census
Specific vocational preparation	DOT; Temme, 1975
General educational development	DOT; Temme, 1975
Race composition	U.S. Census
Sex composition	U.S. Census
Functional foci (data/people/things)	DOT; Temme, 1975
Substantive complexity	DOT; Temme, 1975
Routinization	DOT; see below
Closeness of supervision	DOT; see below
Median income	U.S. Census
Security (employment level)	U.S. Census

ESTIMATING DOT CHARACTERISTICS FOR
CENSUS CATEGORIES

Others have made efforts to use some of the DOT variables,
but, with two exceptions, have either aggregated occupations into
a set of occupations less detailed than the census, ranging from 17
to 221 categories (Bluestone, 1974; Eckaus, 1964; Scoville, 1966);
or generated unweighted averages for occupation categories
(Berg, 1970; Barker, 1969; Broom et al., 1977). The ideal estimates
would use as many DOT occupations as possible, mapped into
the maximum number of detailed census occupation-industry
categories. The desired scores should be estimated by a weighted
average, as some census categories include dozens of DOT
occupations with varying labor force frequencies.

Lucas (1972, 1974) and Temme (1975) followed this approach
for detailed 1960 and 1970 occupations, respectively, in estimating a number of DOT variables. Although Temme estimates a
smaller set of DOT variables, he provides more procedural detail
than Lucas and reports the estimates for both 1960 (N = 295) and

1970 (N = 584) classifications. In sequence, we will treat the scores developed by Temme, then generate the estimates for the remaining DOT indicators.

The item descriptions and metrics for DOT variables are given in the Appendix. For all DOT variables, the scores were assigned to base titles by Department of Labor occupational analysts, based upon detailed DOT job descriptions. The more populous 4000-5000 DOT occupations, which include the vast portion of the labor force, were then checked in situ to validate the scores. The "sample" of jobs in firms was one of convenience and availability rather than a probability sample of a defined population. The DOT was conceived and constructed primarily as an aid to employment counseling. Accordingly, the procedures used in scoring variables are available more in the unpublished memoranda of the Department of Labor than in the written word (except for U.S. Department of Labor, 1956, 1965, 1968, 1972; also see Fine, 1968; Fine and Heinz, 1958; Scoville, 1972).[1]

Scores for involvement with data, people, and things, General Educational Development (GED), and Specific Vocational Preparation (SVP), were estimated by Temme (1975: 174-183). A transformation matrix (of DOT codes by census lines) and weighting source for the estimates were provided by the October 1966 and April 1971 Current Population Survey (CPS) data. These CPS samples have respondents' current occupations independently coded into 6-digit census codes and 9-digit DOT codes. With the DOT code, the data, people, and things ratings were available. GED and SVP scores were merged into individual records from available sources (U.S. Department of Labor, 1956). The estimate of each variable for each census category is an average across persons in DOT jobs and in a given census line, weighting each person's scores by the sample design weight from the CPS.

By way of evaluation, Temme (1975: 181a) performed a one-way analysis of variance on the distributions of CPS scores for data, people, and things, GED, and SVP. The independent variables were the 1960 (295 occupation) and 1970 (584 occupation-industry) census categories. For the 1960 classification the between-category variation (η^2) ranges from 68.5% to 74.8% (and the within-category variation or "error" from 25.2% to 31.5%). For the 1970 classification the between-category variation ranges from 72.0% to 77.1% for the 5 variables. Whether these figures are high or low depends upon the research purpose.

Finally, Temme (1975: 214-227) estimated a "self-direction" score for detailed census lines using a regression prediction procedure (Duncan, 1961; Siegel, 1971). Data from a national sample of 3100 employed men were used to construct the criterion self-direction score.

Kohn (1969) conceptualizes self-direction as bounded by closeness of supervision, routinization of work, and substantive complexity. Temme (1975: appendix B) constructed subscales for these variables and computed an overall index of self-direction. For Kohn's data the overall "self-direction" index is dominated by the substantive complexity of work subscale (r = .927). Moreover, the regression equation that was used predicts the substantive complexity scores (R^2 = .635) just as well as "occupational self-direction" (R^2 = .628). On this basis we treat Temme's self-direction variable as a measure of substantive complexity of work.

MEASURES FOR ROUTINIZATION AND CLOSENESS OF SUPERVISION

The choice of indicators is influenced heavily by the work of Kohn (1969: 153-160). Kohn's measures are taken from individuals for their particular job situations. While this degree of specificity is not available in the DOT information, several of the "Temperament" variables, alone or taken together, permit the development of indicators. Each Temperament variable refers to different types of situations to which workers must adjust and was scored dichotomously (present, absent) for base titles using detailed descriptions and in situ samplings of DOT jobs. As indicators for routinization in work we use DOT Temperament items 1 and 2, and we use items 3 and 4 for indicators of closeness of supervision (U.S. Department of Labor, 1965, Vol. 2: 649-656). The items are reproduced in the Appendix.

The estimation procedure here follows Temme (1975) and Lucas (1972). The approach takes binary pieces of information for DOT occupations and distributes them to census categories, weighting the information to give input to the pieces in direct proportion to the number of labor force individuals they characterize. The indicator information for DOT occupations is taken from the master file of DOT information provided by the Department of Labor. The April 1971 CPS provided a transition matrix and a weighting source. The April CPS contains 60,441 respondents, of whom 53,438 (88.4%) had sufficiently detailed current job information to permit detailed DOT and 1970 census coding. Of the 13,000-plus DOT base titles, 4517 empirically occur in this sample. As a number of observers have noted, the DOT is perhaps overly detailed, as only one-third of its codes occur in even the larger probability samples of the labor force.

The estimates are obtained by arraying a matrix with rows equal to empirically occurring DOT codes and columns equal to most of the unique 1970 census occupation-industry categories as defined in the PC-series subject reports (U.S. Bureau of the Census, 1973). The categories include 421 occupations (across industries) and 174 industry breakdowns for 9 occupation categories.[2] Sample design weights for each CPS record are entered into the appropriate cells of the matrix by virtue of the joint DOT-census codes.[3] After merging the 4 binary indicator scores from the DOT master file (on a row by row basis) and the CPS sample design weights (on a cell by cell basis) the estimates are simply the weighted average (.00-.99 scale) for the 4 indicators for each column of the matrix.[4]

The remaining task in completing the 1960 and 1970 matrices of occupation scores is to generate closeness of supervision and routinization scores for the 1960 three-digit occupation categories. The 1971 CPS only provides a mechanism for estimating the 1970 category scores. The remaining 1960 scores were available from Temme's work or from published census sources.

The October 1966 CPS data used by Temme (with double-coded DOT and 1960 census codes) were unavailable. As an alternate strategy, we used the Bureau of the Census table of "1970 Occupation and Industry Classification Systems in Terms of Their

1960 Occupation and Industry Elements" (U.S. Bureau of the Census, 1972). The table defines the sex-specific number and occupation-origins of the individuals catalogued in 1960 going to each 1970 category. This information has been used to take a known distribution of 1960 socioeconomic index (SEI) scores and generate the 1970 category equivalents (Featherman et al., 1975). To move in the other direction (1970 to 1960), the matrix is rearrayed, at no loss of information, to reflect 1960 categories in terms of their 1970 category composition. The estimates for 1960 categories are weighted in 1960 labor force frequencies providing comparability to the measures taken from published 1960 census sources and to Temme's 1966 CPS-based estimates for other variables.[5]

Finally, measures were taken from published sources (U.S. Bureau of the Census, 1973, 1963): sex-specific median education and race composition as years of education and percentage white, sex composition as percentage male, sex-specific median earnings in hundreds of dollars, and sex-specific employment level as the percentage of those in the occupation who worked 50-52 weeks per year.

MEASUREMENT ISSUES FOR THE OCCUPATION VARIABLES

In this section we will provide some preliminary evidence on the measurement properties of the occupation variables, an external validation of the new routinization and closeness of supervision variables, and information on measurement slippage between classification systems.

Temme (1975) does not treat these issues, and, for the most part, he takes the reliability and validity of the variables as adequate. Several vocational psychologists have discussed or evaluated some of these issues for selected portions of the DOT (Shartle, 1964; Fine and Heinz, 1958; Fine, 1968; Sainty, 1974). Their conclusions are generally favorable but the levels of aggregation in the analyses (Sainty, 1974), along with the

speculative nature of the discussion, are of little comfort. Lucas'
dissertation and related work (1972, 1974) provide no discussion
of the validity or reliability of the DOT indicators that are used.
Scoville (1966, 1972) has been perhaps the most persistent critic of
both the DOT and census classifications. Nonetheless, his work
uses both systems at varying levels of aggregation in several major
studies. Siegel (1971) and Duncan et al. (1972: 77-79) suggest that
in GED-type intelligence demand scales, occupational analysts
may have been rating the social standing of the occupation rather
than the intelligence (or other aptitudes) required to perform in
the role. Indeed, the correlation reported by Temme (1975: 231)
between GED and his prestige score is .933.

Recent history harbors two traditions on these issues. One
school of thought has been critical of some or all of the DOT
information, and then either proceeds to use the DOT or dismiss
it completely. A second tradition, euphoric over the potential
wealth of information in the DOT, generally ignores issues of
validity and reliability. Lacking such studies, we treated the issues
as unresolved, particularly for the new measures.

First, the weighted and unweighted distributions for all the
occupation variables for 1970 census categories were examined
for kurtosis and skewness. Several of the variables showed
departures from a symmetric normal distribution (level of
involvement with data, people, and things; the indicators for
routinization and closeness of supervision; race composition; and
sex composition). Because the primary interest was in covariance
relationships among the occupation variables and with other
stratification variables, transformations that maximized the
linear association among these variables were sought. A number
of one-parameter transformations were applied to the distributions of scores (including natural logarithm, reciprocal, square
root, exponential, square, dummy variable, and arc sin). The
transformations did not make a consistent or marked difference
in the associations with criterion variables (greater than 1-2% of
total association).

Second, using unweighted distributions with job categories as
the unit of analysis, bivariate scattergrams were examined to

detect marked departures from linear additive association. A few relationships showed a limited amount of nonlinearity (parabolic in form), but they were small and scattered among the occupation variables. (However, future users of these scores are advised to check for such relationships with relevant criterion-dependent and independent variables.) In sum, we found the untransformed distributions workable; note that this is a preliminary assessment.

As sources of evidence in the external validation of indicators, several bodies of data were used, with the occupation scores merged with individual records on the basis of 1960 or 1970 census codes for select jobs (father's, respondent's first, and current). They included the 1973 Occupational Changes in a Generation (OCS) data—a national probability sample of male members of the civilian labor force ($N \simeq 37,500$; see Featherman and Hauser, 1975); the *1972-73 Quality of Employment Survey* data (Quinn and Shepard, 1974)—a national probability sample of employed adults 16 years of age or older ($N \simeq 1,500$); and select information from Kohn's (1969) 1964-1974 NORC data—a national probability sample of employed males in the civilian labor force ($N \cong 3,000$).

Kohn (1969; see also Kohn and Schooler, 1973, 1977) has dealt extensively with job characteristics as measured from individuals, particularly for complexity, routinization, and closeness of supervision. If the measures developed here have interrelationships similar to Kohn's measures, then external validity relative to his variables is established. A comparison of our items with Kohn's measures (Kohn, 1969: 153-160) shows close correspondence, but Kohn's items provide more detail. Table 1 gives the zero-order correlations among our measures for OCG fathers and for comparable measures for NORC fathers from Kohn's sample. The DOT-based measures for OCG fathers should have slightly higher correlations, as, on the average, they have been in the labor force longer, and their scores are occupation-specific and not as subject to individual-level variations in jobs, or measurement error.

TABLE 1
Zero-order Correlations for DOT-Based and Kohn's Routinization and Closeness-of-Supervision Indicators (OCG and 1964 NORC fathers)*

Relationship	Zero-order Correlation		
	Kohn '64	'74[a]	DOT-based
Closeness of Supervision--Routinization	.338	.17	.12
CS3 - ROU1[b]			.358**
CS4 - ROU2			.528**
CS3 - ROU2			.678
CS4 - ROU1			.427
CST - ROU1			.464
CST - ROU2			.689**
CS3 - ROUT			.557**
CS4 - ROUT			.522
CST - ROUT			.539
Closeness of Supervision--Self-direction (SC)	-.546	-.68	-.61
SC - CS3			-.631
SC - CS4			-.548**
SC - CST			-.679**
Routinization--Self-direction (SC)	-.412	-.30	-.32
SC - ROU1			-.160**
SC - ROU2			-.568
SC - ROUT			-.381**

*Correlations for Kohn's measures taken from Temme, 1975:218; n's:OCG = 21,000; 1964 NORC approximately 3,000, and from Kohn (personal communication; n = 687).
**Signs of coefficients have been reflected to correspond to the direction of Kohn's scales.
a. Estimated correlations from measurement model for follow-up subsample of all men.
b. ROU1 = "situations involving variety of duties"
   ROU2 = "situations involving repetitive or short cycle operations"
   ROUT = unweighted linear combination of ROU1 and ROU2
   CS3 = "doing things only under specific instruction"
   CS4 = "situations involving direction, control and planning"
   CST = unweighted linear combination of CS3 and CS4
   SC = substantive complexity of work

With two or three exceptions, this is the case. The signs for all coefficients are appropriate, and the DOT-based measures provide somewhat higher estimates for job characteristic association. But, more importantly, the relative order of magnitude for the different pairwise relationships is approximately preserved. The exceptions are the VARIETY-COMPLEXITY correlation (–.160 versus – .412, –.30, –.32), closeness of supervision-routinization correlations involving REPETITIVENESS (.678 and .689 versus .338, .17 and .12), and the lower values in 1964 and 1974 for closeness of supervision-routinization (.17 and .12). But the latter values depend upon the specification of a particular multivariate measurement model. As a whole, we take the information in Table 1 as corroborative of the external validity of the DOT-based indicators.[6]

The *1972-73 Quality of Employment Survey* (QES) offers a second source of validity information. Respondents indicated the extent to which a variety of characteristics described their current jobs. A number of the items circumscribe the complexity, routinization, and supervision indicators. To the degree that occupation-specific measures capture variance in jobs as individuals experience them, then we expect covariation between these measures and individual measures of job characteristics.

Correlations between occupation-specific measures and individual measures are likely to be lower than might be expected for external validity correlations, for several reasons. First, the occupation-specific and individual measures are not measures of the same construct. For occupation-specific measures, the true score refers to the level of a characteristic for a population of incumbents of a given occupation. For the individual-level measures, the true score is defined as the expected value of the characteristic for a particular individual in a particular job. The measures are nonequivalent in this respect. To the extent they are nonequivalent, the variation is subsumed in the error component for the occupation-specific measure. Second, the presence of equivalent measures is also lessened by the absence of strict wording comparability between items. Therefore, for these data to reflect positively on an external validity judgment, we expect correlations that are (a) of appropriate direction or sign, and (b) of modest size—less than expected under parallel forms (.6 to 1.0) but larger than what might be considered small for validity studies (.15 to .20).

Table 2 provides the correlations for the current jobs of 1013 QES males. Several conclusions are warranted. First, the signs of the coefficients are in the expected direction for every item except one (i: R has immediate supervisor). A check of the data shows this is a poor measure with little variance, as 94% of respondents report having an immediate supervisor. Second, the magnitude of the correlations, while not high, is reasonable for REPETITIVE, ROUT, SPECIFIC INSTRUCTION, CONTROL, and CST (we ignore complexity at this point). ROUT and REPETITIVE are most highly related to individual's assessments of having to keep learning new things, being creative, making one's own decisions on the job and doing a variety of different things. This is consistent with what should be expected for indicators of routinization, although item g, which explicitly mentions repetition, was a disappointment. The closeness-of-supervision indicators are most highly defined by the same variables, and additionally by the extent to which the job allows the respondent to make decisions on his own, and whether R supervises others as part of the job. These patterns are consistent with epistemic definitions of concept-indicator relations.

In general, the closeness-of-supervision measures bear slightly higher relationships to individuals' job assessments than do routinization measures. Consistent with other evidence (Spenner, 1977: 106-126), the weakest indicator is VARIETY. The indicator does not appear to be contaminated. A check of its relationships to a large number of other variables in the OCG-II and QES data shows small-to-modest—not large—coefficients. Other than its association with REPETITIVE ($r = -.641$ for OCG fathers) the highest association of VARIETY with any other variable is with Specific Vocational Preparation (SVP) for OCG fathers' occupations ($r = .472$). Finally, as expected, the overall measure of substantive complexity of work bears a consistent, moderately

TABLE 2

Zero-order Correlations between the Characteristics of Respondents' Current Job and Closeness of Supervision, Substantive Complexity, and Routinization (QES males; n = 1013)

Characteristic of Job*	Role Routine Variable**						
	ROU1	ROU2	ROUT	SC	CS3	CS4	CST
How much does your job (require that you) ...							
a) ...have to keep learning new things?	.196	-.390	.330	.414	-.353	.275	.361
b) How much freedom does it allow you as to how you do your work?	.041	-.217	.143	.244	-.183	.124	.175
c) ...require a high level of skill?	.158	-.357	.289	.342	-.358	.216	.325
d) ...allow you to make decisions on your own?	.163	-.398	.314	.431	-.323	.346	.394
e) ...require you to be creative?	.190	-.498	.346	.447	-.412	.325	.425
f) ...allow you to do a variety of different things?	.243	-.419	.373	.351	-.356	.301	.381
g) ...require you to do things that are very repetitious (do things over and over)?	-.082	.228	-.173	-.246	.220	-.147	-.209

TABLE 2 (Continued)

h) ...allow you to take part in making decisions that affect you?	.136	-.341	.267	.354	-.273	.331	.359
i) R has immediate supervisor	-.039	.030	-.039	-.086	-.002	-.082	-.051
j) R supervises others as part of his job	.170	-.360	.299	.432	-.313	.434	.448
(...how true you feel each is of your job....)							
k) the work is interesting	.170	-.365	.300	.356	-.315	.252	.327
l) I am given a lot of freedom to decide how I do my own work	.100	-.238	.190	.279	-.243	.229	.275
m) I am given a chance to do the things I do best	.125	-.306	.241	.292	-.246	.238	.283

*Items a–h had as response alternatives "a lot, somewhat, a little, or not at all." Items i and j involved "yes" or "no" responses to questions of whether the Respondent has an immediate supervisor and whether R supervises others as part of his job. Items k–m had as response alternatives "very true, somewhat true, not too true, not true at all."

**All QES items are scaled in a positive direction (i.e., a high score indicates a high level on the characteristic content of the question (or a "yes" response for dummy variables). ROU1 (situations involving variety of duties), ROUT (unweighted linear combination of ROU1 and ROU2), SC (substantive complexity), CS4 (situations involving direction, control and planning) and CST (unweighted linear combination of CS3 and CS4) are scaled such that "desirable" outcomes (high substantive complexity, low routinization, low or freedom from close supervision) are represented by high scores. Only ROU2 (situations involving repetitive or short cycle operations . . .) and CS3 (. . . doing things only under specific instruction . . .) in their original metrics (used here) are reverse scored (a high score indicated high levels of routinization and closeness of supervision).

high relation to all items except the problematic "immediate supervisor" measure.

In sum, we adduce from the evidence presented that the new indicators for routinization and closeness of supervision are reasonable ones that may be used further. Validation is an ongoing and continuous process; not unlike legal adjudication and argumentation, evidence is presented and a judgment is made, but it is open to appeal and new evidence.

MOVEMENT BETWEEN OCCUPATION CLASSIFICATION SYSTEMS

Several sources of error are intrinsic to using and moving between occupation classification systems. The most general source of error is the lack of, or misplacement of, detail in the DOT and census classifications. Of the 595 1970 census categories, some contain a large number of individuals with heterogeneous job situations (in 1969 labor force frequencies, 1.45 million elementary school teachers, 2.36 million retail sales clerks). Other categories are heterogeneous in having a large number of DOT categories mapped into them (e.g. N.E.C. categories). Other than using as much detail as available, or making industry breakdowns, very little can be done to remedy this error except to create a new system; it only can be monitored.

Two other sources of error in the use of classification systems are in the elicitation and reporting of jobs, and in coding the information. The first type, indexed by test-retest measures of job, can be held to very minimal levels ($r = .85-.95$) for data sets using the CPS-census format of information elicitation (Hauser and Featherman, 1977). The second type of coding and mechanical recording error can be minimized to near zero with the use of appropriate procedures (see Featherman et al., 1975).

An additional source of error that might affect the quality of inferences pertains to movement between the DOT and census systems—as we have done freely—and between 1960 and 1970 census classification systems. This error is implicit when comparing studies or outcomes based on the respective systems.

The QES and OCG-II data provide some indication of the quality of the interface between the classification systems. The QES occupations were independently coded in 7-digit 1970 census scores (occupation-industry-class of worker) and 9-digit DOT codes. Using the DOT code, which contains the degree of involvement with data, people, and things, individual records were enriched with GED and SVP scores. Using the census code, we added estimates for occupation variables from the detailed 1970 matrix. Thus, for 5 variables there are 2 independent sources of estimates for respondents' current jobs. Table 3 provides the zero-order correlations between the two sources, along with means and standard deviations for QES male respondents. The results are encouraging. Means for the 5 variables are virtually identical. As expected, the standard deviations based on census categories are systematically smaller than those based on the DOT, ranging from 23% smaller for data to 11-15% smaller for other variables. Finally, the correlations between the pairs of variables are uniformly high. Assessed against social science standards for measure-to-measure correspondence, this suggests that the DOT-1970 slippage is not serious.

The OCG data offer a similar opportunity to assess the 1960-1970 census slippage for occupation variables. Respondents' occupations were coded independently into detailed 1960 and 1970 categories. Table 4 gives the means, standard deviations, and correlations between the occupation variables for OCG respondents' first occupations. The results are also positive. The variables taken from published census sources (education, sex and race composition, earnings and employment security) should be treated separately as the coefficients represent true means, dispersions and stabilities for 1960 and 1970. For DOT-based variables the means and standard deviations are virtually identical, with the dispersions for 1960 slightly attenuated due to the smaller number of categories. The correlations, which index the retention of information between the 1960 and 1970 classifications, are acceptably high in all cases, although SPECIFIC INSTRUCTION and REPETITIVE are more sensitive to movement between the two systems. Of the census variables, sex

TABLE 3

Means, Standard Deviations, and Correlations between Data, People, and Things; GED; and SVP Based on DOT and 1970 Occupation Classification Systems (QES, n = 1013)

Variable	Occupation Classification System				$r_{DOT, 1970\ CNS}$
	DOT		1970 Census		
	$\bar{x}$	s.d.	$\bar{x}$	s.d.	
DATA	3.40	2.87	3.29	2.21	.944
PEOPLE	6.36	2.36	6.35	2.04	.871
THINGS	5.10	3.11	5.14	2.66	.907
GED	3.83	1.12	3.81	1.00	.890
SVP	5.96	1.99	5.79	1.71	.893

TABLE 4

**Means, Standard Deviations, and Correlation Coefficients
for Occupation Variables Based on 1960 and 1970 Census
Classification Systems (OCG-II, respondent's first occupation)**

Variable	1960		1970		$r_{1960,1970}$
	$\bar{x}$	s.d.	$\bar{x}$	s.d.	
DATA	4.43	2.22	4.44	2.24	.91
PEOPLE	7.05	1.67	7.05	1.70	.93
THINGS	5.03	2.38	5.07	2.40	.90
GED	3.32	1.01	3.33	1.02	.92
SVP	4.85	1.72	4.85	1.74	.88
COMPLEXITY	7.69	6.77	7.70	6.88	.93
SPEC INSTRUC	.26	.27	.30	.32	.80
CONTROL	.15	.28	.16	.29	.89
CST[a]	.89	.45	.85	.51	.87
VARIETY	.38	.33	.39	.35	.87
REPETITIVE	.30	.29	.35	.34	.82
ROUT	1.08	.56	1.05	.62	.87
MEDIAN EDUCATION	10.93	2.49	11.93	2.20	.92
SEX COMPOSITION	79.61	22.54	78.05	23.51	.82
RACE COMPOSITION	89.00	9.52	89.09	7.69	.77
MEDIAN INCOME	43.89	20.05	68.24	34.38	.90
EMPLOY. SECURITY	63.97	17.08	67.62	15.11	.78
n	21,428		22,308		21,264

a. CST = unweighted sum of CONTROL and SPECIFIC INSTRUCTION; ROUT = unweighted sum of VARIETY and REPETITIVE.

composition, race composition, and employment security show the most sensitivity or change between 1960 and 1970 categories.

In sum, we generally find some loss of information in the movement between classification systems. Information slippage is slightly larger between 1960 and 1970 census systems than between the 1970 census and the DOT, but these differences are very small. Estimates of means and standard deviations show little evidence of serious measurement slippage. Moreover, this state of affairs equally characterizes detailed occupation characteristics such as those used here, and molar scores for occupations (for example, Treiman, 1977, reports correlations of .86-.92 for his prestige score between variations of the International Standard Classification of Occupations and the 1960 3-digit occupation categories).

DISCUSSION

Several areas in the social sciences show an increased interest in detailed features of jobs. The measurement of work-role characteristics is often based upon the use of census or DOT classification systems. The work reported here suggests that a wealth of job information may be available for these systems. When appropriately estimated for detailed job categories, the measurement slippage involved in moving between the systems—necessary for score construction and implicit in comparisons of studies using different systems—appears to be minimal for a variety of role characteristics. Moreover, the initial validity evidence for the new estimates of routinization and closeness of supervision is generally favorable.

The availability of a larger set of job characteristics for census classification systems expands the range of extant data sets that can be used to examine research questions.[7] The more promising issues include the social organization or dimensions of jobs and careers, perhaps making more operational popular themes that deal with the quality of work life (such as dual labor markets), race and gender variation in work ("equal pay for equal work") and specifications of the molecular constitution of overall features of roles such as socioeconomic status.

NOTES

1. Detailed training and procedure documents exist for Department of Labor Field Center operations. The unpublished documents obtained from one field center include a

"Guide for Job Verification," a "Manual for Rating Training Time," "Suggestions for Reviewing Work Performed and Worker Trait Rating in Job Verifications," and a substantial handbook of "Procedures for Evaluating Job Analysis Source Data for Combination."

2. Census occupation categories that were delineated by industry were: officials and administrators, public administration, n.e.c. (3 categories); inspectors, except construction, public administration (3); managers and administrators, n.e.c. (36); clerical workers, not specified and miscellaneous (7); foremen, n.e.c. (13); inspectors, n.e.c. (3); mine operatives, n.e.c. (3); operatives and machine operatives, not specified and miscellaneous (62); and miscellaneous and not specified laborers (44).

3. It might be expected that each DOT code maps into one and only one census category. This is not the case. Each DOT code that occurred more than once or twice mapped into an average of 2.5 census categories. Most DOT codes map into 1 or 2 census categories, and a small portion into 3-8 census codes—the number decreasing sharply as the number of census categories increases.

The "unreliability" may lie between the classification systems. Recall that the 2 sets of codes were assigned independently. The measurement of jobs in the CPS is generally excellent. All coders were well trained. We are told that the intercoder reliabilities for census and DOT coding were in an acceptable range of .85-.95.

An inspection of some of the apparent ambiguities reveals a possible explanation. Without access to the original CPS questionnaires—using the numeric codes—the multiple census codes for a given DOT code show that the same raw job information (such as job title, industry, major activity) resulted in the same DOT code, and, at the same time, in very similar, but nominally different, census categories. A typical example finds 46 CPS individuals assigned the DOT code that corresponds to an "architect" or "marine architect." The census codes for the same individuals show 41 of 46 were assigned the architect code, and one each the codes of accountant; urban and regional planner; draftsman; designer; and manager and administrator, n.e.c. The slightly different wordings and job descriptions that may have been given by the 46 respondents could result in a reliable coding from the standpoint of each system taken separately, but less than trivial slippage between the systems. The designer and the draftsman may well have been architects as much as they were a designer and a draftsman from the standpoint of the rules of one system. But from the standpoint of another system that is perceptually attentive to different components of work roles and activities, the 46 individuals are all equally architects.

4. The April 1971 CPS did not include 10 census occupations. They were (1970 employees in the civilian labor force [ECLF] persons in parentheses): health practitioners, n.e.c. (721); therapy assistants (2907); clerical assistants, social welfare (1309); molder apprentices (674); painter apprentices (1760); plasterer apprentices (682); milliners (2343); miscellaneous and not specified operatives, not specified manufacturing industries (19,237); miscellaneous and not specified laborers, not specified manufacturing industries (2715); and lay midwives (963). Following Temme (1975: 182-182a) the source of estimates was the next highest level of aggregation (i.e., for plasterer apprentices, a weighted average for all craftsmen).

5. Two minor points of noncomparability (with Temme, 1975) in weighting procedures should be mentioned. First, the variables taken from Temme for 1960 categories were generated from 1966 labor force sample design weights; the weights for the other 1960 variables reflect 1959 labor force frequencies. Second, the April 1971 CPS is a sample of the total labor force, and this is reflected in the estimates for occupation

variables. The 1960 estimates for routinization and closeness of supervision were generated twice using male and female labor force frequencies.

6. Using procedures developed by Jöreskog, I attempted to estimate a measurement model that was consistent with the work of Kohn and colleagues (Kohn and Schooler, 1973, 1978), for substantive complexity of work, closeness of supervision and routinization. Thus far, the efforts have not been successful. Models were attempted using several large bodies of data for samples of men and of women, under a variety of specifications including random and nonrandom errors among the indicators, and constraining the covariance structure among constructs to the values reported by Kohn and colleagues. The maximum-likelihood solutions that were obtained were characterized by poor fit and implausible parameter estimates (i.e., negative error variances). Where solutions were plausible, they implied very high construct correlations (greater than r = .9 for substantive complexity-closeness of supervision).

There are at least four explanations for the failure to replicate: (1) there is something wrong with my measures; (2) there is something wrong with the Kohn measures; (3) the model is misspecified (see Miller et al., 1979: 72); and/or (4) the model and both sets of measures are without problem; rather, because the Kohn measures are taken from individuals and mine are taken for occupations, the latter set of measures provides a more highly correlated picture of reality. I do not have sufficient evidence to reject one or more of the explanations. I suspect the fourth explanation will weigh heavily in any final resolution. A correlation matrix is available from the author for the interested reader.

7. The scores used here are available for research uses from the author (Center for the Study of Youth Development, Boys Town, NE 68010).

REFERENCES

BARKER, D. G. (1969) "Factor analysis of worker trait requirements." J. of Employment Counseling 6: 162-168.

BERG, I. (1970) Education and Jobs: The Great Training Robbery. New York: Praeger.

BLUESTONE, B. A. (1974) "The Personal Earnings Distribution: Individual and Institutional Determinants." Ph.D. dissertation, University of Michigan.

BROOM, L., P. DUNCAN-JONES, F. L. JONES, and P. McDONNELL (1977) "Worker traits and worker functions in the DOT." J. of Vocational Behavior 11: 253-261.

DUNCAN, O. D. (1961) "A socioeconomic index for all occupations," pp. 109-138 in A. J. Reiss (ed.) Occupations and Social Status. New York: Macmillan.

——— D. L. FEATHERMAN, and B. DUNCAN (1972) Socioeconomic Background and Performance. New York: Seminar.

ECKAUS, R. (1964) "Economic criteria for education and training." Rev. of Economics and Statistics 46: 181-188.

EDWARDS, A. M. (1933) "A social-economic grouping of the gainful workers of the United States." J. of the Amer. Stat. Assn. 28: 277-287.

FEATHERMAN, D. L. and R. M. HAUSER (1975) "Design for a replicate study of social mobility in the United States," pp. 219-251 in S. Spilerman and K. Land (eds.) Social Indicator Models. New York: Russell Sage.

FEATHERMAN, D. L., M. SOBEL, and D. DICKENS (1975) "A manual for coding occupations and industries into detailed 1970 categories and a listing of 1970-basis

Duncan socio-economic scores." University of Wisconsin-Madison Center for Demography and Ecology. 75-1.

FINE, S. and C. A. HEINZ (1958) "The functional occupational classification structure." Personnel and Guidance J. 37: 180-192.

FINE, S. A. (1968) "Use of the Dictionary of Occupational Titles to estimate educational investment." J. of Human Resources 3: 363-375.

GOLDTHORPE, J. H. and K. HOPE (1974) The Social Grading of Occupations (Oxford Studies in Social Mobility). Oxford: Clarendon.

HACKMAN, J. R. and E. E. LAWLER, III (1971) "Employee reactions to job characteristics." J. of Applied Psychology 55: 259-286.

HAUSER, R. M. and D. L. FEATHERMAN (1977) The Process of Stratification: Trends and Analyses. New York: Academic.

KALLEBERG, A. L. (1977) "Work values and job rewards: a theory of job satisfaction." Amer. Soc. Rev. 42: 124-143.

KOHN, M. (1969) Class and Conformity. Homewood, IL: Irwin.

——— and C. SCHOOLER (1978) "The reciprocal effects of the substantive complexity of work and intellectual flexibility: a longitudinal assessment." Amer. J. of Sociology 84: 24-52.

——— (1973) "Occupational experience and psychological functioning: an assessment of reciprocal effects." Amer. Soc. Rev. 38: 97-118.

LUCAS, R. (1974) "The distribution of job characteristics." Rev. of Economics and Statistics 55: 530-540.

——— (1972) "Working conditions, wage rates and human capital: a hedonic study." Ph.D. dissertation, Massachusetts Institute of Technology.

McLAUGHLIN, S. D. (1978) "Sex differences in the determinants of occupational status." Sociology of Work and Occupations 5: 5-30.

MILLER, J., C. SCHOOLER, M. KOHN, and K. MILLER (1979) "Women and work: the psychological effects of occupational conditions." American J. of Sociology 85: 66-94.

OTTO, L. B., V.R.A. CALL and K. I. SPENNER (1979) "Design for a study of entry into careers." Boys Town, NE: Boys Town Center for the Study of Youth Development.

QUINN, R. P. and L. J. SHEPHARD (1974) The 1972-73 Quality of Employment Survey. Ann Arbor: University of Michigan Institute for Social Research.

SAINTY, G. E. (1974) "A validation of the worker trait groups in the DOT." J. of Vocational Behavior 5: 173-176.

SCOVILLE, J. (1972) Manpower and Occupational Analysis: Concepts and Measurements. Lexington, MA: D. C. Heath.

——— (1966) "Education and training requirements for occupations." Rev. of Economics and Statistics 47: 387-394.

SHARTLE, C. L. (1964) "Occupational analysis, worker characteristics and occupational classification systems," pp. 285-309 in H. Borrow (ed.) Man in a World at Work. Boston: Houghton Mifflin.

SHEPARD, J. M. (1977) "Technology, alienation and job satisfaction," pp. 1-22 in A. Inkeles et al. (eds.) Annual Review of Sociology, Vol. III. Palo Alto, CA: Annual Reviews.

SIEGEL, P. M. (1971) "Prestige in the American occupational structure." Ph.D. dissertation, University of Chicago.

SNYDER, D. and P. M. HUDIS (1976) "Occupational income and the effects of minority competition and segregation: a reanalysis and some new evidence." Amer. Soc. Rev. 41: 209-234.

SPENNER, K. I. (1977) "From generation to generation: the transmission of occupation." Ph.D. dissertation, University of Wisconsin-Madison.

STOLZENBERG, R. M. (1975) "Occupations, labor markets and the process of wage attainment." Amer. Soc. Rev. 40: 645-665.

TEMME, L. V. (1975) Occupation: Meanings and Measures. Washington, DC: Bureau of Social Science Research.

TREIMAN, D. J. (1977) Occupational Prestige in Comparative Perspective. New York: Academic.

U.S. Bureau of the Census (1973) Subject Reports: Occupational Characteristics, PC(2)-7A. Washington, DC: Government Printing Office.

——— (1972) "1970 occupation and industry classification in terms of their 1960 occupation and industry elements." Technical Paper 26. Washington, DC: Government Printing Office.

——— (1971) Alphabetical Index of Occupations and Industries. Washington, DC: Government Printing Office.

——— (1963) Subject Reports: Occupational Characteristics, PC(2)-7A. Washington, DC: Government Printing Office.

——— (1960) Alphabetical Index of Occupations and Industries. Washington, DC: Government Printing Office.

U.S. Department of Labor (1977) Dictionary of Occuational Titles (4th ed.) Washington, DC: Government Printing Office.

——— (1972) Handbook for Analyzing Jobs. Washington, DC: Government Printing Office.

——— (1968) Selected Characteristics of Occupations by Worker Traits and Physical Strength: Supplement 2 to the Dictionary of Occupational Titles (3rd ed.). Washington, DC: Government Printing Office.

——— (1965) Dictionary of Occupational Titles (3rd ed., 2 vols.). Washington, DC: Government Printing Office.

——— (1956) Estimates of Worker Trait Requirements for 4,000 Jobs. Washington, DC: Government Printing Office.

APPENDIX
SUMMARY OF DOT JOB CHARACTERISTICS

The following notes summarize select job characteristics available for the approximately 13,800 unique 6-digit DOT codes. For more detail on the full set of DOT variables, the reader is referred to Volume 2 of the DOT (U.S. Department of Labor, 1965: 649-656). We have quoted freely from the appendices to the DOT.

RELATIONSHIPS TO DATA, PEOPLE AND THINGS

"Data" refers to "information, knowledge and conceptions related to data, people or things, obtained by observation, investigation, interpretation, visualization, mental creation; incapable of being touched; written data take the form of numbers, words, symbols; other data are ideas, concepts, oral verbalization." "People" refers to "human beings; also animals dealt with on an individual basis as if they were human." "Things" refers to "inanimate objects as distinguished from human beings; substances or materials; machines, tools, equipment; products. A thing is tangible and has shape, form, and other physical characteristics."

DATA	PEOPLE	THINGS
0 Synthesizing	0 Mentoring	0 Setting up
1 Coordinating	1 Negotiating	1 Precision working
2 Analyzing	2 Instructing	2 Operating-Controlling
3 Compiling	3 Supervising	3 Driving-Operating
4 Computing	4 Diverting	4 Manipulating
5 Copying	5 Persuading	5 Tending
6 Comparing	6 Speaking-Signaling	6 Feeding-Offbearing
7 No Significant	7 Serving	7 Handling
8 Relationship	8 No Signif Relat	8 No Signif Relat

TRAINING TIME

General Educational Development (GED) "embraces those aspects of education (formal and informal) which contribute to the worker's reasoning development and ability to follow instructions; and . . . acquisition of "tool" knowledges, such as language and mathematical skills. It is education of a general nature which does not have a recognized, fairly specific, occupational objective. Ordinarily such education is obtained in elementary school, high school or college. It also derives from experience and individual study." (There exists a 6-point training scale that ranges from 1= "apply common sense understanding," to 6= "apply principles of logical or scientific thinking.") Specific Vocational Preparation (SVP) refers to the "amount of time required to learn the techniques, acquire information, and develop the facility needed for average performance in a specific job-worker situation . . . may be acquired in a school, work, military, institutional or vocational environment . . . does not include orientation training required of every fully qualified worker . . . of any new job." (SVP embraces 9 levels, from 1= "demonstration only," to 9= "over ten years.")

TEMPERAMENTS

The DOT defines this factor as "different types of situations to which workers must adjust." It is scored only if characteristic of the job; present-absent scoring.

1. Situations involving a variety of duties often characterized by frequent change (VARIETY).
2. Situations involving repetitive or short-cycle operations carried out according to set procedures or sequences (REPETITIVE).
3. Situations involving doing things only under specific instruction, allowing little or no room for independent action or judgment in working out job problems (SPECIFIC INSTRUCTION).
4. Situations involving the direction, control, and planning of an entire activity or the activities of others (CONTROL).

Kenneth I. Spenner is a Research Associate at the Center for the Study of Youth Development, Boys Town, Nebraska. At present, he is collaborating with Luther B. Otto and Vaughn Call on a multiyear project investigating career entry. Spenner is a co-author of Volume I of the Entry Into Careers series, Design for a Study of Entry Into Careers *(Lexington, forthcoming).*

120919

DATE DUE

300.724
B677s
1981
Social measurement: current issues.

Ohio Dominican College Library
1216 Sunbury Road
Columbus, Ohio 43219

DEMCO